Amy Raphael has worked for *The Face*, *Esquire*, *Elle*, *NME*, *Rolling Stone* and all the British broadsheets. Her books include *Never Mind the Bollocks: Women Rewrite Rock*, *Danny Boyle in Conversation with Amy Raphael* and *Mike Leigh on Mike Leigh*. She co-wrote *Easily Distracted*, Steve Coogan's autobiography, and worked with David Hare on his memoir, *The Blue Touch Paper*. She was born in London and now lives in Brighton with her daughter.

A SEAT AT THE TABLE

INTERVIEWS WITH WOMEN ON THE FRONTLINE OF MUSIC

AMY RAPHAEL

virago

VIRAGO

First published in Great Britain in 2019 by Virago Press

1 3 5 7 9 10 8 6 4 2

A CIP catalogue record for this book
is available from the British Library.

ISBN 978-0-349-00982-7

Typeset in Goudy by M Rules
Printed and bound in Great Britain by
Clays Ltd, Elcograf S.p.A.

Papers used by Virago are from well-managed forests
and other responsible sources.

Virago Press
An imprint of
Little, Brown Book Group
Carmelite House
50 Victoria Embankment
London EC4Y 0DZ

An Hachette UK Company
www.hachette.co.uk

www.virago.co.uk

For Bonnie.
Speak. You will be heard.

CONTENTS

INTRODUCTION

It is 26 August 1994, and I am watching Hole on stage at Reading Festival. It is their first gig since Kurt Cobain's suicide four months earlier, and no one knows what to expect. Even with Love on stage, wearing not black but gold, the rumours persist. Is she high? Will she collapse? Will she mention *him*?

I am not here for the drama, but for the music. I drink warm beer too quickly and let Love's cracked, desperate and sometimes tender voice sear through me. I close my eyes as she asks somebody to kill her in 'Miss World' and sings about burning witches in 'Softer, Softest'.

I know all the lyrics from *Live Through This*, the Hole album released a week after Cobain's death. I know what people said when it came out: that Cobain had written it. Just as, the following year, some would insist that Damon Albarn had written Elastica's eponymous debut album because singer Justine Frischmann lived with him.

I look up at Love on stage. She is intense, emotional, feral. Performing might be cathartic, but she is ruined by grief. Between songs, she growls into the mic. 'Oh yeah, I'm so goddamn brave.' And, sarcasm turned up to ten, 'This is like a hobby for me.'

The next evening, as the sky darkens, I am in Love's hotel in west London. I have been commissioned by Virago Press, feminist publisher, to write my first book, a series of interviews with female musicians to be recounted in the first person. Love knows that I need her voice in *Never Mind the Bollocks: Women Rewrite Rock*; in fact, my contract depends on it. I know she likes to talk because I interviewed her before, for *The Face* magazine, in Seattle in late 1992 and I met her again the following summer, when interviewing Nirvana in New York.

And yet, even as I'm in Love's suite, chatting to Hole guitarist Eric Erlandson and his nineteen-year-old girlfriend Drew Barrymore, I expect Love to send me away. She hasn't given an interview since her husband died, and I wonder if I should offer to cancel. But no, Love wants to talk. And talk. Non-stop, for two hours. She is brittle, angry, tearful and yet great company. She talks about *Backlash*, Susan Faludi's bestselling book about the anti-feminist backlash in America. About Hole drummer Patty Schemel being the first woman to appear on the cover of *Drum World*. About wanting to play with Elastica.

I ask about Reading Festival. Love knows damn well what everyone at the festival, both backstage and out in the audience, was saying. It was too soon. She looks at the music and style magazines scattered across the floor of her suite and sighs. 'Well – and I hate to sound reactionary, because I really don't go round saying "sexist" at everything – but I really truly believe that's sexist. That music is a lot more vital when you're a boy. But if it wasn't for my baby [Frances Bean Cobain] and my music, I wouldn't even be here on this planet. I'd be gone – fast.'

Both dazed and euphoric at the end of the interview, I get

a black taxi back to Reading at 3 a.m. because I want to see the rest of the weekend's bands. I spend a decent chunk of my book advance in doing so, but I don't care. Sitting in the back of the cab, I realise that Love will survive. After all, she has already been accused of murdering her husband, poisoning her baby in utero with heroin and of being, well, mad. A crazy witch.

Yes, she can be a pain in the arse (she was days late for *The Face* interview, despite insisting that I fly out to Seattle on Boxing Day, and at times her stream of consciousness is tough to fathom), but that's not important. What is important is this: Love never asks for permission to speak. When she speaks, she expects to be heard.

So that they might speak freely in our interviews, I offered all the women in *Never Mind the Bollocks* copy approval. I transcribed the interviews, edited them into first-person narratives and sent them back to each artist. When I started work on this book over two decades later, that same collaborative approach seemed even more felicitous: in a climate where women's testimonies are mocked by men in high power, we surely need their stories more than ever.

The mid-nineties now seem not like a different country, but a different universe, not only in terms of politics, but also in terms of technology: although Tim Berners-Lee invented the World Wide Web in 1989, it took a while for everyone to have access to email.

Thus, one particularly bright morning in the late summer of 1994, the bulky grey fax machine at the foot of my bed churned into action at 6 a.m. and I watched as Debbie Harry's foreword pushed through from New York to London. I remembered my first boyfriend saving up to buy me a vinyl copy of

Parallel Lines in 1978, when I was eleven – still the best present a boyfriend has ever given me. And Harry singing 'Heart of Glass' on *Top of the Pops* the following year in a pink and yellow stripy dress and tie. Those cheekbones. That insouciant pout that predated Instagram by over three decades. Like all my friends, male and female, I fell in love.

Throughout the autumn of 1994, I was periodically woken by the fax machine spewing out its shiny, thin paper at ungodly hours. Blurry-eyed, I found annotated chapters from the American artists in *Bollocks*: Kim Gordon, Kristin Hersh, Tanya Donelly, Liz Phair, or Veruca Salt's Nina Gordon and Louise Post. At least the UK-based artists – Björk; The Raincoats' Gina Birch; Echobelly's Sonya Aurora Madan and Debbie Smith; Doll's Pam Hogg; Sister George's Ellyott Dragon; Huggy Bear – returned their chapters when I was awake.

I was right up against a deadline, with Virago wondering if Love's chapter would ever be returned, when a FedEx package arrived from Seattle. My mouth dry, I pulled the perforated strip off. There were Love's notes, written in black biro and blood-red lipstick. I was so relieved to have them in my hands that I only later considered the lipstick. In another three or four years, she would have sent the notes by email, minus the lipstick. Sometimes I miss the pre-internet world, when FedEx packages were rock 'n' roll.

Looking back on *Never Mind the Bollocks: Women Rewrite Rock*, I remember Huggy Bear, the pioneering British riot grrrl band, being spiky as hell, but then that was their shtick. I described them in the book as seeming like 'snotty, prissy kids'; apart from anything else, their distrust of journalists led to us being banned from their gigs and it took months of cajoling before the band agreed to be interviewed for *Bollocks*.

Huggy Bear certainly had their place in the story of the mid-1990s – their idea of inviting women to stand at the front at gigs is still used by bands such as Dream Wife today – but they didn't have the wild charisma of, say, X-Ray Spex singer Poly Styrene, nor any songs as urgent and thrilling as 1977's 'Oh Bondage Up Yours!'.

So the interviews for *Bollocks* may not always have been easy, but once an artist agreed to be in the book, I was generally given amazing access – very much in keeping with the end of the golden age of journalism. I conducted all the interviews in 1994, a year which, in the indie/rock world at least, was defined by Kurt Cobain's death. Just days after Cobain's suicide, I flew to the East Coast of America to interview Sonic Youth's Kim Gordon, widely regarded as a key influence on riot grrrl, the punked-up feminist protest movement which originated in the early 1990s in Washington state.

The mood among such indie rock royalty was sombre. Gordon talked tearfully off the record about her good friend Cobain. Back on, she said two things that I still remember. The first was this: 'In America, the mainstream doesn't consider you if you're a woman making what they see as annoying music.' And the second: 'I hope my daughter grows up to feel that she can do anything she wants to do.'

Decades later, little has changed. Mothers still worry about being positive role models to their daughters and about passing on the notion that their daughters can make their own choices and succeed on their own terms. Beyoncé, for example, is still talking about the importance of her daughters being self-empowered. In a rare interview published in the September 2018 issue of *American Vogue*, she said, 'My mother taught me the importance not just of being seen but of seeing myself. As the mother of two girls, it's important to me that they see themselves too – in books, films, and on run-ways. It's important to me that they see themselves as CEOs, as bosses, and that they know they can write the scripts for their own lives.'

However, it's much easier to talk about self-empowerment as a loose concept than it is to actually define what the word 'feminism' means right now. Beyoncé should know. She famously performed 'Flawless', a song which samples a TED talk by Nigerian writer Chimamanda Ngozi Adichie, with the word FEMINIST writ large on the stage behind her during the Mrs Carter Show World Tour (oh, the irony of using one's married name).

TIME magazine decided it was the moment where 'a word with a complicated history [was] reclaimed by the most powerful celebrity in the world'. Others dismissed it as 'feminist lite'.

Beyoncé later explained her reasoning to *Elle* magazine. 'I put the definition of feminist in my song and on my tour, not for propaganda or to proclaim to the world that I'm a feminist, but to give clarity to the true meaning. I'm not really sure people know or understand what a feminist is, but it's very simple. It's someone who believes in equal rights for men and women.'

Since the word *féminisme* was coined by French utopian socialist and philosopher Charles Fourier in 1837 – even as early as 1808 he wrote that the development of any civilisation could be judged by the extent to which its women were liberated – it has been assigned multiple nuances. It's been disregarded as a dirty word, as the f-word.

Presidents who think it's okay to boast about grabbing women 'by the pussy' are scared of women and terrified of feminists. But what kind of feminist are you? A fourth-waver or a fifth-waver? The Women's Equality Party holds 'Feminism 5.0' camps because its members feel that a fifth wave is necessary as 'a gender-equal future looks more fragile than ever before'. If you go on a Women's March in the US or the UK, as a woman or a man, does that automatically make you a feminist?

What is clear is that it's not enough to label oneself a feminist, whether 4.0 or 5.0. We have to look further than our own experiences. The *Guardian* published a piece in 2017 saying that no one knows exactly what intersectional feminism means, but to my mind Professor Kimberlé Crenshaw's term can be understood thus: feminism isn't just about white, middle-class women. It needs to be inclusive and that means considering the impact of class, race, disability, gender identity and sexual orientation. Put in its simplest terms, my experience of the world as a white woman is obviously not the same as that of, say, a Hispanic woman.

Crenshaw, a law professor at UCLA and Columbia, saw black women as being 'legally invisible'. She argued that the legal system saw sexism as injustice to all women and racism as injustice to people of colour – ergo, it failed to take into account that women of colour face both sexism and racism.

And all this when, as Beyoncé says, we're still fighting for equal rights for men and women. *All* women.

Progress may be slow, particularly given the present incumbent of the White House. But there are small victories. In 2017, the Me Too movement galvanised women to speak up about sexual aggression, and the American online dictionary Merriam-Webster declared 'feminism' as the most looked-up word of the year (apparently spiking following news coverage of the Women's March on Washington, DC in January that year, and driven by *The Handmaid's Tale* on television and *Wonder Woman* on the big screen).

And yet not everyone likes a label (or a hashtag). When

I interviewed Viv Albertine for *Esquire Weekly* around the same time as the publication of her acclaimed memoir *Clothes, Clothes, Clothes. Music, Music, Music. Boys, Boys, Boys*, she told me that The Slits and many of their contemporaries were against *any* kind of label. 'It would have made it all too easy for the establishment to pack us into boxes – "feminists", "punks", "louts", "degenerates" – and dismiss us. While they couldn't work out what we were, we still had a chance of being listened to.'

Like my mother before me and my daughter after me, I am a feminist. But I understood what Albertine was saying. There's no point in being a feminist if no one is listening.

Not all the women in *Never Mind the Bollocks* directly referenced feminism. They might not have willingly given themselves that label, but I would argue that their actions were those of feminists. Some, however, were more reluctant to take on the issue of gender than others.

In her *Bollocks* chapter, the wonderful Björk reminisced about growing up in Iceland. She mentioned meeting a lover when she was sixteen who was poor but had around ten thousand books. 'I was really lucky,' she recounted. 'I could stand up and say, "Listen, I want to read something that's kind of like, hairy and dangerous with a nice female character". And it'd be like, "Here you go" ... I've read heavily ever since. The ones I liked most were those which made me realise I wasn't mad.'

When asked about her experience of being a woman in the music industry, Björk said, 'I guess I've taken being a woman for granted and decided early on that the only thing for me to do was ignore it. People used to say, "Wow, she can do all this *and* she's a woman!" That upset me – fuck you! Also, when I was growing up and making music, I never wanted to work with people because they were boys or girls ... All that female thing bored me to death.'

I understood what Björk was saying. It shouldn't be about choosing to work with boys or girls, it should be about who's best for the job. But equally I felt slightly disappointed that she was apparently swerving the very real issue of the misogyny – casual and explicit, occasional and everyday – that is ever-present in the music industry.

Imagine my delight, then, when I read Björk's *Pitchfork* interview with American critic Jessica Hopper in early 2015. Entitled 'The Invisible Woman', it was the interview I wish Björk had been ready to give for *Bollocks*.

She was essentially talking to Hopper about her new album, *Vulnicura*, and its intimate response to her break-up with a long-term partner. But there was more: Björk said that women are the 'glue between a lot of things', and that 'it's invisible, what women do'. She talked about her love of Kate Bush, Chaka Khan (particularly a remix album from the 1980s), Joni Mitchell's *Hejira*, widely agreed to be one of the most feminist albums ever made, and working with Venezuelan producer Alejandro Ghersi, aka Arca.

It was originally widely misreported that *Vulnicura* was produced by Arca instead of being *co-produced* by Björk and Arca. Björk admitted to *Pitchfork* that, for a decade, she didn't want to talk about that kind of thing – until finally, in 2006, she clarified her regular co-producing role on her website (it's worth noting that until he went into the studio with Björk, Arca had never made an album, whereas she had already recorded eight).

Journalists still insisted on giving the credit to Arca. Björk's response? 'I have sometimes thought about releasing a map of all my albums and just making it clear who did what.'

Without Hopper having to push, Björk went even further: 'I want to support young girls who are in their 20s now and tell them: *You're not just imagining things.* It's tough. Everything that a guy says once, you have to say five times.'

Björk recalled the time M.I.A. complained to her about not being recognised for her own work in the studio. Björk's advice? 'Just photograph yourself in front of the mixing desk in the studio and people will go, "Oh, OK! A woman with a tool, like a man with a guitar." Not that I've done that much myself, but sometimes you're better at giving advice than doing it yourself. I remember seeing a photo of Missy Elliott at the mixing desk in the studio and being like, *a-ha!*'

From time to time in the decades following the publication of *Never Mind the Bollocks*, Virago had suggested I update it. Reading Hopper's excellent article, I wondered if it might be the right moment.

In various ways, *Bollocks* has stayed in my life in the two decades since it was published.

Of all the books I have written – collaborative biographies with Mike Leigh and Danny Boyle; collaborative autobiographies with Steve Coogan and David Hare – *Never Mind the Bollocks* is still the one that elicits the most attention. I'm not mentioning this because it makes me feel good: my point is that the women's stories held within its pages meant something to people, ten, twenty years on from its publication. I still get emails from young women whose lives were made better in some small way by *Bollocks*; it's on various university reading lists and is referenced in several academic books.

Following his death in 1997, Jeff Buckley's mother Mary Guibert put a list of his book collection on jeffbuckley.com and there is *Bollocks*, happily sandwiched between Germaine

Greer's *The Female Eunuch*, Craig McGregor's *Bob Dylan: A Retrospective* and Webster's *Ninth New Collegiate Dictionary*. (I interviewed Buckley for the *NME* in the spring of 1995, but I doubt he made the connection; I think it's just a happy coincidence.)

Ten years on, in November 2017, *Publishers Weekly* ran a list of '10 Essential Music Books' and there, alongside Lizzy Goodman's brilliant *Meet Me in the Bathroom: Rebirth and Rock and Roll in New York City 2001–2011* and Greil Marcus's *Mystery Train: Images of America in Rock 'N' Roll Music*, is *Never Mind the Bollocks*.

The following year, The Quietus published its 'Top 40 Books About Music' and, to my surprise and delight, *Bollocks* was there again, alongside *England's Dreaming* by Jon Savage (for many people, including me, the best book on punk and 1970s Britain) and *The Sex Revolts: Gender, Rebellion and Rock 'N' Roll*, a super-smart book by Simon Reynolds and Joy Press.

The Sex Revolts came out the same year as *Bollocks*: if both are on a hotlist in 2017, perhaps people really do still want to read about music and gender.

Of course, being a writer, I procrastinated.

I read Rebecca Solnit's 2014 book *Men Explain Things to Me*, the title taken from her 2008 essay of the same name. In 2003, Solnit was at a party in a chalet above Aspen, Colorado, when the host summarised a book he had recently read a review of, ignoring Solnit's friend's attempts to alert him to the fact that Solnit herself had written the book. This essay is credited as inspiring the term 'mansplaining' and, later, 'manspreading'.

The introduction to Roxane Gay's collection of essays, *Bad Feminist*, is alone worth the cover price. She writes of the world changing 'faster than we can fathom in ways that are complicated', and of the cultural climate shifting. 'Feminism is flawed, but it offers, at its best, a way to navigate this shifting cultural climate ... Feminism has helped me believe my voice matters, even in this world where there are so many voices demanding to be heard.'

So, why a 'bad feminist'? Because Gay is flawed. She is human. She is not 'terribly well versed in feminist history'. As a younger woman, she disavowed feminism. 'I was called a feminist, and what I heard was, "You are an angry, sex-hating, man-hating victim lady person." This caricature is how feminists have been warped by the people who fear feminism most, the same people who have the most to lose when feminism succeeds.'

Over time, Gay – by her own admission – grew up and adjusted her expectations. Feminism, she writes, is a choice; even if a woman doesn't consider herself a feminist, Gay will still fight for her rights. She adds her voice to the call for a more intersectional kind of feminism, writing that women of colour, queer women and transgender women need to be 'better included in the feminist project'. Part of the reason Gay wasn't a feminist through her teens and twenties is because she didn't think that, as a black woman, it was for her. She concludes that 'when you can't find someone to follow, you have to find a way to lead by example'.

Feminism is complicated.

I turned from feminist tomes to memoir.

I reread *Just Kids*, Patti Smith's frank and fascinating account of her friendship with the late Robert Mapplethorpe, set against a backdrop of late 1960s and 1970s New York and winner of the 2010 National Book Award for Nonfiction in the US. I was drawn to the honesty in Tracey Thorn's bestselling

2013 memoir, *Bedsit Disco Queen: How I Grew Up and Tried to be a Popstar*, in which she describes both the trickiness of the music business and the pull of motherhood. I read a collection of Hopper's work, wryly entitled *The First Collection of Criticism by a Living Female Rock Critic*, Kim Gordon's *Girl in a Band* and *Hunger Makes Me a Modern Girl*, the moving memoir by Carrie Brownstein, one-time singer with the excellent Sleater-Kinney.

These books felt like a small revolution.

Women have published memoirs before, of course. When I interviewed Courtney Love for *The Face* in December 1992, she randomly opened her copy of Peggy Caserta's *Going Down with Janis*. 'This is the sort of biography I want written about me. I'll read out the first sentence: "I was stark naked, stoned out of my mind on heroin and the girl lying between my legs was Janis Joplin . . ."'

But these new memoirs were different. Caserta was Joplin's lover, a woman privy to Joplin's excesses – but she wasn't inside Joplin's head. These new memoirs not only refuse to reinforce the cliché of the rock star – the cliché that is, let's face it, mostly male – but also let the reader access their stories in a very personal manner.

Inspired, perhaps, in part at least, by Caitlin Moran's gamechanging and hugely successful 2011 memoir *How to Be a Woman*, in which she writes about masturbating, Viv Albertine explains in the first pages of *Clothes, Music, Boys* that she has never masturbated. It shouldn't now be shocking that women masturbate (or don't), but somehow everyone thought it was: go online and you'll see that Moran is still partly defined by it.

Clothes, Music, Boys is, of course, about so much more than minor details like masturbation or the fact that Sid Vicious dotted his 'i's with little circles. It's about how The Slits navigated punk and how Albertine herself handled relationships, survived cancer and the deaths of her friends. It's about life in all its 3D glory, but it's also about righting a wrong.

Even as recently as 2016, a celebration of punk at the British Library included a primer that read, 'Groups such as Sex Pistols, The Clash and Buzzcocks stimulated a nationwide wave of grassroots creativity'; Albertine crossed out the three band names on the primer and replaced them with The Slits, X-Ray Spex and Siouxsie and the Banshees.

Albertine added, 'What about the women!' and signed her name. It was very punk; but also, yes, what about the women?

These unconventional memoirs were tipping the balance away from male artists, but it was clear that there were more stories to be told.

It seemed a very long time since the 1995 publication of *Never Mind the Bollocks: Women Rewrite Rock* and its American counterpart, *Grrrls: Viva Rock Divas* (the name changed because, as my American editor explained, 'the term "bollocks" is not commonplace at all in the US'). So much had changed (technology), and yet very little had changed (women still aren't equal to men in the music industry).

By 2017, when I actually began work on the follow-up to *Bollocks*, it was twenty years since I'd started using the internet at home. In those two decades, the music industry had imploded and social media had exploded. With the huge drop in physical sales (vinyl may be cool again, but it doesn't pay young musicians' bills) and the advent of streaming services such as Spotify, which often pass on even less of the profit to musicians than record companies, all but the biggest artists (Adele, Beyoncé, Rihanna, Cardi B, et al.) know that if they want to make money then they have to tour.

The internet gives and it takes away: for journalists in the field of popular culture such as myself, it's been strange to watch the decline of the printed press and the rise of the blog and the idea that everyone can be a critic. Bands once reliant on record company deals can now release their own music to the public via Bandcamp; subscription services such as Spotify and Tidal have made everything available to everyone and the satisfaction of searching out rare vinyl is a dying hobby.

Even Spotify, it should be noted, has jumped onto the feminist bandwagon: on International Women's Day in 2018, it partnered with Smirnoff (when did the branding of *everything* happen?) to launch Spotify Equalizer. This new tool shows the gender breakdown of the artists you listen to. I got 81 per cent men to 18 per cent women (the shame), but was told I listened to more women than average. I equalised my Spotify playlist using a slider and a new playlist was created.

The monetising of feminism aside, the infrastructure of the music industry has, effectively, changed almost beyond all recognition. *Bollocks* was basically a series of interviews with female indie rockers. Now, indie is no more, at least not in any meaningful sense. In fact, thanks to Spotify's Playlist facility, in which you can pick your favourite song from an album and create a never-ending Best Of list, genre no longer exists in the same way.

My fourteen-year-old daughter doesn't differentiate between Cardi B, Blur, The Beatles, Beyoncé or Bowie (and that's just the Bs). A great song is a great song. Nor is her generation of digital natives particularly tribal; I would never be able to tell what her mates listened to from the way they look, whereas all my peers knew I was a new wave goth into Soft Cell, Siouxsie and the Banshees and The Cure when I was the same age.

I'm not on Facebook, and I spend less and less time on

Twitter (it's too angry, too divisive), but I love Instagram and am fascinated by how female artists use it as a platform not only to sell their work, but also to express themselves freely.

Patti Smith, who joined Instagram in March 2018, is almost unrivalled in her ability to write elegant, poetic posts, whether about Martin Luther King, Kirsten Dunst, the Renaissance painter Raphael, Stanley Kubrick, her two grown-up kids, creative people's gravestones or her set list for that night's show. She isn't on Instagram to sell records, but to communicate. It's almost a lost art.

Smith has 150,000 followers at the time of writing. A big hitter like Adele has 33 million (and follows no one). In April 2017, she posted three videos of herself dancing like crazy in front of her TV as she watched Beyoncé play Coachella. Those three videos, all without sound, racked up an astonishing 18 million views.

When Adele posted a screenshot of Ibeyi's second album, *Ash*, it got nearly half a million likes (and elicited an ecstatic response from the duo, who are Adele's labelmates: 'We are fucking twerking out of joy!'). When Adele wished Beyoncé a happy birthday ('We love you like no other'), the post got over a million likes.

Beyoncé herself is on another level with 117 million followers at the time of writing (she too follows no one). When she posted a photo of herself on the front cover of US *Vogue*'s September 2018 issue on Instagram, 2.5 million people liked it in twenty-four hours. A further 18,000 commented on it.

The same day as Beyoncé's *Vogue* post (6 August 2018), I looked at Cardi B's Instagram. Nearly 30 million followers and lots of photos of her husband Offset's cereal addiction. The most recent post was in fact a repost: '@iamcardib is now the ONLY artist of 2018 to have three songs sell over 500,000 pure copies in the US!' There were 1.6 million likes within twelve hours and 15,000 comments.

The trolls love Cardi B. They write of her 'crazy, funny, fake personality' and the 'fact' that she can't 'rap for shit'.

(It's worth a digression here: a former stripper from the Bronx, Cardi B is an easy target, a singer who got rich very quickly after the global success of 'Bodak Yellow'. People might be streaming her music in their millions, but she isn't given an easy ride. In April 2017, she visited UK hip-hop DJ Tim Westwood's show: he spent virtually no time discussing her music and randomly focused instead on her nails, her favourite weaves, her 'attitude to white chocolate', how many inches she likes, the number of men she's slept with, stripping ... I could go on, but he's not worth the effort. In May 2018, in an interview with *The Breakfast Club* radio show in America, controversial rapper Azealia Banks dismissed Cardi B as a 'caricature of a black woman', and added: 'I don't understand how we go from Beyoncé and Solange and Black Lives Matter to this [Cardi B]. I know we're not monolithic, but come on ... I just don't understand the extreme lack of couth. I've never seen that at the forefront of female rap. I didn't know the bar would be lowered so much. It was kind of like a culture shock.')

Whatever you think of Cardi B, it's a huge shame that, as much as social media gives women their own agency, it also takes it away. Female musicians are called names. Belittled. Insulted. Issued with death threats. With rape threats. Mostly by anonymous people (the majority of whom are probably men, let's face it) hoping no doubt to intimidate these powerful women into silence.

It's just not the same for male musicians: Liam Gallagher, with nearly 700,000 followers, posts a photo of himself jiggling a tambourine at the start of August 2018 and gets 43,000 likes and 285 comments. Scrolling down, I could only find this: 'You're getting more like Phil Collins by the day'. And it might not even be trolling.

Either way, it's clear that one of the central current issues for musicians, especially female musicians, is not only how they *use* the internet, but how they *protect* themselves from it.

Deciding on a title for the follow-up to *Never Mind the Bollocks* was the easy bit.

Although *A Seat at the Table* is obviously the title of Solange's powerful, political and personal 2016 album, the phrase is one that has resonated with me since I was a kid. Having a 'seat at the table' has always meant being part of the conversation. If you have a seat at the table, you have a voice. If you have a voice, you can effect change. As for the subtitle, the notion of an ongoing battle is implicit, but it also refers back to a message Tanya Donelly sent me after the publication of *Bollocks*: 'Thank you for being on the frontline'.

It goes without saying that I wanted to talk to Solange for this book, but she wasn't available for interview. Some reviews of *Bollocks* asked why certain women weren't in the book. I am sure the same question will be asked of *A Seat at the Table: Women on the Frontline of Music*. But here's the thing: if a woman isn't in either book, the chances are that I tried to get an interview with her. Some of the women declined on the basis that they are intensely private, others on the basis that they don't want to be in a book with other women. Fair enough. I wish there wasn't still a need for women to be given the opportunity to talk freely in their own space, but I personally think there is.

I sent many, many emails to many, many publicists. I took

my chances and sent direct messages to female musicians on Instagram. I asked those on Twitter to follow me back so that I could send a direct message. I nudged. I nudged again. I even did it the old-fashioned way – I picked up the phone. Sometimes a manager would be interested and then, a few months later, his or her artist would go global and silence would inevitably follow.

I get it: these artists are protected more than ever before by managers, agents, publicists, PRs and so on. Their interview schedules are based around promoting their records and world tours, not appearing in someone else's book. I would have loved the opportunity to talk to Beyoncé without any limit on time. Ditto Janelle Monáe, an artist as exciting as Prince and as determined to push the notion of gender as David Bowie was before her.

I understand that Britain is a small island (about to get smaller), and why engage with a book – of all things – for a relatively small publisher when 18 million people watch your funny Beyoncé dance?

I quickly realised that, even if I had access to a Knowles sister, my time would be ridiculously limited. The fact that the A*-listers were inaccessible turned out to be a blessing in disguise; it gave me the opportunity to curate a list of women whose music I loved, some of whose stories haven't yet been widely told or who are overlooked because they aren't a big presence on social media. It was oddly liberating to have the freedom to pull together a group of immensely talented women who have compelling stories to tell about how their backgrounds shaped them and their identity defined them. As working-class women, gay women, women of colour or older women. Or, simply, as women.

As genre no longer really exists, I no longer had to worry

about it. I could talk to Alison Moyet, a pop star whose career has spanned a breathtaking four decades, who has sold over twenty million records and is making some of her best work now. On the title track of her 2017 album, *Other*, Moyet writes, 'So I cut out whichever shape I need . . . I'm as free as I've ever been'. It's a sentiment that would surely resonate with the other women in the book, women who both shape-shift and demand freedom.

I could interview Dream Wife, making a name for themselves on the post-punk London scene; or Georgia, an extraordinary young drummer who was too nervous to go into the school music room at lunchtime because it was full of boys; or Catherine Marks, voted UK Producer of the Year at the 2018 Music Producers Guild (MPG) Awards – not Female Producer, but Producer.

I could talk to Jessica Curry, the BAFTA Award-winning composer of the score for the game *Everybody's Gone to the Rapture*, and CHVRCHES' Lauren Mayberry about their frankly terrifying experiences of being trolled online. To Kalie Shorr, about how she and kindred young female musicians in Nashville dealt with the entrenched sexism in the capital of country music by forming Song Suffragettes, a songwriting collective for women. To Nadine Shah, who writes brutally honest lyrics of love and loss, but who is also unashamedly political. Her most recent album, *Holiday Destination*, was about the plight of displaced people and the global shift to the right. Her next album will be about 'issues specific to women', including gynaecological issues rarely discussed in public, never mind on records.

I met French-Cuban twins Ibeyi at XL Records in Notting Hill as the sky was turning an apocalyptic orange at midday. I sat there, helpless, as tears were shed when they talked about their late father, a member of Buena Vista Social Club. I met

Maggie Rogers – made famous overnight when a video of Pharrell moved to tears when listening to her song 'Alaska' during a masterclass at NYU went viral – at an Airbnb in east London. She was generous with her time, but it was clear how hard it is for a fiercely creative and independent woman to be catapulted into the limelight by a man.

Emmy the Great shared wonderful stories about growing up in Hong Kong, moving to East Grinstead and the difficulties of making a living from music in the early twenty-first century. She introduced me to Mitski, a singular artist born in Japan and now living in New York, but only after living in a dozen other countries in between. Tracey Thorn talked of the feminist books she 'hoovered up' when arriving at Hull University to study English, and of having no control of her public persona when she became famous.

It was summer 2018 by the time I met Radio 1 presenter Clara Amfo in a rooftop restaurant in Soho, where she talked about her strong and stubborn Ghanaian mother; her assumption, as a kid, that she was equal to her brothers and how 'UKIP Dave' tweeted his disapproval when she started DJing at Radio 1.

Norwegian pop star Sigrid, then just twenty-one, was in such demand that I didn't get enough time with her to write a chapter, but no matter – her experience of the music business mirrors that of plenty of women in *A Seat at the Table*, and can be encapsulated in a few choice sentences. 'Don't Kill My Vibe', her debut single which became a global hit, was inspired by an earlier songwriting session with two men. In the song she writes about being shut down and treated like a child. She sighed as she explained, 'I felt like my opinions weren't respected. Maybe because I was young as well as female. I wrote the song as a universal message: don't just smile, speak out. Say when something isn't okay. "Don't Kill My Vibe" is so aggressive because I had that anger in me. It was good to get it out. I'm very happy if young women relate to the lyrics, especially if it gives them permission to be angry.'

Other young artists on the brink of success were also pushed for time because everyone else wanted to talk to them too – which augurs well for the future of women in music. Poppy Ajudha made a huge effort to meet me at a Brighton restaurant during the Great Escape music festival between giving several radio interviews and performing live. She talked about growing up with a mother whose family are from Britain and a father whose family are from St Lucia and India ('I know what it's like to be objectified as a mixed-race woman'), about coming out on Instagram ('I still cringe a bit') and Cardi B's complex character ('whether she's a feminist or not, she illuminates a more modern way of expressing the female voice').

Kate Tempest, meanwhile, arranged to meet on an abandoned sofa in a large south London park. I found her there with Murphy, her husky, and, aware that she isn't keen on interviews, was surprised she was happy to talk for almost three hours. Forced off the sofa by the noise of an industrial lawnmower, we moved to a park bench, where we were briefly interrupted by a jogger desperate to tell Tempest that she is a genius poet and performer (she blushed). And then, finally, on to a cafe to drink tea among the local yummy mummies (Tempest apologised in advance).

She talked, at length, about books, music, sexual capital and everything in between. Sometimes wary of giving too much of her private self away, Tempest surprised me with her honesty: 'As a woman, the temptation is to go out onto stage – and I've done it so many times – and try to be liked. You need them to like you before they'll listen to you. You need them to relax in your company. The best thing you can do as a woman is make yourself look a bit stupid and unthreatening. You are effectively saying, "I've worked really hard and I've got lots to say, but don't worry, I'm still a woman and still stupid".'

One of the last women I interviewed was Natalie Merchant, former singer of 10,000 Maniacs and, since the early 1990s, a solo artist. In the scorching summer of 2018, she sang for over two hours in a local church in my hometown of Brighton, opening with interpretations of Victorian and modernist poems, receiving rapturous applause for 'Motherland' and 'Texas', and unexpectedly climbing the stairs to the balcony and leading the audience in a singalong of tunes from Lionel Bart's *Oliver!* soundtrack.

After the gig, I was taken backstage to meet Merchant by her female tour manager. She sat on the sofa drinking tea as her guitarist, Erik Della Penna, packed up the tour van. Merchant has been in the music business for thirty-five years, not all of them easy. As she explains in her chapter, she has found a way of remaining true to herself, through both the music she is now performing and the work she has done for the past two decades as a community organiser and volunteer.

But the first woman I interviewed for this book stayed in my mind as I got on with interviewing all the others. It seems a long time since I battled the high winds of Storm Doris to meet Héloïse Letissier in her east London hotel room in February 2017. As her alter ego, Christine and the Queens, she had already released *Chaleur Humaine*. Watch her dance and, like her idol Michael Jackson, you'll see that she *is* the music. She sings in English and French, often flipping seamlessly from one to the other in the same song. She identifies as pansexual, but that matters less than the music – as her sexuality is in the music, so the music *is* her sexuality.

In 2018, Christine cut her hair short and returned as Chris. Listen to the Jackson-esque funk of *Girlfriend*, the first single from the second album, *Chris*, and you won't be able to keep still. Watch the video, in which Chris is macho and feminine at the same time. Be reminded that two decades into the twenty-first century, gender is no longer just about male vs female, but about all the incremental states of being a woman.

When I met Letissier, I was ready to talk about Solnit, Gay and the new wave of feminists. Apologetically, she said she hadn't read them. And there it was: the women in this book might or might not read Solnit, but you can be sure they know what mansplaining is – after all, they work in the male-dominated music industry.

I decided, in Letissier's hotel room, that feminist theory didn't matter. She was doing her own thing – pushing away perceived notions of identity like Bowie before her – and what a glorious thing to be doing. I didn't want *A Seat at the Table* to be a clickbait book in which women gave knee-jerk responses to feminism. I was more interested in the impact on their lives of social media, Spotify and Bandcamp. In how these women try to support each other rather than compete against each other. In how they are trying, finally, to drop that ancient female habit of trying to be liked by conforming to a stereotype. Or in superstars like Cardi B, how they are challenging and subverting the old-fashioned notion of feminism.

In every interview I did, I was reminded how much has changed since the first book. In *Bollocks*, I lamented the lack of women featured on the cover of the *NME*; now the music weekly only exists online and has none of its previous influence. As I am writing this, Janelle Monáe has just posted an image on Instagram of all the women of colour who have recently graced fashion magazines – including Beyoncé on the cover of *Elle* and Rihanna on the cover of the September 2018 issue of British *Vogue*, the first time a black woman has been on the cover in the magazine's 102-year history.

More female musicians than ever are coming through – so many that I have been in a panic every day for two years about missing out on one great female musician or another – but there need to be more, especially behind the scenes. It shouldn't be a surprise that Catherine Marks was Producer of the Year, but in 2017 the hard fact is that only 6 per cent of the Music Producers Guild's members were women.

I wanted to know, above all, how these women have got to where they are today – what their childhoods were like, how easy or challenging it was to get into music, what their expectations of the music industry were, how they have been treated and how they have found their voices.

I let the women in *A Seat at the Table* talk. And talk and talk. Eighteen of them, in all, talked to me between February 2017 and October 2018. They have, inevitably, released albums, or made big creative decisions, since I interviewed them. Christine became Chris after Letissier had approved her chapter. But time will always march forward, and my hope is that each of these women's oral histories not only captures a moment in our very fast-moving times, but will resonate in some meaningful way for the reader.

So, after eighteen months of talking to women with a kaleidoscope of experiences, I went away and transcribed the interviews, edited them and sent them back to each woman for approval.

Here are their stories, told in their own words. Not all of them identify as feminists, but when they speak, they expect to be heard.

Amy Raphael, Brighton, August 2018

CHRISTINE AND THE QUEENS

Héloïse Letissier was born in Nantes, where her father is an English professor at the university and her mother a French and Latin teacher at a local school. Letissier started theatre studies in Lyon, but didn't complete her course. In 2010 she went to London, where she hung out with drag queens and started to tentatively sing. Christine and the Queens, both an alter ego and a stage name, was born. The first album, Chaleur Humaine, *was released on Because Records in the UK in 2016. A single, 'Girlfriend', came out in May 2018, this time by Chris and the Queens. One day, she has said, she might simply be 'C'. Chris, the album, was released in September 2018.*

As a kid, I wrote short stories that used to creep my mum out. At first she assumed that these were stories I'd found on the internet. But they were from inside my head. Perhaps my parents were too liberal: they let me watch films like *The Elephant Man* when I was nine. I also read books early, such as *Belle du Seigneur*, Albert Cohen's terrifying book about love and relationships. And Dickens. The Brontë sisters. French poets. Heavy stuff.

Love felt doomed before it had even started. The love letters I wrote at the age of ten were like me writing to Rochester.

The boys' responses were simple. 'I just don't get it . . . what about your tits?'

Me: 'Don't you want a connection through life and time?'

Boys: 'No, I just want tits.'

I was maybe too intense. It's not a problem, it just made me think differently. In a way I'm thankful because it gave me a strong interior life and I became obsessed with freaks and acceptance and how to relate to others. On the other hand, it made it hard for me to connect to kids my age because I was immersed in this different, older world. I was lost in literature and movies.

I was always more interested in writing material to perform myself. It's what I'm doing now; it makes more sense for me to do everything because I'm not so good at interpreting people's words. So I realised I could write plays and stage them, which was always about shaping a world for myself to be comfortable in. Or finding a way of expressing myself properly.

I am fully aware that I'm a control freak. I even developed a fixation about having a face and a body that I didn't choose. I'm obsessed with Michael Jackson, but even if I wouldn't do what he did, I could understand this idea of wanting to redefine everything, including your physical self. Sometimes I'm infuriated at how I didn't get to choose . . . At the same time, I have this body forever and I will grow old with it.

Christine is more than a stage character. It's about embracing what I have. It's a survival technique. By choosing 'Christine' as a name, I am reconnecting with everything I actually am. My face, my muscles, my desires, the dick I don't have, the pussy I do have. Having a stage character makes it more confusing for people because they often think it's about becoming someone else and actually, for me, it's kind of the opposite. I'm allowing myself to be utterly naked, exposed and bare.

I know how appealing it is for people to imagine that Christine is some other person, but it's just me. A totally unfiltered version of me. I honestly feel that sometimes the character is me in everyday life. I spent a very long time censoring myself; I was terrified of just appearing in the daylight, of being judged all the time.

I was loved as a kid, so I can't blame my upbringing. I'm just a strange person.

I sometimes wonder how different my life would have been if I was a guy. I was utterly and totally receptive to the shame inflicted on girls quite early on. There are so many different ways to be ashamed of everything. Smells, hair, not pretty enough ... I was even receptive to that shit at junior school. I got poisoned by all the self-hatred that can float in the air. Every girl deals with it differently; I was suffocated by it.

France is still a pretty macho culture. I was raised exactly like my brother and I could express all my desires and wishes at home. But it wasn't okay, outside the home, to *want*. Women are the ones who are *wanted*. I couldn't understand that shit. I didn't know how to be wanted. I didn't understand the parade of it.

It's hard to tell how I might have reacted to the critical success of my first album had I been a male performer. I react really well to rejection – it's a dynamic I've been engaged with for years. Suddenly my music was being widely embraced and I was like, 'Oh shit, they love me.' What should I do with all that love coming my way? I was concerned that critical and commercial success might kill something. Or diminish the energy. But, then again, there are so many more things to do with Christine. There are so many things to be done in terms of representing female performers in pop music and in terms of how one can exist as a woman.

I don't find any of the extracurricular activities easy. I over-analyse everything.

As an artist, I am forgiven for having terrible social anxiety and disliking parties. But I don't know how to behave when I meet fans. When I really admire an artist I am always really scared of meeting him or her in a social situation. I want them to stay on stage. I am afraid when people ask me for a selfie; I am sure I'm going to ruin the moment. I tell them they are meeting Peter Parker and not Spider-Man. Maybe I should start wearing glasses off stage.

It's easy to understand the difference between Peter Parker and Spider-Man, but as soon as I was successful in France, I had to repeatedly explain who Christine is, who I am, how we relate to each other. I'm not saying the UK is like a fantasy land, but me being a young queer woman was immediately more understood. In France I had to say things over and over. They thought I could be more feminine. 'Why don't you embrace your femininity with a dress?' Oh dear. Let's go back to the beginning. Let's explain how I don't relate to gender.

People know me now in France, but at first it was tough and some of the feedback I received was incredibly violent. Strangely enough, not homophobic, as I don't look that threatening as a pansexual girl. I'm not butch. I don't look like I'm going to threaten the patriarchy. 'Oh well, she's fiddling around with girls and touching pussies sometimes.'

The abuse was about me not being feminine enough. Not fuckable enough. It's insane. After one of my first gigs, a guy came up after and said, 'Do you really think you're interesting enough to look at for forty-five minutes? You're not even fuck-able.' This is where we fucking are!

It's as though I don't belong. I'm not allowed to exist as *me*. If you don't play the game you immediately face more resistance. I want to bend the rules. This is why I love the metaphor of being a virus: how can I go there, fuck it up a bit and start a domino reaction? This is why I'm interested in the pop vector. If you make a great pop song, people have to remember it and then they're fucked because they have to check you out on Google and then they're exposed to you. If you can say just one sentence that can fuck things up a bit . . .

It was ever thus: just think about Bowie in the 1970s. I watched *In Bed with Madonna* again recently; it came out in 1991, but it's still really modern. I was freaked out! We still need Madonna now, fucking things up a bit. I don't see nearly enough progress. I often wonder: am I fucking things up as much as I wanted to? Am I really going to change anything, or am I just going to pass by?

Maybe I can inspire one girl.

Or ten girls.

It will be enough.

Christine was born out of the most sexist thing that ever happened to me. I wanted to be a theatre director and I was crushed. Violently. It was the first time I properly realised that being a woman would be a problem if I wanted to be a boss.

I entered theatre school in Lyon in 2008, when I was twenty. I already knew I wanted to be a stage director. I was committed. I began to notice as the year wore on that male and female students were treated very differently. Women were encouraged to be naked on stage as a way to be more at ease. Guys were encouraged to direct plays. It was always insidious, as sexism is. It always makes you wonder if *you're* the problem.

During the course of the year, two guys wanted to stage plays and were allowed to do so. I had written a play and wanted to stage it. The course leaders told me I wasn't ready. I asked if there was a system to evaluate my work; they couldn't answer any of my questions. I realised they were douchebags.

I decided to stage my play anyway and to invite them to the production.

When they heard I was rehearsing for a play, they called me in and told me to leave the course. I wanted to know which rules I had infringed, but they wouldn't discuss it.

It was the most violent thing that has happened in my life. My craft is my shit. I couldn't process it. I stopped eating for a week. I was furious. The students started a petition to get me reinstated in the school; no one understood why I'd been thrown out.

And then I got dumped. Jesus, that was a shitty year. I couldn't write any more. I wasn't really living. I was suicidal. I hope I never, ever go back to that place and feel that way again.

I wanted to somehow disappear, so I left for London with heavy make-up hiding the stress rashes on my face. My father took me there as a kid and it always felt like a welcoming, diverse city. My father, an English professor, didn't talk to me in English when I was growing up, but we did sometimes listen to the BBC and he passed on his love of British culture.

I thought I was doing something really rock 'n' roll, but I sat on Eurostar on my own thinking I had lost it. When I arrived in London, I was too scared to even take a bus. I stayed in a house belonging to a friend of my father's and I was so unbalanced that everything felt like an extension of the chaos in my head, even the messy rooms packed with piles of things.

I thought leaving Lyon might be enough, but I was still fucking miserable. I had rashes in London instead of in Lyon. I was gasping for air.

Then, one night, I went to Madame Jojo's, the Soho nightclub which closed in 2014. I'd been reading Professor Judith Butler's book *Gender Trouble*, and seeing the drag queens take on female identity was really exciting. They in turn recognised something in me, coming up to me after the show, looking at me with their big eyes and asking if I was going to be okay. I knew, at that moment, that I would eventually be safe.

I clung desperately to the queens. They took me back to their home and I spent time with them. They showed me things, such as a documentary called *Paris is Burning* about the vogueing culture and finding your own family, finding the people that soothe you. For the first time, I decided to stop pleasing people, to just be myself. I started embracing everything I used to hate. I was so moved by drag culture: a flaw is immediately seen as a bonus; your weird nose becomes your greatest feature. It was so empowering. Every scar is a jewel. You are not dirty, you are superbly dirty. It's fabulous.

Jean Genet, one of my favourite writers, said, 'I am going to be called the great whore'. After meeting the queens, I thought, 'I'm going to do the same thing. I'm going to create my own legend.'

As soon as I wrote Christine's name down, I gave a name to my anger.

And, in the same moment, I discovered how to sing.

I hated my voice. I still don't really like it, but I make myself work with things I don't really like because it makes me more efficient.

The queens encouraged me to sing. Louder! Louder! They were the first ones who thought I had a good voice. I was whining a lot, telling them how envious I was of their stage performances. They didn't indulge me; it was kind of tough love.

They told me I could sing, but I just sighed and insisted I couldn't. They kept saying, 'Just sing.'

'No, I can't . . . '

'JUST SING.'

'I can't. I hate my voice.'

'Just shut the fuck up and sing.'

Eventually I started to sing and they said, 'You have a good voice. Use it.'

It distracted me from my sadness and it gave me a new obsession. I was only in London for three weeks, but the queens educated me, partly by the documentaries they showed me, but also by telling me to sing – and to sing louder.

I haven't seen the queens since. Some journalists called them and it made me feel so fucking bad. When I did my first French TV, they wrote to me saying, 'Oh wow, you were really serious about singing!'

So serious! I discovered how soothing it is just to sing. It can be primal but melodious. It's so intimate; you can't really cheat with your voice.

I started singing in English because it allowed me to be incautious. The first songs in English were quite raw and defiant: 'iT' and 'Be Freaky'. 'iT' because the capital 'T' makes me think about a dick. I fantasise about having a dick in the song.

It was fantastic to write again. After the shock of theatre school in Lyon, the words came back to me. Oh my dear Lord, thank you.

Was it something that arrived, or blossomed, or that I finally looked in the eye? Despite overanalysing everything all the time, music is still mysterious to me.

Maybe I shouldn't question where it came from. Anyway, the songs arrived quickly. I self-produced them in a lo-fi style using GarageBand, and my theatre school friends, who had been worried about me, listened to them. They said they were good, so I posted them on the internet.

Les Inrocks, one of the main French music magazines, had an online contest. I posted three songs and immediately got into the finals. I didn't even have the time to want it.

I started doing gigs. When I showed up on stage in my crappy customised H&M suit, there were ten people in the audience, so I could do my own shit. I felt really present, which doesn't often happen to me. I wanted to do it again immediately, to recapture that feeling of being in the moment. Nothing else mattered. It made me feel I could belong.

I brought a crazy amount of energy to my live shows, but equally I hadn't mastered how to do them: my computer would crash on stage and I'd shout, 'That's okay! I'm going to tell you a story.' I was almost drooling with energy! The audiences were half freaked out and half empathetic. I could see them thinking, 'What is she even doing?'

Sometimes I would go on stage and stare at the audience without saying anything. French dudes just wanted to see a live gig and there I was, offering them silence, dance moves and a computer. People were intrigued by it. They didn't know what was happening. It was more like performance art or cabaret than a pop show. And there was always one dude shouting, 'Get naked!'

Those early shows were like an installation of Tormented Young Girl Doing Pop Music. I always used to say that I was playing the role of pop star and then I became addicted to the idea of *being* a pop star.

I often reference Andy Kaufman because I'm intrigued by the way he dealt with performance. When I started out, I had this manic energy and Christine was more defiant than she is now. I wanted to play on how uneasy seeing a young girl on stage can make people feel. I was pushing the awkwardness and the uneasiness. When I stood on stage without talking, I felt like Andy Kaufman.

At least I could dance! Even when I wanted to stage plays, I was interested in dance. I loved Pina Bausch and Maggie Moran. And, of course, Michael Jackson. Even my dancing wasn't properly understood in France at first. And now they're all dancing in video clips! Not that I launched a trend . . . it was just that I was seen as being a bit weird because, instead of playing an instrument, I was dancing.

I fell in love with Michael Jackson when I was really young. I was obsessed with him. He was everything and nothing. Black, white. Female, male. Mainly a dancing energy. It was more than a love story, though: the groove in his music stopped me from getting too much into the *chanson française* vibe. *La chanson française* is basically talking with three notes behind it. There's *no* groove in it; it's words with a hint of music. In my opinion, anyway. I don't think anyone can deny that the French language and pop music have always had an odd relationship. It's not a happy marriage. Luckily, hip-hop has become the new pop, and hip-hop sounds great in French.

But when I said I was going to work on a French pop record, there was a sharp intake of breath. *Chaleur Humaine* is sung in both English and French. You might think French sounds sexier, but it's the opposite for us. Plus there's the issue of being immediately understood, of being heard in the UK and in the States.

I wanted to look beyond France; I signed to Because Music because it's an Anglo-French label. I liked the fact that they would get my musical references. Equally importantly, they didn't want me to be sexy. A&R people had been saying to me, 'I love what you do, but you should be sexier.' My response? 'You don't get me. See you later.' Shame on them.

Because Music wasn't even sure *Chaleur Humaine* would sell. They took a bet on me and it paid off. Sometimes talking about my story freaks me out because it sounds a little like a fairy tale. The queens urged me to sing. I got into the finals of a competition. I slowly got into the music business by doing more and more gigs. I put a band together and signed to a record label. I didn't even have time to think of it as a job or something that could make a living at some point. I got really lucky.

I wake up every day and think, 'Fuck, how did I get here?' It's a delicious feeling.

The release of the first album was so interesting for me in terms of how Christine was perceived. I love to read the comments below the line for hours, especially the French ones. Especially this idea of being fuckable enough, of being in or out of the male gaze. They don't want me to be sexual in *that* way. Oh, I'm going to be *so* sexual.

My obsession is to redefine what everything means. I want to be sexual in my own way. If I can't escape the male gaze, maybe I'll use it, deflect it, make something out of it. Confuse people.

Why do we ever think we can escape politics? Everything is political. My stardom is that of a young, white, queer French woman. I would have written something different if I was a black guy. People ask me if a pop star can be political today and I'm always saying, the choice *not* to be political is a political act.

The music industry and the media are as sexist as they ever were. I've stopped counting the number of times people have assumed that a man wrote and produced my songs.

'You produced this shit?'

'Yeah?'

Man falls off chair in response.

Or:

'Some fucking great tunes, man. Who's writing for you?'

'Listen to the fucking lyrics. Do you think someone else could write those for me? Do you?'

There is no one way to be a woman. There's no one way to be a man. I could say that there's no one way to be anything. The question of identity for me is really problematic because I do relate to my female body – I don't feel like I'm trapped in my body – but equally I feel like I'm a constant stream of possibilities. That includes being an old man, a young boy, a young queer woman, a horny pansexual woman. It's a constant flow.

I grew up with narrow and unimaginative versions of what a woman could be. I knew many strong women, but not the many different ways of defining yourself as a woman. For example, when Lorde arrived with acne scars and great lyrics, she was so different to anyone who had come before and it made me realise how much we lacked diversity of any kind. Thank god she arrived! I wish she had been around when I was younger.

I read about being a black woman: you grow up and you see films with blonde girls all the time. You never see yourself.

There is no one for you to identify with. It's like growing up as a lesbian and being surrounded by heteronormative movies: you're always having to trick yourself into finding the one character you could maybe identify with.

When I thought of Christine, I wanted to fit in a space and just exist.

I see artists experimenting with many ways of playing the female part, but not really subverting it. Lady Gaga was quite interesting when she was playing with a freaky idea of what it means to be sexy, almost in a cyborg-creature way. I had a Björk phase before high school, when I was about twelve. I loved the fact that she was a creature creating sounds that didn't exist before. She was birthing a new thing.

Sometimes on stage I say, 'Hi, I'm a young boy dreaming of being Beyoncé', because it's a distortion. I don't see myself as being the ultimate sexy woman in the male gaze. Beyoncé *is* very much in the male gaze but she uses it to be powerful. In fact, Beyoncé is using the shapes given to women to empower herself: she is both sensual, sexy and very much in control of everything she's giving you. That's a way to claim back your power as a woman.

There are women – feminists, even – who think Beyoncé shouldn't 'flaunt' her sexuality. You can't tell a woman to own her own body and then shame her for doing so. In France I've been called a good feminist and role model because I wear clothes. Christ, they don't get it. Maybe I'll be butt naked on a future album . . .

I've always said that I want to be political, sweaty, dirty, high-tempo, really sad. I am always sad. I try to be less sad, but you can't defy your deep nature. I do feel I have more strength these days, which is good.

The truth is, I don't know what it means to be myself or to be someone else. I have a fragmented notion of identity. I always wanted to be a star, but sometimes when you *are* a star, you actually don't exist any more. People project on to you all the time. You can only have control over what you say and do; the rest of it is out of your hands. If you think about it too much, it's truly bizarre: people remember you for something you don't even know you gave them.

IBEYI

French-Cuban twin sisters Lisa-Kaindé Díaz and Naomi Díaz grew up in Paris, but regularly spend time in Cuba. Their late father was the famed Cuban percussionist, Anga Díaz, who received a Grammy for his work with the Latin jazz band Irakere and was also a member of Buena Vista Social Club. Their mother, who is also their manager, is French-Venezuelan singer Maya Dagnino. Ibeyi, who take their name from the Yoruba for 'twins', released their debut eponymous album on XL Recordings in 2015. Their second album, Ash, was released two years later. Lisa-Kaindé plays the piano and is primary songwriter and singer, while Naomi sings backup and plays the cajón and Batá drum, traditional Peruvian/Cuban percussion instruments.

Naomi Díaz: We come from a very arty family. Our mother took us to shows in Paris: hip-hop, soul, jazz. Not so much rock. Our maternal grandfather is a painter – he's crazy, but we love him. Our maternal grandmother was a teacher who worked with refugee children.

Lisa-Kaindé Díaz: Our paternal grandmother sang in

church and our paternal grandfather was a saxophone player. Our father was a genius percussionist. Our mother is a musician without an instrument; she has an amazing ear and she writes lyrics with me.

We were raised by two incredible, strong, independent women, our mother and our grandmother. Naomi and I were taught that we could do anything we set our minds to if we worked like crazy and really went for it. We were lucky. We grew up in a house where art was given to us as the answer. 'If you feel sad, go and see that movie.' 'Oh, you feel like that? Go and listen to this album.' It's the biggest gift our parents gave us. Art and music to make us feel better and to make us better people.

In fact, our family considered music so important that we were put in music school when we were seven to study classical music. Our childhood memories are dominated by music; we used to fall asleep at our grandmother's listening to the audiobook of *La Flûte Enchantée* [*The Magic Flute*] by Mozart. Not just the musical parts, but the whole story.

Naomi: Our grandmother's sofa was shaped like a boat and we were put on there to listen to the audiobook, but inevitably we fell asleep.

Lisa-Kaindé: Grandmother used to sing us lullabies, too, which are now part of the world we have created in our music. When we were fifteen, our mother took us to a Yoruba choir to finally sing the songs we had been listening to during our childhood.

Naomi: At first we didn't want to go!

Lisa-Kaindé: We really didn't! It was on a Friday afternoon, when we'd just finished a week of school and we were two grumpy teenagers: 'Oh god, we don't want to go and sing with old people.' But the minute the choir started singing, we changed our minds. We could feel it.

Naomi: Instantly.

Lisa-Kaindé: Yeah. And then we went every week. Yoruba comes from Nigeria and Benin and when the slaves were shipped to Cuba, the culture remained there. It's a huge part of Cuban culture. And it's a huge part of our lives and our music. When journalists ask us to describe our music, we say we make 'contemporary Negro spirituals'. It's the closest thing we have found to describe it: a mix of Yoruba prayers and hip-hop beats, electronic sounds, rhythms and voices.

Our father unconsciously influenced us: he was never afraid to mix different types of music in order to create his own! And through his legacy, his albums and videos, we learned that it was important to have no boundaries when it comes to creativity.

Our mother put everything she could at our disposal: as well as music, there were books, so many books, both fiction and non-fiction. Photography books. Art books. Music books. One day our mother laughed because Naomi came up from her room and said, 'Mama, I just discovered an incredible new artist. Do you know Janis Joplin?'

Naomi: I was only twelve. It was very funny, though.

Lisa-Kaindé: Our family could see the excitement we had about hearing an artist for the first time. For example, I cried the first time I heard Nina Simone's version of 'I Put A Spell On You' when I was fourteen. I was at music camp and it was my turn to perform a song. Someone handed me a set of headphones to listen to a track and it was Nina Simone. I was watching all these kids running around and then they just kind of vanished and all I was aware of was the song.

It was the first time I had an out-of-body experience while listening to music. I feel very emotional simply talking about that moment. Nina Simone somehow made sense of the world for me. I didn't need to look like someone else, I could just be me.

I started singing the song and I could see the effect it had on people. I believed every single word that came out of my mouth.

Suddenly I had an identity. Previously I was always someone's best friend, only invited to a party because of the people I hung out with. I always felt clumsy and not quite able to fit in. I was always 'Lisa who?' until I started singing, and then I became 'Lisa the singer'.

I had no particular interest in being famous for the sake of it; I idolised Ella Fitzgerald, Meshell Ndegeocello, Björk and Frida Kahlo. Though, in the case of Kahlo, I am disappointed by how much such a freethinking woman was slowed down by love.

Anyway, even when I sang 'I Put A Spell On You' at music camp, it still didn't occur to me that I could be a singer.

Naomi: I saw a change in you when we went into the studio for the first time. I don't think I'd ever seen you trusting your instincts before. It was so powerful. Being in the studio for the first time was really powerful for me as well. I felt free, I knew what I wanted – and you and Richard [Russell, owner of XL Recordings] trusted my judgement 100 per cent. I realised that I had an ear and a love for producing.

Lisa-Kaindé: We were recently asked in an interview what we thought of sisterhood and I said that it was one of the most important aspects of being a woman. We are encouraged to think that there can only be one woman at the top of her game in any genre, and of course that makes women compete against each other. The women at the top tend not to help the next generation because they are scared of it.

Naomi: Scared the younger woman is going to take their place.

Lisa-Kaindé: I heard a famous black model telling a younger black model that she didn't help her because she was constantly being told that the younger model would take her place. Whereas in fact it's so important to embrace young people and help them because, guess what? The reality is that there are not enough women at the top. And of course there is space for more than one! The only way women can get to the top is by helping each other.

I'd say that, on the whole, female artists do help one another. Although we have it easier than our mother's generation – if only because we are expected to work as opposed to stay at home and raise a family. We also have to deal with things like social media. As a famous woman, the messages you receive every day are truly disgusting. We need to feel strong and support each other so that we can fight.

I can't imagine not helping another female artist, but then I can't imagine not being a feminist. There are as many ways to be a feminist as there are to be a woman. I ask myself every day, 'Do I want to appear in this video naked because it's going to sell records? Or might I consider it because it's what I want to do?'

No matter what the question, if the answer is 'It's what I want to do', then I am being a feminist.

Naomi: I totally agree. There are so many ways to be a feminist, and mine is to know what I want and what I don't want. To be 100 per cent myself. To never settle for what other people want or believe.

Lisa-Kaindé: If you could succeed as a pop star without sexualising yourself, then a lot of young girls would follow your example. You don't have to be perfect.

My friends and I don't dress the same. For me it all comes down to diversity. Don't commit to the mould they made for you. Also, you can sexualise yourself in thousands of different ways.

It all relates to how you are represented. When we were growing up in France, we weren't represented. The only poster I had was of political activist Angela Davis; she was one of the few black women at that time with natural hair. One of the best messages I've had from a fan said, 'My daughter is so happy to rock her natural hair because of you'. My god! Me accepting my hair helped a girl accept herself. It took me years – so many years – to realise how beautiful an Afro is. I couldn't see people rocking it, being proud of it.

If you can see someone in the public eye doing something as ostensibly simple as rocking an Afro, you too can wear your hair naturally.

Lisa-Kaindé: It was amazing to grow up in two countries and with two cultures. Being French-Cuban means many things to us, but perhaps most significantly that we are totally unafraid of anyone who is different to us.

Naomi: We grew up among rich people and really poor people in Cuba. It was beautiful to spend time with everybody, regardless of their backgrounds.

Lisa-Kaindé: I guess when you're a kid, you develop an aptitude to be happy anywhere and to connect with anyone. It's a really important lesson because life is like that. Which is not to say we don't lead very different lives; Naomi and I remember a close friend telling us that she was pregnant at the age of sixteen. Whaaat? We half-European women tend to get pregnant when we're much older because we have things to do!

Naomi: Like party.

Lisa-Kaindé: Like change the world. Travel. Be a woman. *And* party.

Naomi: I've wanted kids forever, but we're not only here to have kids! People seem to forget that sometimes. We have work to do. However, our friend is raising her son so well – he will grow up to be a good man.

Lisa-Kaindé: I read a James Baldwin book which included the famous letter he sent to his fifteen-year-old nephew in 1962. He wrote, 'Know whence you came. If you know whence you came, there is really no limit to where you can go ... There is no reason for you to try to become like white men and there is no basis whatever for their impertinent assumption that they must accept you.'

He told his nephew – also James – that not only did he not have to worry about being accepted by white men, but it was also vital he accepted himself. It's an amazing thing to say to a child. Much as we might like to think otherwise, we all try to fit in. Like when your mother comes to pick you up at school and she's a little bit weird compared to the other mums.

Our father came to pick us up once and Naomi didn't want anyone to see that he had dreadlocks. You try so hard – insanely hard – to fit in.

Naomi: He was so good-looking, too! Poor Dad.

Lisa-Kaindé: Imagine being James Baldwin's nephew and being told as a teenager that you don't have to fit in. That it doesn't matter what other people think. The movie that most helped me understand being an outsider was the film *A Woman Under the Influence* by John Cassavetes, which came out in 1974. I saw it when I was really young because our mother is such a huge Cassavetes fan. I fell in love with Gena Rowlands and to this day she's one of my favourite actresses.

Her character is totally different from anybody else; she is weird in her own special way. The problem is not her, it's her husband. He loves her the way she is, but he feels embarrassed by her eccentric behaviour when there are people around. At the end of the movie, he finally accepts that she is different. He no longer cares about other people's opinions.

It helped me to understand that if I didn't fit in when I was older, I would just have to find someone who would love me the way I am.

Naomi: It wasn't always easy for us to fit in at school because none of our friends wanted to talk about deep things.

Lisa-Kaindé: Whereas we were talking about deep things really early on; I remember Naomi and I talking to our grandmother for hours when we were eight. After our father's death in August 2006, Naomi and I probably became even more serious, for a while at least.

I didn't feel that my friends at school understood me. I was telling someone recently that I felt very alone as a child – close to my family, but lost in society – and he asked if I had ever felt suicidal. I certainly felt as if I needed to play a character in order to fit in. I started to wonder why, if I felt so alone, I had never felt suicidal. I realised very quickly that it was because I had a twin. I had Naomi. I was never totally alone.

Naomi: But why, Lisa? Why? Why did you feel alone at all? I remember you buying candy for people . . .

Lisa-Kaindé: I gave all my candy away and then bought more and gave that away too. I wanted people to like me.

Naomi: I don't understand. It really hurts me.

Lisa-Kaindé: I know you hate it when I talk about it. Do you remember Mother once asking if I ate the chocolate bread she gave me every day? She's incredible; she knows everything. I had to admit that I was giving it to my friends, in the hope that they might love me. She said, 'Baby, you don't buy people's love.'

Naomi: It's too heartbreaking.

Lisa-Kaindé: I wasn't sure I was enough.

Naomi: Neither was I, but I didn't give all my food to so-called friends!

Lisa-Kaindé: You're tougher than me. Your attitude was, 'Either they love me or fuck them'. I'm not like that.

Naomi: It depends. The kids at school did horrible things to you, like steal your keys and hide them behind a toilet. While you were crying, the girl who hid your keys was pretending to look for the kid who had stolen them.

Lisa-Kaindé: That girl needed to feel like she was the most powerful in the class. Meanwhile, I wanted to talk to adults. When I was thirteen, they didn't listen; by the time I was sixteen, they were interested in what I had to say. I had read books, I had opinions.

Naomi: I didn't feel that because I had a boyfriend who was four years older, very intelligent and cultured. I'm adaptable; I can sit in the street in Cuba and talk about hair for four hours without any problem. Lisa can't do that.

Lisa-Kaindé: No; I'd feel empty. I need people to feed me knowledge or I get bored, which isn't great. All my friends are older than me.

Naomi: So we were both drawn to older people! I didn't feel such an outsider at school, but we went to dinner in Paris a few months ago with school friends who are now at university. It was terrifying.

Lisa-Kaindé: Other than our two close friends who were hosting, everyone was so blank. They were all doing marketing and weren't engaged with anything *real*. They were the embodiment of this society we find ourselves in that doesn't want to feel. I felt so disconnected from them. They were in their microworld of college and weren't concerned about the wider world. At all. The world is not your marketing class.

I suppose the contrast between our lives was more extreme because we'd just come off tour; we'd been travelling around the world and talking to fans about their life experiences.

Naomi and I are the opposite of complacent. We need to take down walls. We articulate that in our song 'Ash': 'We can see through the walls/Through the ceilings and the floors'. At least listen to the other person and her story.

Naomi: Yes! Stop living in your own head.

Lisa-Kaindé: I do live in my head too much. It's really bad. Well, I love being in my head because it saved me. When I was feeling alone and had no friends and everyone asked what I'd done at the weekend, at least I had something to say: I wrote a song.

Naomi: You had something to say about the world. If you put your songs out there and people you respect admire what you do, then it stops you from feeling as though you're alone.

Lisa-Kaindé: Richard Russell, who produced both our albums, saw a video of us on YouTube when it had only had three hundred views. He was one of the first people to see our work when it was made public – except maybe our grandmother, who probably clicked 'play' 299 times. The internet has served us well in that sense; it not only led to our record deal with XL Recordings, but we were also later encouraged on Instagram by Adele and Beyoncé. Two incredible female artists at the top of their game, who are free to do what they want because they are in control.

We were truly happy and honoured to be part of the visuals for *Lemonade*. It's such a wonderful, important album and it created such a sense of pride in the black community. Working with Beyoncé and film-maker Kahlil Joseph on the visuals was a beautiful experience, and confirmed to us that there is no need to compromise your art or your message if you want to make it to the top.

Beyoncé watched our show from the side of the stage at Coachella in spring 2017, which made us feel incredibly supported. What a wonderful gift!

Naomi: So, two albums in, we know that the music business is like a war, but it's one we're happy to fight in.

Lisa-Kaindé: It's true! You have to work your ass off.

Naomi: At the same time, we're really lucky; we know women in this industry who have it much worse than us.

Lisa-Kaindé: One of our biggest strengths has always been finding the right person to work with. We work with loads of women – two female managers and a female product manager just for starters – but also with some great men. Richard has talked about how he's always been surrounded by brilliant women and, of course, he's not threatened by them. Nor is XL a label that defines you by the colour of your skin, your gender or the type of music you make. If they sign you, they believe in you as an act.

For me, the hardest thing in this industry isn't being a woman of colour, but being 100 per cent myself. Making choices which I hope I'll be proud of in thirty years. Staying true to myself when we are in an industry that is so hard.

Naomi: At least we were tough right from the start. We knew what we did and didn't want.

Lisa-Kaindé: That's true. But what has been specifically challenging for me as a woman of colour – though not because of our record company – is image. For example, we asked video directors for their visual interpretation of a song we wrote called 'Deathless'. The lyrics are about the time a very aggressive French cop arrested me when I was sixteen and assumed I was a drug dealer because of the colour of my skin: 'He said, he said/You're not clean/You might deal/All the same with that skin.'

I read twenty video treatments and they were *all the same*: going back to Africa, playing on drums and dancing. At one point I was defeated by it all, but I was convinced there was another way to go. Thank god we called Ed Morris, a hugely talented visual artist we had worked with before.

Naomi: He also directed 'River', 'Mama Says' and 'Ghosts' for us.

Lisa-Kaindé: Ed's great. He found another way for us to portray our lyrics visually: we were to lie on the floor in long red dresses, repeatedly birthing each other.

Naomi: The industry was determined to put us in a box, but they couldn't. Not musically and not visually. Why would we want to film a video in Africa? Because we're black? Oh, I see. Do they have no imagination?

Lisa-Kaindé: For a long time, black artists couldn't go back to their roots. But once they realised that a video filmed in Africa could work, it became the go-to idea. It's just annoying that they roll the same idea out over and over again. You can't be completely yourself; if you dare to try, there's a big chance you won't get to the top. If you want to be as successful as possible, you have to somehow dilute yourself.

Lisa-Kaindé: We felt powerless while touring the first album, as though we couldn't change anything. Why even try? And then, by contrast, making the second album made us so hopeful. I knew we were doing something small – we might not change the world, but it felt good. We were in control. Powerful.

Perhaps if everybody performed a small act of kindness, we could get it right.

Even just by getting people to sing along to our songs at our gigs it was as though we could feel the strength of human beings marching in the same direction.

Naomi: Until the world started changing so rapidly with Trump's election, we didn't even know how reactive our songs were.

Lisa-Kaindé: It's not really conscious. It always comes through. We have always been committed to politics with both a small and a big 'p'. We've always talked to our grandmother about women, about equality, about race. When I was tiny, about eight years old, I went to see Grandma.

I said to her, 'I think I want to be the next President of France.'

She didn't say, 'Hmmm, I don't think it's going to happen.' Or: 'Be a ballerina instead.'

She simply said, 'You have my vote.'

She's still alive. She's in her mid-seventies, but she looks sixty-five. She was the head of an association that worked with refugee children. For example, she went to Guatemala when the country had been suffering for decades. She went to Palestine. She'd go into camps and encourage kids to play and then teach parents how to play with their kids once she'd gone.

Naomi: She got the kids painting – and the images were terrifying.

Lisa-Kaindé: We wouldn't be the same without our grandmother or mother. We were lucky: we had incredibly strong female role models. We saw our mother working her ass off every day and come home to us. It was inspiring. Grandmother was free for her generation. She travelled without being married in countries that were still very conservative.

Naomi: Our grandmother has always got something to say about our videos. 'You're too fashionable! You're wearing too much make-up!' Sometimes she even emails our crew, telling them off for letting us dress a certain way. She's amazing.

Lisa-Kaindé: She even wrote to our record label, telling them that she wasn't pleased with an interview we'd given. But I think she's pretty proud of us!

Naomi, you just talked about our songs being reactive: probably our proudest moment so far is Michelle Obama agreeing to let us use one of her quotes for our song 'No Man Is Big Enough For My Arms'. She said it in response to Trump bragging about sexually assaulting women in the Access Hollywood tape and his utter lack of regret: 'The measure of any society is how it treats its women and girls'.

In fact, it's not even about being political any more. It's just about having basic respect for all women.

KATE TEMPEST

Kate Tempest: poet, playwright, novelist, rapper, spoken-word artist. Tempest was born in south London, attended the BRIT School for Performing Arts and Technology and then went on to Goldsmiths, University of London. In 2013, Brand New Ancients won the Ted Hughes Award for New Work in Poetry and the following year she was named as one of Britain's twenty Next Generation poets. Her albums Everybody Down and Let Them Eat Chaos have both been nominated for the Mercury Prize, and she was nominated for Best British Female Solo Performer at the 2018 BRIT Awards.

As far back as I can remember, I remember reading. I used to carry a book with me everywhere I went. Also, music was always a massive part of my life. Whenever music played, I couldn't help but sit down and shut everything else out and listen to it. It was never background sound.

My mum was into Tina Turner, The Beatles, Annie Lennox, Tracy Chapman. My dad grew up in the 1960s, so he was into all that 1960s soul and R&B, as well as Bob Dylan, Cream, Jimi

Hendrix, Keith Jarrett, Miles Davis. They played classical music, too. Tchaikovsky and Beethoven. I'm the youngest of five kids, so I was listening to all my elder siblings' music. They were into everything from Nirvana to Take That to speed garage. Books-wise, I loved Ursula Le Guin's Earthsea trilogy, which was like magical feminist sci-fi. I loved Brian Jacques' Redwall series of books that were essentially *The Lord of the Rings* but with mice. I was *really* into books about animals. I wanted to be a vet when I grew up. That was the kind of kid I was – happier talking to a dog than to a person. Glasses the size of my entire face about three inches thick. Reading books about dragons.

The first album that I deeply, passionately loved was Michael Jackson's *Bad.* I loved it *so* much. I learned every word. I thought about the music all day. I memorised the lyrics. The next album I felt that strongly about was *The Miseducation Of Lauryn Hill,* which came out when I was about twelve. And then Mos Def's *Black on Both Sides,* which came out a year or two later. Books I was reading around this time were things like George Orwell's *1984,* Gabriel García Márquez's *One Hundred Years of Solitude.* Lao Tzu's *Tao Te Ching.* John Irving's *The World According to Garp.* Milan Kundera's *The Unbearable Lightness of Being.* Aesop's *Fables.* Things like that.

I liked school when I was very young, but I stopped attending lessons when I was about thirteen because I was having a tough time there and I didn't want to go in any more. I spent lots of time sitting in the park, reading and listening to music instead. Hanging out with friends. Writing terrible poems.

Growing up in south-east London has been crucial to my development as a musician and as a human being. I feel extremely lucky to have grown up so close to black British culture and to have learned so much from it, both musically and politically.

In a city like London, there are so many styles of music and ways to engage with sound, all of which are available to discover if you're passionate and curious. As soon as I was able to start getting out to parties and raves and sound clashes, I was all about it. I suppose I was fourteen when that happened. I used to attend dub raves with my childhood friend and, to this day, close collaborator Kwake Bass. If we went with his mum, Dawna, we usually got in okay.

I absorbed a *lot* of knowledge from those days – hanging out, listening to new sounds and feeling the pressure of bass in my body. We used to climb up on top of the speaker stacks of Jah Shaka's sound system and record the sets on Kwake's MiniDisc player so we could listen later. He was making beats at the time. I wasn't rapping yet. At that age, I was just absorbing. I thought I was going to be a beatmaker like Kwake, until one day he said to me, 'Sis, you got to find your own thing.'

I think I was fourteen when I went to my first Notting Hill Carnival and it blew my mind. My friends had been going since they were young children but my family had never gone. It was a new experience for me. The sound system I loved most was Channel 1, with Mikey Dread at the controls. This was also the year I got my first job in a record store. It was in Lewisham market, around the back, in a hip-hop and soul shop. It enabled me to investigate everything I needed to investigate about styles and sounds. It's mad to think it now, but this was before streaming. If you wanted to hear an album, you had to go and physically get hold of it.

I was listening to everything when I was at work. From Buju Banton to Biggie Smalls. From Mary J. Blige to Elephant Man to D'Angelo to Bahamadia to Organized Konfusion. I was just lapping it up, and every time someone came in to ask for something I hadn't heard of, I'd find it and play it. This was the time when I discovered some of my favourite rappers: Pharoahe Monch, Gravediggaz and Chester P.

Outside of the shop, I listened to nothing but hip-hop for two solid years, but then I got into drum 'n' bass and jungle through friends and I started going raving to faster, harder music. I always loved what massive stacks of bass and drums do to rooms full of people but, until I went to a jungle rave, I'd never really seen how intense it could get. The London DnB scene was a huge part of my musical education. I fell in love with it. We used to go to nights like Valve and Renegade Hardware at old London clubs like Fabric and The End. I think I was about sixteen when this all kicked off and, for a good few years, I was out every weekend. My favourite emcees were Skibadee, Det and later, Eksman.

At this point in my life I'd been around a lot of rappers, but I'd never contributed to the sessions. I hadn't connected the writing I was doing privately in my notebooks with the music I was out dancing to or the lyrics I was listening to my friends spit when we were hanging out. Instead, I was making beats on a little sequencer and playing guitar.

Kwake and I got into the BRIT School, a Croydon-based music college. It had a recording studio and a radio suite and rehearsal rooms with pianos in them. I'd never seen anything like it. All the kids there were these larger-than-life characters – dancers and gospel singers and drummers, people who were studying production and knew how to rig lighting and all sorts. It's free to go there but you have to audition to get in; I played a bit of Spanish guitar at my audition because, at the time, that was what I was into. Miraculously, they let me in. It was an amazing moment for me, because I'd not really been going to school for a few years and suddenly this felt like an opportunity to sort myself out and really commit to something.

I started writing rhymes, but I kept it secret. I wanted to share my lyrics but I was too afraid to. I just kept practising on my own. Then, one day, I bit the bullet and called up a good friend, a kid called Budgie who was a rapper I really admired and I spat this lyric I'd written down the phone to him. And that was it. That's how it began. Literally a few days later I was at Deal Real, a hip-hop record store in Carnaby Street that hosted parties on Friday nights, jammed with rappers. It was an exhilarating environment. There would always be some big names that would pass through if they had shows in London, like Ghostface Killah or Mos Def or Skinnyman or Blak Twang. It was definitely a place where people were serious about lyricism.

As I remember it, this friend that I spat my rhyme down the phone to took me up to the front and I reached for the mic and the host looked at me as if to say, 'Are you sure?' But he gave me the mic and that was the first time I spat bars in front of people. I was sixteen. It was a crazy experience. The whole place went nuts. I was this dweeby-looking girl/boy. Ginger hair tied back, big glasses, I used to rock this massive duffel coat with a paperback in each pocket. I looked so young and I wasn't sleeping much at the time because I was writing all night, so I had these crazy bags under my eyes. But people just went nuts for it because I think they recognised the love I had for the art, or because they were surprised that I wasn't as shit as they thought I was going to be. Who knows? The point is, I felt I'd found it. The *thing*. My thing. And so, that was it. I had a purpose.

Usually when I walked into a room I would get confused stares from people, and the eventual 'What are you?' because they couldn't work out my gender. But as soon as I got up the front with my lyrics, I felt the shift, my position in the room changed. Like any teenager, I was hungry for acknowledgement and status. After that first performance, I felt like I'd found my place in the world and after that, any time I was anywhere where it might have been possible for me to rap, I was like a dog with a bone.

I couldn't go raving any more without pestering the MCs to let me on the mic. I couldn't be at a party without rapping. I'd plug headphones into the mic-jack of a mixer and rap down the headphone because, at that time, no one had a mic. I couldn't pass by a group of kids hanging out on the street without rapping. I used to rap for people I met on trains and buses – strangers. It was a compulsion. My friends called it 'rap attack'. They used to laugh at me for it. If I went missing at a party, or something, they'd be like, 'Where's Kate? Oh. Rap attack.' But I had to share my lyrics. I had to overcome the surface impressions that people may have had about me and get to a place that felt truer, and deeper. I had to connect. I lived for it. It was all I could think about.

Kwake Bass made the beats, I wrote the lyrics. We had our unit. We formed a crew with two others, and we called ourselves ITAL. ITAL was Kwake on production, me rapping, another rapper named Confucius MC and a vocalist, pianist and saxophone player who went by the name of Arise. Confucius was a real mentor to me at this time. He was like my lyrical soulmate and I still rate him as the one of best MCs this country has produced. I feel extremely blessed to have had his friendship.

These were our formative musical experiences. We were seventeen and eighteen and trying to get out there. We weren't ready yet, and we had a lot we all had to go through before we would be ready. But to have connected so deeply with like-minded others at such an important age is something I am always grateful for, and the strength of that foundation is one of the reasons I'm able to keep building.

I finished at the BRIT School after two years and I got a job doing street fundraising. A year before, my sisters had taken me to a very small festival, full of hippies and mushrooms. It was the first time I'd been around that kind of thing. I loved it, and I'd blagged a gig for the following year. The festival was called The Big Green Gathering. I got some mates together to play with me. We ended up with a fifteen-piece band, which we called the New Cross Philharmonic Orchestra and, after that gig, we basically played hippy festivals and squat parties in airport hangars for a solid year.

I had no idea how to go about getting better gigs. We played in between punk bands, techno DJs and circus acts. We did a five-night tour of Cardiff. It wasn't intentional, but I kind of drifted away from the hip-hop scene and found myself rapping at free parties instead.

I was hungry to learn, but hadn't thought about university as an option until one afternoon I went into Goldsmiths, which was down the road from where I lived, and discovered something called Professional and Community Education. You could do evening classes three nights a week and it cost about £200 to do a module for the whole term. I just went in and spoke to a guy there who was the head of the PACE department. I explained what I was interested in and he enrolled me for evening classes.

Over the next two years, I did several short courses, everything from an introduction to anthropology, to a politics module, to a film course. One course I took traced the Oedipal myth in literature from Sophocles to Freud. I was so blown away by it that I transferred over to do a degree in English literature. There had only been about ten of us in each of the evening classes, and they were grown people with kids and jobs who were really keen to learn and not afraid of saying the wrong thing. The discussions we had in seminars were always interesting. I was reading academic books for the first time in my life. Authors like Roland Barthes and Michel Foucault and bell hooks.

When I transferred over to full-time, I didn't connect with it in the same way. Everyone felt too cool for me. But I loved having access to the library; it was open till midnight and I lived just across the road so whenever I wasn't gigging or writing or recording, I'd be in there, reading.

I was pushing as hard as I could with my music, but I kept hitting brick walls. The only way I knew to make progress was to get out to gigs and get up on stage. But I couldn't work out how to move the gigs forward, make better demos, get played on the radio or anything like that. I was still playing with a band, I loved live music and I wanted my music to be live, with live instrumentation.

South-east London was full of musicians. My band used to rehearse in my front room, but I got served with a couple of noise complaints so we had to stop doing that. It's expensive booking out rehearsal space, which was why the squat scene was so brilliant. We could rehearse in a squat all day and all night for a fiver. All those squats are closed now. It makes me wonder how any of us would have managed to pursue a path in music the way we did if we'd been born a decade later. (A whole bunch of people I used to play with back then I still play with today. They are professional musicians, session players, or touring with their own bands.)

Although, saying that, there's a load of new musicians

coming out of south-east London, so I'm probably just seeing the past through the back-in-my-day rose-tinted glasses. One of the amazing things about those years is that we got to experiment with styles and jam for hours on stage with no pressure. Nothing was public in the way it is now. We shared our music in gigs and in sessions. But after the session, that was it. On to the next thing. At the time I was desperate for success but I'm really glad that, for all those years while I was finding my voice, I had the space and the privacy to get things wrong and learn from my mistakes.

I think I was twenty when a friend of mine invited me to an event she was going to. It was a poetry slam. I'd never been to one before; I don't think I'd even heard the word 'slam'. But I went along with her and signed up. When it was my turn, I just spat my lyrics a cappella and ended up winning it. I remember the prize being something massive, like a hundred pounds, but I may be mixing memories there. For sure, this was my introduction to poetry, and that night I met some of the poets who would go on to teach me what spoken word was, and what it could be for me.

I found myself on stage jamming with Ferry Lawrenson and Archie Marsh at a party one night and it seemed to work well. The three of us started a band which we went on to call Sound of Rum. We had our first rehearsal on a Wednesday night, and by the end of that weekend we'd played three gigs. Initially I had invited four others to come and rehearse with us, but we were the only three that turned up, and so we decided to make it a trio.

I finished my degree at Goldsmiths in 2008. I was twenty-two. I decided to throw myself full-time at my poetry and music and see if I could make my living. I'd met a few people on the poetry circuit who were spoken-word educators and were using it as a way of engaging school kids with literature. As a poet, you could get a workshop gig and the fee could be anything from £80 to £250 a *day*. So I was convinced I could make things work. There was an organisation called Apples and Snakes based out of my local theatre and community space, the Albany in Deptford, and they helped poets get workshop placements and things like that. If I could get two school gigs a month, my rent was covered, which meant I was basically free to make music for the rest of the time. After food and bills, everything I made at gigs I could put back into my projects.

Since that first performance on the mic at Deal Real, getting in front of crowds has been the way I've made my name. So, as Sound of Rum, we just kept doing it – crossing the country to play to ten people in a pub and remembering to be grateful for the opportunity. We got a few bookings on tiny stages at festivals, no billing on the flier, no fees, but tickets in and (hopefully) petrol covered. We spent a full summer busking by food stands, in campsites, in any relatively quiet spot, in as many festivals as we could get into. We always managed to draw a crowd.

It was a fun, knackering summer, and by the end of it we had enough money from CD sales to pay for studio time to record a proper demo. I still meet people at gigs who say, 'I saw you busking up a tree at a festival in 2009.' It's a good feeling when people know that you've put the work in.

So I came to poetry the wrong way round, really. I had always listened to lyrics very intensely and, as a kid, I used to write them out so I could study them. Rappers I worked with when I was a kid, like Confucius MC, would say, 'You're a poet, you know', and I would get annoyed with them because I thought it was an insult.

But, almost without wanting to, I found myself enjoying poetry. I was gigging at spoken-word nights more and more, and I started to enjoy having the space to really dig into my lyrics when I was performing. I started being more adventurous with my approach to writing, and to take myself more seriously as someone who was a writer. I met some poets who I found inspiring, like Polarbear, David J, Inua Ellams, Ross Sutherland, Angry Sam, Zena Edwards, ShortMAN. The list goes on and on and on. After a couple of years of going out there and performing as much as possible, I started getting commissioned by different organisations to write pieces, and pretty soon I was a poet for hire.

There seemed to be more opportunities to earn a living in poetry than in music, which is strange. I suppose the world of touring bands is so oversubscribed. Trying to make a dent in the music industry without representation or style is incredibly hard. I was all substance and no fucking style! In music, people took one look at me and said, 'No way, you're never going to make it.'

I did get a deal eventually. I put an album out with Sound of Rum on Rob da Bank's record label, Sunday Best. We gigged like crazy. We managed to get a bit further up the bill at festivals. We got a little residency at a London pub. We got a few support slots and learnt a lot about the music industry. I thought all we needed to do to make progress was make an album and get it out in the world, but it wasn't that simple. We wanted to be full-time musicians but we needed to work our other jobs to pay the bills. So we'd meet after work and ram all the gear into the car and drive all over the place to play, then drive back.

It was around this time that a theatre director who'd seen me gigging my poetry got in touch and offered me a commission to write a play for his theatre company, Paines Plough. I felt elated, terrified, out of my depth and amazed to be asked.

The experience of writing that first play was probably the most important experience of my writing life. It changed everything for me. It opened my brain up to dialogue, narrative. To understanding that, if a line works when I speak it but dies when it's spoken by someone else, it means it's a weak line. I realised I could push through difficulties in form if I could just stay focused on story – writing a play taught me about plot in the same way that my life as a rapper taught me about flow.

And one of the most important lessons it taught me was that writing isn't just something that pours out of you, it's something you have to work at, craft, struggle with. Cultivate. You have to put yourself in situations where you are extremely uncomfortable if you are ever going to give your writing a chance to surprise you. You have to actively open new routes in your brain for your ideas to flow down. And you will only find your voice once you've lost it a few times.

It was definitely hard graft being in a band, gigging as a poet, going into schools to teach kids whenever the bookings came in and writing a play all at the same time. But it was my big passion, and I was electrified by the fact that things seemed to be moving. It was all I'd ever wanted to do, and so many other people I knew had turned away from their passions because they had to focus on real life. I knew what an incredible blessing it was that I had the opportunities I had to keep making work, getting gigs, being booked for things.

Eventually, I finished the draft I was working on and *Wasted* had its first preview. (In theatre, before a show is ready to be publicly seen, there are previews, which allow the cast and crew to get their heads around what needs to be done to get the show ready. It's like a step up from a rehearsal but not quite a proper performance.) The first preview of the first play I ever wrote went on at Latitude Festival at midnight with 850 people in the audience and loads more outside watching on a screen. Some of the lines just made my stomach heave, I was so ashamed of them. But I was proud of what we had produced as a team. Theatre is about collaboration, and that's beautiful. My old mate Kwake had created an incredible score for it and he was playing along, live.

Because of all the work I was doing in poetry and with *Wasted*, I was invited to take part in a residency at the Battersea Arts Centre, a theatre near Clapham Junction, where I was given space to write. It was so incredible to not have to be anywhere, just to sit down and write. I sat at a desk in a little room in the back of the theatre and I began to write *Brand New Ancients*.

The musical community I was a part of in south-east London was all about the DIY mentality. White labels, printing T-shirts, putting on our own gigs. I realised that I should be applying the same ethos to poetry. I couldn't get my poetry published, so I started a publishing house. Self-publishing is frowned upon in the literary world as a vanity project, but the music world is different. Starting up your own label and putting your own music out is completely standard. In fact, it's the best way of doing things. I knew people wanted to buy my books, but nobody wanted to publish me. So I found a printing place in Deptford, teamed up with my childhood friend Luke Eastop who was an artist, and we made some books.

We did an initial run of 300 and that sold out. Then a second run of 300 sold out. They were beautiful books that came in boxes with a hologram front and a hand-sharpened quill and some fake tattoos. We wanted them to be more alive than just a book. Like a performance of some kind.

By 2012, we'd made enough money from the small print runs to do a large run of 1,000 books. *Everything Speaks In Its Own Way* – a line from James Joyce's *Ulysses* – was a collection of the spoken-word poems I'd been gigging, alongside poems I'd never spoken out loud. Ones that were more intimate, less multi-rhythmic. Plus a DVD and a CD. Kind of all-you-can-eat Kate Tempest with a pretty cover.

A friend of mine worked at the Old Vic Theatre and she told me they had no shows on for a week in the summer and were inviting different artists and musicians to put shows on for one night. So we launched the book in a 1,000-seat theatre in the centre of town and we didn't have to pay them anything upfront. They just took a cut of the door. I invited a bunch of artists I loved to perform with: Hollie McNish, Chester P, Zia Ahmed, John Berkavitch. We sold it out. It felt like such an audacious thing to do. A big 'fuck you' to everyone who sneered at spoken word. It was a joyous night. We put a few settees on stage and, after their performances, everyone just chilled out on stage and watched. It felt like we were all in it together. It was one of my proudest moments.

I didn't know it at the time, but Don Paterson was in the audience that night.

By this point, I'd been doing poetry solidly, pretty much, for four years. I had my issues with the 'scene'; I didn't want to get stuck in poetry any more than I did in squat parties or festivals or UK rap. Every scene felt too small. Don Paterson sent an email to our 'publishing house' saying that I was obviously doing very well on my own but, if ever I wanted an editor, he was poetry editor at Picador and I was welcome to submit some poems. I couldn't believe it.

If this all sounds like it's overlapping, that's because it was.

Everything was happening at the same time. It was always the case that I'd be working on three different things at once. I started previewing *Brand New Ancients* at the same time as publishing *Everything Speaks* and finishing redrafts of *Wasted*. *Brand New Ancients* went on tour and did very well. It won the Ted Hughes Award for New Work in Poetry in 2013. It won a Herald Angel Award and it transferred to New York. It was a turning point in my writing and in my performance. I felt I had spent all these years in training to be able to deliver this story. It was my most ambitious project, and it set the pace for the projects that would follow. Like, 'If I could do that, I can do this'.

Another turning point was meeting Dan Carey. He came to watch a Sound of Rum gig in a pub – I think he was one of four people in the audience at that particular one. Still, we played some of our best gigs to rooms with barely anyone in them. It felt more important to play well because, whoever those four people were, they had come. Dan and I connected so deeply from the minute we met. It took a few years, but eventually we got into the studio together.

What ended up happening was this weird critical mass: the amount of work I was doing in music led me to poetry; the amount of work I was doing in poetry led me to theatrical writing; the amount of work I did in the theatre led me – strangely – back to music, through *Brand New Ancients*. The music industry eventually took notice because of all the work I'd been doing in other areas.

By the time we made *Everybody Down* and signed with Big Dada, I'd been working full-time on my craft for six years. I'm really glad that things took the time that they did. That I was twenty-eight before *Everybody Down* came out and I had as much work behind me as I did.

*

As a woman, the temptation is to go out on stage – and I've done it so many times – and try to be liked. You need them to like you before they'll listen to you. You need them to relax in your company. The best thing you can do as a woman is make yourself look a bit stupid and unthreatening. You are effectively saying, 'I've worked really hard and I've got lots to say, but don't worry, I'm still a woman and still stupid.'

If I had more sexual capital, it might have been a flirtatious thing. But because I don't have that, because I have the little sister role in the audience/performer exchange, I used to come on and be a bit goofy and a bit sweet. As I've grown into myself, I've realised that it makes me feel fucking gross and I hate doing it. It's received behaviour. And it's actually kind of manipulative. I feel much stronger in my stagecraft now than I ever have. I have huge respect for the audience. Because I've spent the best part of fifteen years rapping in smelly rooms with ropy equipment, when I get decent monitors or an amazing stage, or a dedicated crowd, I don't take a second of it for granted.

When you're performing, it's for the audience, it's a connection you're conducting. But when you're writing, it's not for anyone but the idea. It's not you. It's not really anything to do with you. In fact, the more involved you get with it, the more difficult it will be. You have to work your entire life to hone your skills, improve your craft, expand your reach, so that when an idea comes you can facilitate it as best you can, aware that it's not *yours*. You didn't create that. You just have to do your best to get it down from out of the sky above your brain and through your clumsy, clichéd hands and down onto the paper without killing it completely.

ALISON MOYET

Born in Essex, Alison Moyet sang in a handful of punk bands before forming Yazoo with Vince Clarke in 1981. They disbanded only two years later, in 1983, after a string of hits including 'Only You' and 'Don't Go'. Moyet's first solo album, Alf, went to number one. In the winter of 2017, she took her ninth studio album, Other, on a world tour, playing fifty-nine shows in fifty-eight cities. Her records have sold in excess of twenty million copies.

In 1977, when I was fifteen, I got on stage with two school friends at the Roundacre in Basildon on the promise of a free lemonade. Soft drinks didn't usually happen for us, so it was a good deal. We started singing an a cappella version of 'My Friend the Sun' by Family and almost immediately got booed off.

'Fuck off!'

'We're only here to drink beer!'

Fair dos. We were only there to drink lemonade.

A year later, the same two friends and I decided we would form a punk band.

It was about hanging about with your mates, making a noise and feeling that noise inside your body. It was about having something to do on a Friday night. A do-it-yourself movement was happening, which suited those of us that could afford nothing else. But none of us played any instruments. Well, I played oboe, but that didn't really fit. And then we met a band who assumed we were more than an idea and invited us to support them at a gig they were doing in a hotel in Leigh-on-Sea.

We agreed before thinking it through: we had no material at all for a gig in two weeks' time. It was reason enough to start writing, for want of a better word.

We constructed a collection of mostly improvised songs quickly and pulled a band of sorts together. We knew a boy called Rob Allen in the year below at school who played guitar. I said to him, 'You're playing with us.' It wasn't a question. We got some rehearsal space in a school art room, the four of us, but one of the girls couldn't get to grips with the guitar at all. Before the gig she went to her art teacher and got her hand set in plaster of Paris so she could pretend she'd broken it as an excuse not to play.

We did the support gig. Kim, in a cast, who was supposed to play guitar, sang backing vocals. Rob played freestyle guitar and Sue played the bass, mostly sliding one finger along the fretboard. We picked up a drummer on the fly, which was always quite easy. They were mostly pulled from the bar or the smattering of regulars watching. We managed to keep two of those drummers for a good few weeks. They'd have no idea of the songs; it was just a matter of shouting, 'One, two, three, four!' and then you told them when to stop, unless their sticks had flown off beforehand.

I was inspired by Poly Styrene's shrill and unorthodox

styling, so I really gave it volume. We got rare respect getting up on stage, just going for it.

I recently saw a fanzine review of a gig we did in front of a wall of skinheads who came up to the front of the stage to intimidate us. That's how it was in town. Punks, Teds and skinheads, all at odds. It was one of those situations where you couldn't look scared because then you'd be in trouble. I vividly remember picking up the mic stand and just flying at them with it. Wheeling it like a scythe. There I was, some mad adolescent in army greens with her hair cropped, swinging at them with a mic stand. You could see them thinking, 'She's barking, I'm not going there'.

Most of us were in at least one band in the late 1970s. We'd book a school hall, get hold of an amp and a couple of guitars and play short sets in front of around fifty mates. We had society. Our own scene. This Basildon ended up growing bands that floated. Depeche Mode and Yazoo in particular.

When I was young, I had a strange bravery that was lost in my early famous years. My first nickname was 'Stamina' because I had a strength and physicality that wasn't recognisable in girls of that period. I wasn't particularly fat compared to today's norm, but most others in the 1970s seemed to be a size 6 or an 8, whereas I was a 12 or a 14.

My dad came from a French peasant family, and my sister and I were expected to do the same physical jobs as my brother. Dad was a real patriarch and a scary creature, if only because he was the product of his upbringing in occupied France. He had to shoot his starving dog as a kid because there wasn't enough food for humans, never mind animals; his cousin was mutilated; his neighbours disappeared in the night; his dad was taken away to drive his lorry to Dunkirk, though he managed to escape. He was a street kid left to his own devices in a dangerous world.

My dad finished school at thirteen, leaving by the window, but he was an incredibly clever man. And he gave me the belief that I could put my hand to anything. I'm not talking about ambition or making lots of money, because that wasn't something that was ingrained into us. But I could fix anything if I applied myself – by the age of fourteen, I could hang wallpaper.

My mum, meanwhile, taught all day, came home, cleaned and cooked dinner before working her way through a pile of exercise books. We were left to our own devices beyond the non-negotiable daily household chores and so long as we weren't caught idle, if I said I didn't have any homework, she accepted it. God knows why.

My parents were hard-working and careful. Clothes were handmade. We only ate fresh meat and vegetables, wholegrains and home-made yogurt. I grew up thinking that only rich people ate processed food.

Every summer we drove to see our paternal grandparents in France, where we all slept in a one-bedroom cabin. They had no phones, so this was the only time my dad could see his family and friends and talk to them. On the way, we'd sleep by rivers and in fields, making our beds out of hay, washing ourselves in the rivers and gazing at the stars till we dropped off to sleep under sheet plastic to keep dry of dew.

We didn't have money for many records, but when I was ten, my gran handed me all her original Apple Beatles singles. A fantastic gift! Otherwise, it was a case of the music I was exposed to by the family. My dad listened to Jacques Brel, *la valse musette* and hits from popular westerns, and my mum to Petula Clark and classical music. My sister was into the Faces and soul, while my brother was more into prog rock, The Who,

Led Zeppelin, Melanie, and folk, like Jack the Lad. When I started seriously listening to music myself, it was X-Ray Spex, Buzzcocks and Elvis Costello, whose image was painted on my bedroom walls.

I have always been more of a doer than a consumer. I like making art, but I don't go and see it in galleries. I liked listening to music, but was always more impatient to make it. I write but don't read. I played recorder well when I was young. I was musical, but never learned to read music fluently because I'm so often disengaged.

Leaving junior school, I gained a place to learn the oboe at the Saturday-morning music school in Laindon, where I first saw Vince Clarke. I was sent to register for the theory class, but I couldn't find the room and didn't feel confident enough to ask anyone for help! So I missed out on music theory simply because I didn't know which part of this new school the class was in.

At senior school, as a rare instrumentalist I was enrolled in the 'orchestra'. I went to audition for a role in school musicals but was asked what it was I imagined they'd need me for, and besides, I couldn't sing. I only have one memory of anyone noticing my voice. At that Saturday music school, aged eleven. The guy running a singing group that I attended on one occasion turned round and looked at me in a really quizzical way. Like I stood out, and for once it didn't seem like it was because I had been disruptive. It was the first positive reaction I'd had. I didn't go back.

The friends I grew up with in Basildon didn't have great hope. None of us went to university. It was never a consideration. We were fodder for the local factories; our new town was populated to feed those factories. Kids that tried kept it quiet.

In the meantime, we had to find a way to keep ourselves busy, to entertain ourselves. Even though we'd been booed off the stage at the Roundacre, I knew I had presence. My family were vocal, full-on and aggressive and so was I, which my peers found discomfiting. An aggressive boy is scary, but an aggressive girl is scarier because she is rare and unquantifiable. So much of it was front, self-protection. I always ended up getting attention for the wrong reasons and I had to defend myself. I learned early on how to put on a dead-eyed stare – my variation of a cat fluffing out its body to look bigger. I was scared on the inside, but I didn't show it.

But when I started singing, I had a fighting spirit. I was big and hard-looking and I wasn't intimidated about standing at the front and both taking abuse and giving it. I didn't sing because it was known that I was the best singer in the group. That was irrelevant. The singer was often that because they couldn't play. I had the volume and would write the songs, so it was fitting for me to sing them. I was an attention-seeker.

Later, when I first went into a recording studio, I had no understanding about moderating my voice. Dynamics had not previously been required, so it was a full-on bark. So used to feedback and having no monitors, I was still trying to be my own PA.

I had no ambition to leave Basildon when I left school. I lived off £5 a week, which covered bus fares and perhaps one drink, but we never felt poor because no one had any money. We had a massive gang of mates.

After leaving school, and courtesy of shop jobs, I was going to see Dr Feelgood, Wilko Johnson and endless other local bands, and by the time I was eighteen, I was doing gigs on the pub rock scene in Canvey Island and London, mixing English R&B up with some Billy Boy Arnold and new wave.

At some point I began to appropriate a mid-Atlantic drawl because of the music I was then listening to. You start, effectively, piggybacking someone else's style. I was listening to a lot of Janis Joplin; because she wrote about heartbreak, I fantasised about having my heart broken. Because she drank a lot, I tried very hard to become an alcoholic. I didn't like the taste, but I persevered for a while. I remember going out one night in a T-shirt made out of dishcloths, army green trousers and a mohair jumper with fashionably big holes in it. I arrived home really pissed and realised I'd forgotten my key.

Worried about my authoritarian father seeing how I was dressed, I thought it'd be a good idea to take off the army greens and mohair jumper, then put them in the dog kennel, despite the fact that it was snowing. I was standing there in my T-shirt and boots thinking, 'He's not going to like this T-shirt at all.' So I took that off too.

So it's gone one a.m. and I'm standing there with virtually nothing on, thinking it'd go down much better when Dad answered the door ... I didn't forget my key again for a good while.

I didn't go looking for trouble, but sometimes I found it unwittingly. Around this time, I was doing backing vocals at The Bridge House in Canning Town, which was a big venue for punk and mod bands. The manager of one particular band was there, his Rolls-Royce parked outside. He wanted to have a meeting with me, and I really thought I was made. I borrowed money off my mum to get to the far side of London. I was so excited. I was only eighteen, and this was going to be it!

I arrived at his offices and he immediately said he had a flat next door, where he'd rather take the meeting. I thought nothing of it. Bear in mind it took hours to get there; it wasn't a simple or a cheap journey.

He pointed at the sunbed and asked if I would like a session. I declined. He was surprised. Why wouldn't I take off my clothes in front of this relative stranger and get on his sunbed?

He looked at me and said, 'Well, what do you want?'

I replied, 'I want to sing.'

He said, quite tersely, 'Go away and think about it then.'

That was it.

The big meeting with the big manager. Retrospectively I wasn't sorry he'd had his soft-top slashed outside the gig the night we met.

Funnily enough, a couple of years ago I saw him in Germany with the act he was managing. He was perfectly friendly and I was sitting there thinking, 'You don't remember how you treated me at all, do you?' And I said nothing. I'd forgotten how short he was.

Despite that incident, I only started considering the different experiences male and female artists might have when people started asking me about it. For the most part, I haven't particularly noticed being a female artist – in the sense that it doesn't stop me choosing what I want, and I have never had the male artist experience to measure it against.

Maybe it was because I wasn't considered attractive that I avoided that radar, but no executive ever asked me to lose weight or to be pretty.

I have, however, worked with men of lesser professional status who can't handle the disparity. One collaborator had a way of asserting dominance by disparaging my singing style. He criticised my vibrato. He dismissed my history. He deleted all my takes at the end of the sessions when I had gone. Only to say the next day that it was a shame he had wiped them. That they had been good takes. That experience impacted on my confidence for a good while. Second-guessing is a neutral gear.

I wasn't recognised as a songwriter for the longest time. There has always been the assumption that a man has done it for me. Even in Yazoo, Vince was congratulated for the songs 'Winter Kills' and 'Nobody's Diary', which I wrote, and for 'Situation', which we co-wrote. That's not Vince's doing. People think singers on the whole are merely the muse.

Yazoo had a bit of scratch to it, and that scratch was mine. I wrote it in.

I recently did an interview in which the first question was: 'How important is the producer on an Alison Moyet record?' A producer is obviously important on every record, but they speak as though we are the channel through which travels the greater presence of a more profound practitioner. Icing for a cake that has been very carefully made by someone with greater nous.

I would say this, maybe, is the female issue. The indication that we must fight harder.

But I actually think it's a singer's lot. I see male vocalists dismissed in the same way.

Maybe it's something to do with how records used to be made way back when.

When I went on *Top of the Pops* for the first time in the spring of 1982, I had to borrow money off my mum to get some fabric down Basildon market so that my friend could knock me up a dress. I hadn't even considered how to move to the song. When the music started I thought, 'What should I do with my feet?' I was like a mad Eagle Eyes Action Man, making it up with the cameras rolling.

Back then I did my own make-up, my own hair. Oftentimes

that hair was cut the night before, after too many beers. Hence the hat in 'Don't Go'; it wasn't a style statement, I just got pissed the night before and cut all my hair off. I had to wear a hat because I was marginally bald. But at least we looked real. The girls who were considered to be beautiful in the 1980s would now be seen as the dowdy average girls-next-door. Average women doing their own make-up and their own hair. Bodies more comprehensively covered but truly exposing more of ourselves. Our faces. Our choices. Wank fodder, not an ambition.

We sang live on tape. Three takes and choose the best one. Now anyone can sound like they're a flawless singer, with auto-tune and lovely thighs.

Things happened really quickly for me. My mates would tell you that I wanted to be famous when I was a kid, but my idea of being famous was getting the headline at Dingwalls or the Hope and Anchor. Doing a set and being able to buy a round. Being part of the London pub circuit. Postered.

I had no thought of being a pop star, but I became famous really quickly and jaded pretty quickly, too. The problem with pop music is the assumption that your most significant creativity happens in youth. It's completely wrong. There are songs in my back catalogue that are average at best, but they were hits because I was seen to be in my prime. I had radio's ear. I was that year's name, or one of them. It's impossible to do anything for any amount of time without learning how to better hone your craft, your writing, who you are. Pop music is the only arena in which it is assumed that your creativity decreases as you age.

The assumption for women is that your edge is left at the doorstep when you have babies. I have a soft body, therefore I must have soft sensibilities. I must be malleable. I must be pliant. Or a man-hater.

I felt liberated in some ways when social media came along. As much as it's a poisonous thing, in that it sucks you in and sups on your energy, it has also allowed me to present myself. I don't have to be pleasant, I don't seek to be lovely. People sometimes say on Twitter, 'Alison Moyet is not lovely'. Why the fuck should I be lovely? When did I say I was? Women are expected to be nurturing and loving and I am these things, I'm just not those things in isolation. Loveliness is not a prerequisite for craft.

I want to be able to be ugly when it's right for me to be ugly. Some women, given the right associations, are allowed that. They are rebel souls defined by their audience. A rebel chooses herself.

As I've grown older, I have become far more at ease with pleasing myself. I have, for example, become more entrenched in my Europeanness. I want to sing with my own accent and use the language that I find compelling or pertinent. I'm accused of being pretentious for indulging my own ideas, but how can creativity ever come without pretension? Isn't the point of art to lose yourself in another reality, or to find yourself where you are? I don't care about that kind of criticism. Even when I was very small, I never had approval. I'm not used to it. The lack of it is my tinder stick.

So many people in the music industry are seeking approval. Everyone seems to be scared of making the wrong move, of quoting the wrong name. If there's one thing I can say for myself, I've never been that afraid. My records are getting better because I trust my judgement. I don't need the right society to feel relevant. I am relevant because I have something to say about my now, and I can articulate it.

I've been in this industry for thirty-five years. I've been singing since I was fourteen. There is no one better qualified than me to say whether or not I'm better qualified than I was. I'm telling you: I am better than I was.

I've never felt the need to conform to one shape. No one has ever really claimed me: I've never been cosseted, nor have I been someone's muse. I've stood on my own two feet or I've had no value at all. That's how it was for me. And it really saved me. I have more than my career in my life. When my career is taken away, I am not empty.

I left school unqualified and had no other obvious choices. I sang because it was easy. I liked how it made my body feel. I learned what I liked by doing it. Not by observing. You're going to make some careless moves. You're going to have to pay for them for a long time, and they will hang like rocks around your neck.

I got bored and sold out a couple of times.

I got integrity and turned down fortunes.

I find consistency a difficult thing.

I'm going to fuck up, because I don't have my eyes on a prize. I live in the day.

Sometimes I'm the rarest bird and sometimes I'm a cunt.

I'm comfortable with that.

My music has always reflected where I've been at, and sometimes that means it's been disengaged and disinterested and dull. I have authenticity, and that forgives me my lazy transgressions.

When I click, I simply love me and what I can do.

Doors were always closed to me: I've never seen a closed door as something to stop movement.

Pop is by nature transient. I outgrew my zeitgeist and I frittered away my status.

These, though, are the things that stunt your growth.

To the world I am smaller, but I know otherwise.

I am in my mid-fifties. I am other.

NADINE SHAH

Nadine Shah left the north-east of England for London when she was seventeen. She released her first album, Love Your Dum and Mad, *in 2013 and her second,* Fast Food, *two years later. Her third album,* Holiday Destination, *was released in 2017 and was nominated for the Mercury Prize.*

There is much I've learned to appreciate in recent years. Mum and dad's beautiful house on the clifftops in Whitburn, in the north-east of England, overlooking the North Sea. My dad, who is from Pakistan, playing and singing ghazals, a form of Arabic poetry, in his amazing voice. My mum, who is of Norwegian descent but was born in South Shields and who can just about hold a tune, singing songs by The Shirelles, The Supremes and The Shangri-Las. Our karaoke song of choice is still 'Leader of the Pack', with me on backing vocals.

My two older brothers were in bands when we were growing up. The eldest, Karim, was in a Jimi Hendrix cover band at school called Susan's Marmalade. They used to rehearse at our house and the deal was that, in order to do so, they had to let me sit in and watch. My other brother, Ricky, played drums in a heavy metal band. I wasn't really into Pantera, so he avoided the humiliation of his younger sister attending band practice. The three of us are still super close and all live in London. At any significant show of mine, you can guarantee that they will be in the audience somewhere.

My brothers are close in age and were therefore afforded more freedom growing up than I was. I don't think it was because they were boys. It was the simple fact that they could look after each other. I think people sometimes assume that because I have a Pakistani father I would have grown up with one rule for boys and another for girls. Sure, he was more protective of me when it came to dating, but my girlfriends' English fathers were exactly the same.

I was happy at home, but I found school challenging. Until I was fourteen I attended a girls' school and I hated it. I found all those girls en masse totally restrictive and regressive. When I moved to a co-ed school, I didn't like the way girls were treated by some male teachers – we were definitely objectified. Even adolescent boys were disgusted by that behaviour. They looked so embarrassed every time it happened

In both schools, I was the closest thing there was to a 'foreign kid'. Before 9/11, I loved being mixed race, I loved being different. It made me feel unique and special. I remember studying 'Presents from my Aunts in Pakistan', the Moniza Alvi poem about having both Pakistani and English heritage. My teacher smiled at me between paragraphs because she was excited to see me so unusually attentive. It was one of those small life-changing moments in the sense that the poem sparked my interest in poetry and lyric writing.

It's worth mentioning that I attended a private school. I had an extremely privileged education. People hear my north-east accent and make other assumptions, but I'm not going to lie about it. I am always annoyed when other musicians hide their privileged backgrounds and pretend life has been so hard for them. They should instead be honest and strive to help young people who haven't been afforded the same opportunities they were.

For the record, no child of mine will ever attend a private school. I believe a high standard of education and health care should be offered to everyone, not just those who can afford it. It's the same in the music industry. Money gives people choice. It opens doors. So many hugely talented musicians can't pursue a career in music because they have no financial help from their family. There are so many unheard voices right now because of the fundamental division between those who have and those who have not and, as a result, there is a poorer quality of musical output.

Had I been at a comprehensive school, maybe I would have a different story to tell. Maybe it would have been more culturally diverse. As it was, I was the kid with the Muslim surname at my private school. It wasn't fashionable to be Pakistani or Muslim. Even before 9/11, I was bullied verbally and physically for being Pakistani.

But, after 9/11, the racial harassment was different. People I had previously assumed were liberal suddenly started voicing narrow-minded, venomous, racist thoughts. Racism was everywhere. At the performing arts club I attended. Amongst the kids I'd hung out with. And, of course, at school.

I was fifteen at the time and two years later I moved to London. I was lucky because I had both emotional and financial help from my parents. I moved in with my older brother, who was studying in London. Dad paid the rent. It looks romantic and glamorous on paper: 'She moved to London alone at seventeen to pursue a career as a jazz singer.' But it was pretty scary. London can be an intimidating city and I had zero connections. No one gave two shits about me.

I was never in bands at school. They were a boys' club that I had no interest in joining. I was, however, in many a musical. I was going to say that all evidence has been destroyed, but that's not actually strictly true. My old music teacher, Mrs Blazey, sent me a video of a school musical I was in back in 1995. I remember it well because she wrote a solo for me and the lyrics were really political and poignant. I told her recently that those lyrics have informed my own lyric writing, politics and activism.

Although I wasn't in a band, I always used to sing. I would imitate Mariah Carey and Whitney Houston. All the power singers. Singing for me back then was about vocal acrobatics. Performing was just an opportunity to demonstrate a bag of tricks. Even as a child, I found it overwhelmingly unsatisfying.

Then I heard Nina Simone. Her voice was unlike anything I'd heard before. I love the fact that you can't identify her gender from her voice. Her voice isn't perfect, in fact it's almost ugly at times. It was the first honest voice I ever heard. It gave me the encouragement to explore and use the bottom end of my vocal range, where I'm far more comfortable. It's doubtless vomit-inducing to say this, but Nina Simone helped me to find my voice. She completely shaped the way I sing today.

Before I moved to London, I sang gospel music and I then fell into jazz, but I never sang in public. My mum found an advert in the Yellow Pages for a recording studio in an old pit village outside Newcastle. Mam would come with me to record there. Mick and Denny, the two old fellas who ran the studio, would order backing tracks and I'd record them. It wasn't the coolest thing I've ever done, but I still have those recordings and I'm pretty proud of them. At the very least, I'm glad that I documented the development of my voice.

When I arrived in London, I sang in Pizza Express restaurants all over the capital. I'd get fifty quid, a glass of wine and a main course. I scoffed so many dough balls that the mere mention of them these days makes me want to throw up. I lived on them! I sang all the classic jazz standards from the Cole Porter Song Book. It's a gorgeous collection of songs, which I always performed in a northern accent.

I really enjoyed that time. Of course, I know that I was just background music, which can be pretty tough at times. Especially when someone comes over and says, 'Can you keep it down? We're trying to have a conversation here.' Ouch. But it was good preparation for where I find myself now. It toughened me up.

I continue to be inspired by Nina Simone every day. If I find myself in a tricky situation at work, I think, 'What would Nina do?' I would say that ninety percent of my refusal to take shit from anyone comes from this mantra. But Nina is not my only heroine. The work of Frida Kahlo had a big effect on my writing. I've always admired how brutally honest she was with her work and how she let her audience in. She took us into the bathtub, into her darkest moments and into her fantasies. She is literal in a way that means pretty much anyone could relate to her. I love her.

Three albums in, I feel braver than I used to. I found my voice when I started singing in my own accent and now I'm willing to write ever more literal lyrics and not hide behind metaphors. This is, in part at least, down to the rise in female solidarity in the music industry. I feel less judged than previously and more encouraged than ever.

*

I released my first album, *Love Your Dum and Mad*, in 2013. It was described by some reviewers as the imagined union of PJ Harvey and Nick Cave, but I'd never heard their music when I made the album because I'd been a total jazzhead. After the constant comparisons to both artists, I listened to their work and became a huge fan. How could I not?

The first song I ever wrote, 'Dreary Town', was a direct response to the death of Matthew Stephens-Scott, a very close friend of mine. He was my eldest brother's best friend and he quickly became like another big brother to me. I owe my entire professional career as a musician to him and will be eternally grateful for all the encouragement he gave me while he was on this earth. Writing 'Dreary Town', which is an ode to Matthew, was a cathartic exercise, although of course I miss him to this day. The album title is a reference to a painting he did and that painting is also on the cover of the record.

Love Your Dum and Mad is about love and loss, but the only way I can properly engage with my audience is via pure honesty. Of course, that means having to expose myself emotionally and there are times when I think about my lyrics or about things I've said in interviews and I wish I hadn't been so open. My mother still cringes at how brutally honest I can be, but I can't see that changing anytime soon.

I am not embarrassed by my first album, but some of my early experiences of the record industry shocked me. I met more than one arse-slapping pervert along the way. I found my second album, *Fast Food*, more enjoyable to make. By that time, I was more familiar with the journey of an album from the studio to the press to live shows. I felt more confident in the knowledge that there were people out there who actually liked the music I was making. It was much quicker to make – nothing at all like making the much-discussed 'difficult second album'.

Sonically, *Fast Food* was a departure from the first album. The sound was informed by taking *Love Your Dum and Mad* on tour and wanting to make the audience move around and dance. I also found playing the guitar so much more freeing than being stuck behind a piano. I had fun with the lyrics too. On 'Fool', for example, I reel off a list of reasons why I despise a former partner, but I'm simultaneously poking fun at myself for being exactly the same as him. I speak a lot about failed relationships on *Fast Food*, but I never intended to be cruel. The fact that those relationships failed had as much to do with me as it had to do with them.

I had written about other people's suffering on the first album and received hundreds of beautiful messages from fans expressing their gratitude and opening up about their own mental health issues. It was only fair to open up about my own issues on *Fast Food*, so I wrote about my panic attacks and anxiety in 'Stealing Cars' and again was surprised at the response. People are much kinder than I thought they'd be, which in turn made me feel less vulnerable.

There are so many aspects of the music industry that can seriously aggravate my mental health. During the first album campaign, my anxiety and depression got much worse. There were so many factors that I'd never considered. Social media. The power of adrenaline during performances. The pressures of success and failure. I had to learn to curate my own environment to ensure I could exist in a healthier space within the music industry.

I no longer google myself daily to see what people are saying about me. I take time to let adrenaline settle after a show instead of rushing off to the merch table. Most importantly, I sat and thought about what success might actually mean to me, because I had forgotten about it along the way. I remembered that it was a simple thing: playing an instrument well enough to be able to compose my own songs and to release an album. I had done that and everything else was therefore a beautiful bonus.

I certainly have enough stories to bore the hell out of my grandkids, even if my career should end tomorrow.

There are so many great artists who write the most beautiful love songs, who soundtrack our heartache. There are artists who write music to make us dance and music to allow us to escape. But, when I started writing my third album in 2016, it was virtually impossible to write anything other than a political album.

My brother Karim is a journalist and he'd been documenting the Syrian civil war before it was widely reported. He used to come back to London and tell me about the horrors he'd seen. I was angry and frustrated at my ignorance, but angrier still that it wasn't more widely spoken about. With first-hand testimonies and much research, my third album started to take shape. At the same time, the world finally woke up to the crisis and suddenly it was front-page news. But only because it was happening on our doorstep, in holiday destinations.

We saw refugees and immigrants coming ashore in Greece after making the most harrowing journeys. We saw all the chaos in Calais. We saw images that live with us to this day, including the devastating photo of a police officer cradling a dead child on a Bodrum beach.

As we know, the rise in displaced people coincided with a global rise in nationalism and a severe decline in empathy. There was so much that needed to be said, but I couldn't find many musicians who were willing to address these issues of our time. My frustration grew and grew.

I was initially terrified of making an album as political as *Holiday Destination*. It felt like commercial suicide. But I didn't care. A few other musicians started to write on similar subjects and I felt slightly reassured. I found Kate Tempest's work especially inspiring at this time. The fact that she has never been afraid to speak out made me feel less alone.

When *Holiday Destination* was first released, I said some negative things about musicians not being vocal enough about political issues which I now regret. Social media can be so polemic and intimidating and I now understand why musicians aren't outspoken on certain topics such as refugees. Which is not to say that I regret writing that album. I don't. If I was frustrated, it was because I had an overwhelming sense of preaching to the converted. What kind of real change could I actually inspire?

I have said this before, many times, but I will say it again. I genuinely wish I had written *Holiday Destination* for Adele because she has a huge global audience and can speak to so many more people than I ever could. At the same time, it was beautiful to see the audience reaction when I performed the album live. Watching people leaving a venue with their activism fully charged made me feel like the album was doing something, however small. Being in a room full of people who actually give a fuck was in itself inspiring. I had a sense that I was voicing their frustrations for them.

And then the album was nominated for the Mercury Prize. I was with my band in the middle of a three-day stint of festivals and I burst into tears. It was a beautiful moment. I'd followed the awards since I was young and it meant a lot to me. I was gutted that *Fast Food* hadn't been nominated, but I'm glad they chose *Holiday Destination* instead. Finally, we had the opportunity to speak to a wide audience, one that I wouldn't have otherwise been able to reach. It gave the album a new lease of life and enabled me to spread the message to more and more people. For that I am truly thankful.

I do believe that music can effect change. Musicians are people too and, as I said earlier, it's part of our job to document the times we live in. I just wish I had a larger reach. I was so happy to see Taylor Swift both encouraging fans to vote and promoting a Democratic candidate. It was unbelievably exciting. I have huge respect for her for speaking up. Many people think we should leave politics to politicians, but politics is for everyone and so we have to all speak up. Now more than ever.

I mentioned the arse-slappers earlier. Over the years there have been too many occasions to mention where I've been treated as a woman and not as a musician. I've lost count of the number of times I've turned up to a venue and been asked if I am the girlfriend of a band member. Posters of my face are plastered all over the venue and STILL they ask.

I always feel angry, but I never show it. Every part of my being wants to demonstrate that anger, but I know it won't get me anywhere. Instead I calmly say, 'This is my band and I'm here to do my job and play music.'

I only hope they realise their mistake and don't do the same thing to the next woman who enters the venue.

I was once asked by a journalist if I wrote my own songs. I didn't overturn any tables, but I did walk out of the room.

There have been times when we have approached fashion houses and asked them to clothe me for awards shows. More often than not we have been told, 'Sorry, we don't provide outfits for artists bigger than a size eight.' I am five foot ten and a size ten. I am tall but slight. I've been made to feel ugly, overweight and ashamed by those companies. I didn't realise that female musicians are supposed to be the same size as models. I didn't sign up for any of that. My job is to make music and put on a good live show. I don't give two shits about looking pretty.

The only fashion house I've ever worked with that hasn't commented on my size is Vivienne Westwood. The *only one*.

Now I dress myself. It's simply less demoralising.

I have, in the past, been paid less than male artists for live shows. I can't say if it's because I'm a woman or whether it's because my previous booking agent didn't fight harder for more money. I now have a female booking agent and my fees are considerably higher.

I can talk about these failures in the music industry and in society, but I am not perfect. I am so unbelievably ashamed to admit that there was a time when I was unsupportive of other female artists. I blame this on my own insecurities coupled with the backwards logic of the music industry. When I was growing up, I always felt that there are so many professions in which there's only room for one woman, a notion that forces us to be competitive.

When my first album was released, I found it particularly disturbing that 'female solo artist' was referred to as a genre. It's not a fucking genre! My work shouldn't only be compared to other female musicians. That's super-lazy music journalism and it forces us women to be competitive with each other.

I remember journalists encouraging me to say negative things about Anna Calvi, as though she was in direct competition with me. I never fell for the bait because I respect her far too much and am a proper fan of her music. It had the opposite impact on me, in fact. From then on, I made a point of reaching out to other female artists and forming alliances. It's the best thing I've ever done.

Two of the first people to wish me luck at the Mercury Prize were fellow nominees Lily Allen and Florence Welch. The sisterhood is too strong for men to continue to divide us!

I was signed to 1965 Records for *Holiday Destination*; now I'm a free agent again and it's a lovely place to be. I'm currently writing my fourth album, which takes its inspiration from stories female friends have shared with me. Stories about sexism and issues specific to women. I was, for example, diagnosed with endometriosis in early 2018 and I was surprised to find out how many women live silently with the condition, even though it can ultimately affect your fertility. So I'm writing about that and about the pressure on women to reproduce.

I'm guessing it won't be a global hit, but my female manager doesn't give a shit because she's awesome. I don't care either. These things need to be said and I'm not scared of saying them.

JESSICA CURRY

Jessica Curry is a BAFTA Award-winning composer of contemporary classical music and co-founder of acclaimed games company The Chinese Room (although she stepped down in 2015). She wrote the music for the genre-changing game Dear Esther, won the BAFTA for the PS4 game Everybody's Gone to the Rapture and was awarded the Outstanding Contribution award at Women in Games in 2018. She is a presenter on Classic FM and has collaborated with poet laureate Carol Ann Duffy. Her work has been performed around the world, from the Royal Albert Hall to Sydney Opera House.

I don't come from a musical family. My mum bought me and my older brother a piano in the hope that we'd have lessons. I was four, and fascinated by this contraption that could make amazing noises. I started lessons with an incredible teacher, who I saw every week until I was eighteen, but I never did any grades. She said, 'Just love music. Play what you want and we'll explore it together.' She was so nurturing.

I was in the school orchestra and choir. I sang madrigals. I played the cello. I did a music GCSE, but still avoided formal grades; I wasn't bothered about the traditional level of attainment. I just wanted to play and enjoy it and was lucky to have teachers who weren't trying to push me to achieve for the sake of it.

I didn't initially think about doing a music degree or pursuing it as a career because the composers we learned about at school were all dead white men. I know it sounds really stupid, now that we have access to the internet and can learn about a huge variety of composers, but back then, in the 1980s, we only had access to library books and they really were full of dead white male composers.

I read English literature at UCL, but I missed music. When I left, I was completely unemployable. After many rejections, including a job as a server at Dunkin' Donuts, I got a job in the Warner Bros store. My lovely late stepdad, who was an avid *Guardian* reader, cut out an application for the National Film and Television School (NFTS) and said, 'You're wasting your talent. Just apply for this – you might get in.'

I applied for the postgraduate diploma in screen music and managed to talk my way in. I'm very passionate, and I was this big whirlwind of enthusiasm, so I suppose they took a punt on me. I had no idea what I was letting myself in for! It was so male-dominated and some of the men were really, really misogynistic. I met with one on the first day and was brimming with excitement. 'I really love music and I'm so ready to do this . . . '

He sat me down and said, 'The only reason a woman should be in my office is to clean it.'

He was adamant that women couldn't write decent music.

Later that week someone else – a pretty senior figure – came up to me and said, 'We'll never work with a woman composer, so why are you here?'

This was 1995, not 1895! I wasn't clutching a posy and delicately dabbing at myself with a handkerchief.

It was my first real experience of sexism and I was profoundly shocked. I had an incredibly strong working mother. I'd been to a very academic all-girls school which had been started by a suffragette and where female achievement was seen as the norm, and from which many of the girls went on to become brilliant scientists. My English literature course had been dominated by women.

I went from being in female-dominated spaces populated by high-achieving women to being surrounded by entitled blokes at the NFTS who had decided what I couldn't do before I had had a chance to show what I *could* do. I felt like I was spoiling their sacred male space. Not everyone on the course made me feel unwelcome, of course, but the prevailing mood was very macho. I went back there a few years ago to do a talk for the games students, and it's so different now – almost unrecognisable, in fact.

In my final year I was exhausted, and I had to battle it out to finish the course. Among the men in their puffa jackets and backward baseball caps going on and on about making Hollywood blockbusters, there was one ray of light. A female sound artist called Evelyn Ficarra came in to talk and I wanted to cling to her. She was working in the industry I wanted to work in and she gave me the confidence to keep going. She saved my life, creatively speaking.

I now mentor quite a few women games composers – it doesn't take much to share your experience and expertise. Often someone will email me asking for advice on something that has happened, or wondering where they should go to meet people. Then there are the three women that I've made a commitment to help longer-term; it gives me considerable pleasure, because I know it's still a massive struggle for women.

Anyway, film school was brutal and it crushed my confidence completely. I have experienced considerable success since then, but I still find myself feeling grateful for being accepted. I still notice when someone is nice to me. Well, why wouldn't they be? I'm really talented. I'm pleasant to work with. I resent feeling as though I have to ask for permission to be successful simply because I'm a woman.

When I graduated from NFTS, it wasn't with a sense of 'I'll show you'. I wasn't that confident. I just felt that there was no place for me in the mainstream film industry. There were so few role models; the only two successful female film composers at the turn of the century were Rachel Portman and Debbie Wiseman. It was a really blokey world. You were either resented for being a female with the audacity to be in their world, or you received pathetic comments like, 'Oh, I just said a swear word. Not in front of the ladies.'

Often you are made to feel like you've crashed the party and that you are somehow weaker.

As a woman, you are labelled 'difficult' if you speak up. If you're not apologetic. If you're not softly-spoken. If you're not girly. If you choose to navigate things differently. I've realised recently that I make myself amenable so that no one can ever level the 'difficult' accusation at me. I would never tell an aggressive journalist that he was making me feel uncomfortable because I know the write-up would be along the lines of, 'Jessica Curry is really spiky . . .'

I've heard stories about male composers who are legendary for their massive tantrums in the studio. Apparently this means they are passionate, in control. They are *auteurs*. I might say, politely, 'The oboe is a bit loud. Could you turn it down?' And guess what? I get an eye-roll and a sotto voce, 'Are you on your period?'

Often I think those men don't know how to behave with a woman, especially in the games industry. With women so rarely in evidence, men get flustered and, because they feel diminished, they become angry.

I worked with Carol Ann Duffy in 2016 on a project called *The Durham Hymns*. A century on from the Battle of the Somme, we marked the anniversary with a work for brass band and choir. Carol Ann, inspired by the true life experiences of County Durham people, wrote lyrics to the hymns to commemorate their sacrifice, courage and endurance, and I set those beautiful texts to music. She was amazing. So inspiring. She doesn't care what people think or what they say. She's all about the work. Society teaches us women that we are mothers, nurturers, enablers and supporters. So actively taking the reins is really uncomfortable for a lot of us because, societally, we've not been taught to do that. All the stress around projects, all the little comments – that's all just white noise to Carol Ann.

I was at a meeting with her and she was asked to do something. She very politely but very firmly said, 'That's not in my contract, so I'm not going to do it.' You could see how taken aback they were, but it didn't bother her. Guys say no all the time without any fuss.

My new strategy is to surround myself with as many non-apologetic, high-achieving, powerful women as I can. So far, it's a strategy that's working well for me.

In some ways, I have had no choice.

My husband Dan Pinchbeck and I set up The Chinese Room, an independent games development studio, so that we could write, produce and design our own games.

That makes it sound very simple. It wasn't.

It all started when it was announced that I was doing the soundtrack for *Amnesia: A Machine for Pigs* in 2013. It was a sequel, and the original soundtrack was both much loved and written by a man. Because it was a horror game, it also had a percentage of a certain type of games fan. And they went for me.

The day my involvement was announced, I got a tweet that read: 'I know your son's name and I'm going to come and slit his throat'. Gamer websites instructed other fans to 'go for this woman'. They rallied and the abuse continued. They fake-reviewed our games both on gaming websites and on Facebook, which effectively destroys your business. They constantly changed my Wikipedia page.

It was a sustained and organised campaign of hatred. The emails and online comments were so extreme. Death threats. Rape threats. Sexual threats. You can block them, but they are gamers, they are tech-savvy. They just find another way of getting to you. I am furious with social media platforms, who could choose to manage this kind of abuse but who want the traffic.

A lot of women leave the games industry because of this kind of abuse. As a mother, you cannot accept abuse aimed at your child. I'm an adult who chose to be in this industry, but my son is innocent. It's scary, and it has definitely changed the way I live. I used to walk freely in my home city, in London and in any given European city. Not any more. I'm more cautious now.

The games industry didn't know – still doesn't know – how to deal with the situation. Most people say, 'Oh, they'll never carry out those threats. All women in this industry get threats. You just need to calm down about it.' When I tell anyone outside the games industry, they are horrified – which shows it's become totally normalised within the industry.

Finally, in October 2015, I wrote a blog post on The Chinese Room website about why I was leaving the company. I explained that I have a degenerative disease that is made worse by exhaustion. The work I had done on *Everybody's Gone to the Rapture* had pushed me to breaking point, but my involvement was downplayed. I have been referred to as 'Dan Pinchbeck's PA' and as 'Dan Pinchbeck's wife'. When Dan himself referred to me as 'the brains of the operation', people commended him for his kindness.

The blog post was written out of desperation. When I look back on it now, I realise I couldn't function for the first time ever. At the time we were having difficult publisher relations, the trolling was violent and endless and I was facing everyday sexism.

So I said to Dan, 'I'm going to write a blog post today. I need to make a big change.' He was really supportive, even though it was almost certainly going to affect the company.

Dan has always been supportive, but my experiences really politicised him and now if he gets invited to do a panel or conference, he always says, 'I'm only doing it if there is representation in terms of ethnicity and gender.' It's so important for men to be vocal about the fact that it's always white, middle-aged, middle-class men being asked for their opinion on everything. If there's no diversity, Dan gives up his place.

I felt very alone at that time. When I read Björk's *Pitchfork* interview about the invisible work female artists do, I cried with relief. It was a very powerful moment: a woman as high-profile and respected as Björk had experienced very similar issues to me. She talks at the end of the article about having a responsibility to other women, and it's something I wrestle with. Since the blog post, I get requests all the time asking me to talk about what it's like to be a woman in games.

I know it helps other women, but sometimes I just want to talk about my work. My male colleagues don't ever think, 'Do I have a responsibility as a man in this industry to be inclusive and tolerant, a responsibility to mentor people?' They just do the work. That's the luxury they are afforded.

In a way, I've let the genie out of the bottle and I can never put it back. If you google me, the blog post is the top story. But then I was telling a woman in the games industry that I regretted writing the blog and she said, 'No! It really inspired me. It was obviously written by someone who is fighting for the right things, someone who will stick up for women. Never, ever apologise or regret doing it because it has inspired so many women in the industry. It has made them braver.'

I learned what is catnip for the trolls and so I navigate my way very carefully through social media now. I am guarded when I talk to people in the games industry. I've become much more neutral, which bothers me because that isn't an honest representation of myself. As a woman you naturally neutralise yourself anyway.

I'm feeling my way around the games industry quite tentatively at the moment. It's a deeply troubled place with deep-rooted issues of racism and sexism. The working hours are brutal. It's got a massive suicide rate.

I feel that my destiny probably doesn't lie within that industry. I've always been fairly peripatetic in terms of the projects I do. I've never restricted myself to composing for just one genre, for film or theatre or games. I'm inspired by people and projects, and by stories. By branching out, I have probably been less traditionally successful but I've loved each and every project that I've done. I don't want to write the score for a massive-budget zombie/slasher game that makes me feel sick when I play it, and I've never been motivated by money.

I now feel as though I want to get on and write the music I know I have in me, without apologising for doing so. I want to enjoy work. I want to work with amazing, positive people who bring me joy and happiness and inspiration and creativity.

Despite my misgivings about the industry, I've been working on my first game since the blog post. I'm trying to prove to myself that it can be a positive experience if you protect yourself carefully. For example, I worked with a female leader of the orchestra on *Everybody's Gone to the Rapture*, which is almost unheard of. The relationship between composer and leader is key during recording sessions, and leaders are almost always men. Clio Gould is one of the best violinists in the world and a fantastic orchestral leader – so I worked with her again on this new project.

After the *Rapture* sessions aired, the musicians came up to me and said, 'It's so rare to have a gentle session. It's so rare to have a female composer in the booth.' They said I was so nurturing, that I saw them as people. I took time to talk to them – even if I was told off for doing so, for wasting time. Too often, composers shout at musicians like they are just robots. And that was a choice I made – to try not to become bitter but to keep being a thoughtful, funny, joyful person. That's an act of resistance in itself because then you haven't let the bullies win and you have retained the best part of yourself. I think this is vital.

Although some of my experience has been incredibly tough, the amazing thing about being an outsider is that you are able to create work that doesn't sound or look like anything else, and that is an incredibly powerful thing. It's only recently that I've started to truly understand what a strength and a badge of honour that is. In an increasingly plastic world, people crave authenticity and a unique voice. My experiences – whether that's ill health, motherhood or being a woman in a man's world – all enable me to write music that speaks directly to people. That's indescribably valuable.

Yes, there are trolls. But I also receive emails and letters from fans every day who value what I do very deeply and who have been profoundly touched by my music. People walk down the aisle to my music. They bury their loved ones to it. And loads of people write to me to say that my music has got them through some terrible times in their life. That is worth every negative experience I've been through and more.

Music has got me through some really tough times in my life, too, and to know that you have done that for someone else – it doesn't get better than that. To know that you have been someone's light in the darkness, that you might restore something within them – for me, that is music's function and power.

I've always loved writing for choirs, and that's something I'm currently doing more of. For me, choirs represent the best of people. When people from different religions, races, political beliefs and backgrounds come together to sing, they create unity and harmony. It's a beautiful concept and it's just so powerful. Every experience you have in life, whether positive or negative, steers you forward in a certain direction. The music I'm writing at the moment is representative of the person that I am as a result of the times I've lived through. Even though it's been hard, I try not to have any regrets because it's made me the person I am now, and I've learned a lot about myself.

*

I do have hope for the future. Younger female colleagues in the games industry seem better able to protect themselves, and they just aren't willing to waste their emotional energy. Perhaps because they are digital natives and have therefore grown up with the internet. Perhaps because they don't seem to need male approval, despite the fact that they have chosen to work in a male-dominated industry. They are doing good work and the rest is white noise which they choose to cut out. I see them asking less and less for permission and I find that heartening. It makes me very happy.

They also laugh in the face of aggression, which is really powerful. As though to say, 'You are irrelevant to me. When you have achieved what I have achieved, then maybe we can have this discussion.' I've learned the hard way that anger is painful; you get angry and you hurt yourself. Laughter and joy are far more powerful tools.

Social media has its uses: it can be very powerful in terms of the dissemination of feminist material. You can find your digital tribes of support, whether it be Everyday Sexism or other female composers. You can align yourself with amazing women who stand up for themselves.

My mum is a writer and she says, 'Just do the work, Jess. Speak through the work.' I do think, increasingly, that she's right. Every time someone says that I didn't deserve to win the BAFTA or get a commission, I have to remember to say to myself, 'I'm going to keep getting better.' I don't have to have a dialogue with the trolls or the execs. I can speak through the quality of the work that I produce.

My life is much calmer now, but talking about what I've been through is nonetheless upsetting. I have to look forward, to focus on the fact that women in games are finding their own powerful world of networks. I used to wonder if women at games conferences were a good thing. Did we really want to be *women* in games? Couldn't we just be working in games?

But it's actually very refreshing and exciting to go to one of those conferences, see that so many women have faced the same problems and realise that they haven't given up. You feel less isolated. You meet inspiring women. You see that the networks that have sprung up are both useful and empowering.

Whether we like it or not, we, as women, have collective responsibility for each other. I feel cautiously optimistic: the world is changing, and I'm proud to be a small part of that.

MAGGIE ROGERS

Playing harp, guitar and piano from an early age, Maggie Rogers released her debut album, The Echo, in 2012 while in her senior year of high school. Her second album, Blood Ballet, was released in 2014, during her sophomore year at the Clive Davis Institute of Recorded Music at New York University. Her breakthrough came in 2016 with the song 'Alaska', which became hugely popular after Pharrell Williams' reaction to it during a college masterclass: he was moved to tears, said she was singular and that he had 'zero notes'. The video, which – as Rogers explains in her chapter – was shared 'without her permission', went viral shortly afterwards. Rogers has since released the EP Now That the Light Is Fading and the singles 'Split Stones' and 'Fallingwater'. Her debut album, Heard It in a Past Life, was released in January 2019.

I grew up in a rural area, about two hours south of Washington, D.C. on the eastern shore of Maryland, in a place called Easton. My little brother has very sensitive hearing, especially with bass frequencies, so there wasn't a ton of music in the house. My sister is only fourteen months older than me, but was never super-interested in music.

Yet music was something I was really drawn to from a very early age. I think it's a sign of how supportive my parents have been that I'm making music now. I had a Mozart music box. I listened to a lot of classical music. I started playing the harp when I was eight or nine. I grew up loving Tchaikovsky and Vivaldi. I remember the cover of my CD of Gustav Holst's *The Planets*. I remember the birthday I got a boom box. I remember the Xmas I got a karaoke machine. I remember getting piano lessons.

Growing up, I wrote poems and songs. I listened to music with my mom in the car on the way to music lessons, when it was just us. Erykah Badu's *Baduizm*, *The Miseducation Of Lauryn Hill*, OutKast's *ATLiens*, Alanis Morissette's *Jagged Little Pill*, The Cranberries' *Everybody Else Is Doing It . . .* The first CD I bought with my own money was a dual purchase of Britney's *Baby One More Time* and the orchestral score to *Harry Potter and The Sorcerer's Stone*.

I read constantly. We didn't have TV. We had dial-up internet until I was in the seventh grade. Probably the most crucial part of my musical development was when I left home. At fourteen, I went to a co-educational boarding school called St. Andrews School in Delaware because there wasn't access to higher education, especially arts education, where I lived.

Every night after dinner I did something to do with music. Monday I sang with a thirty-piece jazz band. Tuesday I played the harp in the orchestra. Wednesday I sang in the choir. We had chapel on Sundays and Wednesdays, so I sang classical music on those days. Thursdays was a cappella practice, and I arranged and sang in the group. Very quickly I substituted required sports for time in this little recording studio that I created. So not only was I practising and playing music for two hours a day, I was also recording and writing songs for two more hours a day. Every day.

All of my friends were artists, many of them painters; they all hung out in the painting studio. One of the teachers had a record player and a collection of records in the studio and it was the first time I heard Bob Dylan, Joni Mitchell, Talking Heads, The Rolling Stones, The Beatles. There was no internet, no cell phones or TVs at the school, so it had this vibe of being stuck in the 1960s and 1970s in the best way.

It was a tough school academically; you couldn't stay in if you didn't want to be there. There were no drugs or alcohol. There were no day students, so nobody was coming in and out. I grew up really slowly in this strange bubble. I was an eighteen-year-old happily playing four square or cards on a Saturday night, or I was in the studio, or running around with friends.

Very quickly, my first band became the other musicians in my class. I played banjo and my two best friends played cello and violin. So, right off the bat, I was writing string arrangements. I was listening to a lot of bands like Vampire Weekend, Bon Iver, Tallest Man On Earth and Sufjan Stevens.

For college, I went to the Clive Davis Institute of Recorded Music at New York University. It had a similar vibe. It had a very specific curriculum; we were being trained in the music industry – in engineering, production, and recorded music history. Because I didn't grow up with music around the house, I showed up at school without any kind of internalised pop music catalogue. I still get nervous around other musicians because there are so many musical references I don't know. But there's something really special about getting to discover classic records at an older age. I didn't hear Michael Jackson's *Thriller* till my senior year of college.

To hear Prince for the first time at twenty-two is fucking awesome. I think I was able to soak in a lot more and listen critically because of it.

The classes at NYU are built to resemble a microcosm of the music industry, so I was the folk girl. I played the banjo. I wrote folk songs. That was me. Next to me was the white rapper next to the manager next to the writer next to the rock boy. I became really interested in synthesizers and focused on taking my production to the next level. I was learning how to properly mix for the first time, stuff like that.

I started this folk band, Del Water Gap, with one of my classmates and we played seriously for a year. It was my first time really gigging and being in a band, and it was a special time. I remember feeling invincible and having this romantic view of being a songwriter in New York.

At the end of the first year, Del Water Gap started to attract the attention of some record labels. I had a panic attack and realized I couldn't sign my name. I was in a duo with a boy and it was slowly feeling more like his band than mine. I was becoming 'just the banjo girl'. I felt like I was boxed in by this instrument, where people expected me to sing harmony and be an accessory to the guitar. I would bring songs to the band and be told that my songs were too girly or not right for our audience. It was supposed to be our band, fifty-fifty, but it very quickly started to feel like I had no creative control.

It was probably the hardest decision I've ever had to make. I left the band and went hiking in Alaska for a month. I definitely wasn't thinking about songs at that time.

This band had consumed my life for a year, and I needed some time to figure out where I was at, who I was, and what I was thinking about.

*

I was punched in the face by New York. I moved there when I was eighteen, having been sheltered pretty much my entire life. I'd never met a person who did not mean what they said or who was manipulative or who had ulterior motives. Although I never understood that way of life, I was of course aware that those characteristics existed. I read about those kinds of people in fiction.

New York was such a vast metropolis compared to the rural area I grew up in. I had spent my whole life up to that point making a huge effort to get to see live music. An adult had to agree to drive me two hours each way, just so that I could go to a concert. To get to a concert we would have to leave at 5 p.m. and get home at 2 a.m. It was a big commitment. It was even more difficult when I was at boarding school because we had class on Saturdays.

Suddenly, in New York, I could go to live music all the time. The culture I had fought so hard for my entire life was there on a plate. When I arrived in the city, I thought I had everything figured out, but then I entered this new world and realised very quickly how different things were.

I needed time out in Alaska. I cut all my hair off; my song 'Alaska' is entirely autobiographical. Cutting my hair off was totally cathartic and empowering and I needed the change. It was about starting anew. This was something I did when I was twelve and seventeen, too. A kind of ritual, a way of marking time.

When I arrived back in New York that August, I felt centred. I moved out of the dorms and into my first real apartment and then found for the first time that I couldn't write music. I had two and a half years of songwriter's block. I put music to one side and started working in journalism and on books. I freelanced for *Elle* and *Spin Magazine* and worked as an intern and then assistant editor with Lizzy Goodman on *Meet Me in the Bathroom*, her oral history of the New York music scene at the start of the twenty-first century, a project that lasted three years.

During the second half of my third year of college and during the ongoing period of writer's block, I moved to Paris to study contemporary art, expatriate literature and French. I fell in with a group of native Berliners and made several trips to Berlin. I didn't have a cell phone, so my friends sort of just took care of me and showed me their world.

It was in Berlin that I heard house music for the first time. I'm so drawn to lyric and melody that I never thought listening to a six-minute house track was something I'd be interested in. Suddenly I started to understand the meditation of it, the slow development and growth. So I'd go clubbing, in Berlin first, then Paris. House music obviously exists in Brooklyn, but it didn't for me when I was eighteen. I was a banjo player getting excited at seeing some acoustic set at Joe's Pub.

I was listening to lots of music in Paris: Pixies, The Breeders, Sonic Youth, The Cure, Ryan Adams (I keep lists of my playlists by season, so I could be even more specific). And yet still I couldn't write a song. I tend to wait until I have something to say rather than actually sit down and write, but even then I tried and nothing came. I wanted to do more than write folk songs. Those always came quickly, in my sleep, like a formula.

I was bored and I wanted to challenge myself. I was listening to Carly Rae Jepsen's record, *Emotion*, and my room-mate said, 'I know you say you don't like pop music, but you should see your face when this record comes on.' She was right: I suddenly realised how much I loved pop music. I started wearing a lot of pink eyeshadow and I had this worlds-collide moment: how can I love pop and pink eyeshadow and also love hiking? Can I be this same person?

I watched a lot of music videos and festival performances from a lot of different artists and tried to understand who I would want as my peers if I was going to make more music. Maybe I found it so hard to write music around this time because I was trying to fit into specific stereotypes. When I wrote folk music I would wear red cowboy boots, denim and overalls every day. The hardest thing was realising that I didn't fit the pop stereotype or the folk stereotype, and I didn't know where that left me. I'd lived in New York for four years and loved it, but I loved going home and spending time outside just as much.

Then I guess I realised that I could just be exactly who I am, and make music that is both pop and folk. I let go of genre and gave myself permission to be me.

As soon as I understood that I didn't have to be in a box that already existed, I felt totally free to create. I stopped censoring myself and started experimenting. I've always been the kind of person who writes ten songs and puts out ten songs. It can take twenty minutes to write a song, or two months. It took two and a half years to write a three-minute pop song about a one-month hiking trip, but of course I had no idea that 'Alaska' would be a catalyst for such a big shift in my life.

At first I didn't like the song 'Alaska' at all. I thought it was too poppy. The melody line at the beginning felt too happy. It didn't feel totally like me – or maybe it was just a me I didn't recognize yet. My last semester at NYU, I was in the advanced production class. It was really just a thesis class where we got studio time to make work and then had to show it to the class and our professors for critique. Eventually it was my day to present my work, and I only had that song, which no one had ever heard.

I didn't think about what I was going to wear to the class. When I'm dressing like my artist self or for performance, I have a way of looking a bit more put together or stylized. But when I'm working as a producer or songwriter, I'm going to work. I'm not going to present myself to the world, I'm going to get my hands dirty. That day, I wore the jeans and T-shirt from my East Village apartment floor, and a necklace made out of some cooking string and two elk vertebrae that I found while hiking.

I couldn't sleep the night before, but I didn't know why; it was just school the next day. It feels weird to say this, but I could feel something happening. As I was walking to class, someone asked me to put on a mic. I was confused. And then I walked into the class and there was a camera crew.

And then Pharrell walked in. Masterclasses happen at least two or three times a semester, but we usually know who with beforehand. I guess it was unusual not to be told who was coming, but I didn't really think about it. It was just my turn, along with two other classmates, to show my work in class. I didn't have much to show, but I did have this one song. I was starting to get into trouble because we were nearing our final project and I hadn't turned in anything in a while. What I had turned in was basically a fake project. Instead of making it hold value in my artistic world, I turned in something to meet the requirements. My professors knew I was totally bullshitting and were starting to get kind of frustrated with me.

I remember feeling very calm. I didn't feel stressed or excited, overeager or anxious. I just felt calm and settled – my heart was racing, but my mind was sharp and clear. I was super-super-present. Having said that, I don't have much memory of actually meeting Pharrell or him being there. But I knew it was important. I felt the gravity of the moment.

I was shocked by what happened. I knew I did things

differently from other people, but I didn't always think of that as an asset. It's very strange, being told that you're that special. I'm not sure I feel that way. For me, the song didn't feel special. It just felt like another song. Just the thing I was working on at the time.

Usually I enjoy making the music without considering how it will be received. But I left NYU that day thinking, 'Well, OK, I've never made pop music before. It's a good sign that what I'm trying to do is translating in the way that I hoped it would.'

I wandered around Chinatown for a while and found my way to my friend's house. I walked in and said, 'Something really weird just happened.' He's a very sweet, kind of dopey friend, like a lovable puppy. He was like, 'Yeah, whatever, man.' And I was like, 'No, I just met Pharrell and he really liked my song.' And he was like, 'That's cool. Want to get lunch?' I was like, 'Yeah, all right, but he *really* liked it.'

I needed to tell someone. But what do you say? We had lunch and then, later that day, I wrote the song 'Better', which ended up on my first EP, *Now That the Light Is Fading*. I just kept working.

I called my mom that night and told her about the master-class. She said, 'That's great, honey.'

I really didn't think anything would come of the meeting with Pharrell.

That whole thing happened at the beginning of March. I wrote him a thank you note and there was a bit of industry buzz, but nothing happened. I graduated on May 20 2016, and on May 31 I moved out of my college apartment and went home to Maryland. On June 1, the video of Pharrell listening to 'Alaska' went viral.

That day I sat at my kitchen table and wrote emails for fourteen hours straight, trying to keep up with the flood in my inbox, texts from friends. It was really crazy, but because of school, I felt weirdly prepared for it. Our final project in school was to make a business plan. I had a three-year timeline, a marketing plan, merchandising designs, stage plot, a list of people I'd want to open for, publishers and labels I was interested in, sync licensing . . .

For a long time I took these meetings with labels and managers alone. I would bring in my business plan and set it on their desk. They would check out my mission statement, my timeline, all the video treatments, all this stuff. I wanted to make sure I was clearly communicating my vision.

And I stated from the beginning that I was serious about the plan – this is what I wanted to do, this is how I was going to do it. So I thought I could actually manage myself for a little while. And I like being in control. What was so good about going to NYU was that I learned how to do this stuff. I'm a producer and an engineer – I figured I could do it all by myself.

It became evident very quickly that I needed help.

I signed with Mick Management that Wednesday. 'Alaska' came out on a Friday. On the same day, I left the country. I was terrified and really overwhelmed by all the attention. My private life became very public very quickly and suddenly there were all these people that wanted me to be this *thing*. And things got crazy, fast. I went to the mountains in France to visit a friend and was in a small mountain town when I read my first *Pitchfork* feature. I got a call and was asked to be in the September issue of *Vogue*. It was nuts. I ended up choosing the mountains instead of the *Vogue* photo shoot, but later that year appeared consecutively in the October and November issues.

It was a really powerful and disorienting level of disbelief.

I had planned this trip to Malaysia before I graduated, to visit my sister. I heard 'Alaska' for the first time on the radio in Malaysia, driving with my sister in Borneo, where she was living. Just super-weird.

There have been so many moments. Like walking past someone wearing a Maggie Rogers T-shirt at an airport and keeping my head down. When I'm not on tour, everything kind of settles. I keep waiting for all this to go away a little bit, because it happened so fast. I haven't gotten attached. But it isn't going away.

I joke with my mom about being a pop star. I'll say, 'This is my pop star jacket.' It reminds me of the kid who used to sing karaoke in the living room. I dressed up as a pop star for Halloween one year and a rock star the next, wearing a plastic 'leather' jacket both times. But the truth is that I don't know what it feels like to be a pop star. With the onset of streaming services, I don't think that concept even exists any more. If we live in an environment where Selena Gomez is sampling Talking Heads, maybe the pop stars are dead.

I have become protective of my family. I don't post photos of my mom on Instagram or Twitter on Mother's Day. I didn't grow up on social media, so it feels like work. I'm trying to become more natural with it, but it feels like this thing that I have to remind myself to engage with. Being recognized and asked for a picture is very difficult for me. It still feels uncomfortable. After a show in Chicago, a boy my age was waiting by the tour bus and we had a really nice conversation. It felt like we were really connecting. Then he asked for a photo and I said no. My mental health was starting to waver, and I was really struggling on tour. The photo stuff made me feel less than human. He looked at me and said, 'C'mon, Maggie, you didn't make it yet.' He walked away and I just stood there on the street.

That moment has stayed with me because I wasn't trying to be a diva. The last thing I want to do is appear inaccessible or ungrateful. I didn't have a choice about the way this happened for me. The Pharrell video captured an incredibly intimate, unguarded personal moment that was shared with the world without my permission. I wouldn't take it back, but it meant that the transition was really fast and hard. I was unprepared. It wasn't calm in any way. I had to deal with the kind of anxiety I'd never had to deal with before. I had terrible panic attacks. Things have settled a little, and I've managed to figure a few things out, but so much fell out of my control so quickly.

It was such a strange, unexpected experience, but at the same time, the video has allowed me to be me. There's no image. No persona. I get lots of messages from people saying, 'I'm so proud of you.' I've never met them and yet they have a sense of investment and personal connection. They are as much a part of the story as I am. It's crowdsourced pop stardom. The most 2016 thing that could possibly have existed.

In almost every article ever written about me, Pharrell is mentioned in the first sentence. It's not so much the 'discovery by a man' element. The frustrating thing is the language used around it: 'Pharrell-approved songwriter'; 'Pharrell protégé'. I understand that it's where the story starts for many people. As a journalist, you tell a story, you have an angle. Also, I haven't put out a lot of music, so there hasn't been a great deal more for me to tell people, realistically. But it completely ignores the fact that I have been writing music for ten years and producing for six or seven.

All of those nights in high school when I wasn't hanging out with my friends, instead I was working in the studio. All those times in middle school I spent alone, teaching myself to play guitar. All the time in college I spent not partying or being part of a fraternity or taking weekends off but spending time at band practice, writing business plans, making music videos. It makes me want to cry. It ignores the fact that I've been doing this for a long time. Even Capitol wrote 'Debut EP by Maggie Rogers'. I had to remind them that it was my third release – I put out two full-length independent records before all this. But that doesn't fit the Cinderella story. It doesn't fit the 'born out of the brain of Pharrell, fully formed' narrative.

It's been a steep learning curve. It's been exciting, but it's also been incredibly uncomfortable. I make music to understand the way I feel. Then I play the song until I feel better. Then I write a new one. I'm as confused and frustrated by the world as everyone else is. I admire songwriters like Leonard Cohen who can tell stories. I love his poetry as well. I love the way it's intertwined. Patti Smith does that too. I'd like to get to a point where I can write the kind of song that people will listen to in fifty years.

EMMY THE GREAT

Emma Lee-Moss was born in Hong Kong to a Chinese mother and English father, and raised in East Grinstead. As Emmy the Great, she has released three studio albums since 2006: First Love, Virtue *and* Second Love. *A fourth studio album was recorded in New York and will be released on Bella Union in late 2019. In 2013, Emmy the Great's original songs appeared on the soundtrack for Sony Pictures'* Austenland *and, in 2017, she composed the original songs for Sara Pascoe's stage adaptation of Jane Austen's* Pride and Prejudice. *When not making music, Lee-Moss is a print and broadcast journalist.*

School is such a crapshoot. You only really have a chance to figure out who you are after the chaos of your school years. I went to a strict Chinese state school in Hong Kong where everyone was Chinese except me and a girl whose parents were missionaries. I was then going to be sent to a convent school, based on the entrance exams all Hong Kong kids take at eleven – you get fed to a school according to your results and, compared to the very high academic standards of kids there, I was floundering.

Luckily for me, we moved back to England that summer and instead of going to an old-fashioned all-girls' school in Hong Kong, I went to a Steiner school in Sussex where we all ran about barefoot and talked about feelings. I never had to work at maths again; I was top of the class until I was fifteen, pretty much based on what I'd learned in Hong Kong.

We moved back because my parents had always agreed that they would return to England, and Dad was feeling a hunger for home. Lots of our friends were also leaving in the summer of 1995, partly because in July 1997 sovereignty over Hong Kong was going to be returned from the UK to China and nobody knew what was going to happen.

We always felt like an English family. We spoke English at home. My mum, as was the tradition, yelled at me in Cantonese when she was cross. And I spoke Cantonese at school in Hong Kong. I went through a period of rejecting it after we moved to England – I was trying really hard to blend in with other kids, and I didn't want them to think I was different. Nowadays, my Cantonese is fluent again. When I go to China, the language I've filed away in a part of my brain returns, almost overnight. It's so strange. Language is the most interesting thing.

I have always listened to music in both languages. There was a big alternative American rock scene in Hong Kong and bands like Fugazi and Weezer were popular. The culture was very international, but of course American culture was always dominant.

I listened to a lot of Cantopop, the style of Hong Kong music that was the leading Chinese pop of the 1990s. It had a highly commercial, sometimes syrupy style of production, but something about the Cantonese dialect gave it life. The big stars of the genre were not afraid to bust taboos. Artists like

Anita Mui and Leslie Cheung played with ideas of gender in their performances, elaborately orchestrated stadium affairs that even Madonna might have balked at. Faye Wong, also known as 'the Chinese Björk', is still one of my favourite artists. I love her collaborations with the Cocteau Twins – she pushed creative boundaries in a way that no other Cantopop artist has attempted.

Most of the kids of our family friends went to international school in Hong Kong, so I had this kind of secret world in which I listened to Cantopop on my own (it wasn't deemed cool), and then this other world where I talked about Nirvana or Green Day with the international school kids. A boy would often say a record was cool and eventually I'd agree.

When I arrived in England, I switched my allegiance to Britpop. I remember sitting in a group of people at my new school and everyone was talking about the kind of music they liked. I said something like 'Metallica'. Everyone in the group happened to be into indie music so I suddenly felt scared and said, 'I think I mean Radiohead. And Blur. And Sleeper.' I guess I was a typical teenage kid, trying to get into the tastes of the time and seeing how they defined me. I gradually moved on to Belle & Sebastian and Glasgow music, then the lo-fi singer-songwriter post-Daniel Johnston world of The Microphones and Mirah.

My main musical influence was my babysitter, who I spent all my weekends with when I lived in Hong Kong. She was four years older than me and she's still my best friend – I'm godmother to her son now. At least I had her taste to balance out the maleness of Britpop: she played me Nirvana, but also the Cranberries. Even then, I only became really confident in my tastes when I started discovering music entirely on my own: I got into The Moldy Peaches, Kimya Dawson and

Joanna Newsom, and singer-songwriters such as Joni Mitchell, Sandy Denny and Leonard Cohen.

The discovery of music wasn't, for me, a conscious thing. It was rather a constant conversation, especially in those fertile teenage years when I was forming my musical identity. Because I lived in two countries, I discovered music in a different way to other people. Sleater-Kinney and Bikini Kill I only discovered at university. I was, however, really into Ani DiFranco before she was more widely recognised. A friend who had moved to America sent me a song of Ani's on a mixtape and then I went and bought all her stuff. The inventiveness of her songwriting, the fact that she self-distributed and that her label was called Righteous Babe all had an influence on me at the time. I still respect her, even though I couldn't tell you what kind of music she was releasing now.

A defining musical event was Fiona Apple's speech at the MTV Video Music Awards in 1997, a few days before she turned twenty. She went up to get her Best New Artist award and started ranting about her image. 'This world [the music business] is bullshit, and you shouldn't model your life around what we think is cool and what we're wearing and what we're saying. Go with yourself . . . and it's just stupid that I'm in this world.' I thought it was an amazing speech.

When I went to the University of Westminster to study contemporary music, I discovered Diane Cluck, who is also self-distributed. I found an album of hers in a record store that she had placed there with her own hands. A handmade album. I fell in love with her.

So I think the women who influenced me most profoundly in my youth were all fiercely independent, which was a huge part of why I loved them.

At the same time, I am totally and utterly a girl of the 1990s, and as such, I've been shaped by the conditions of the 1990s. I didn't picture myself being a musician on stage; I pictured myself befriending a musician. I was worried about my appearance – I was convinced I was overweight, even when I became emaciated from an eating disorder. I thought I had to act in a certain way in order to be cool. All that stuff fell really hard on me at the time. Then, suddenly, songwriting just happened. It wasn't something that I could consciously control. I just reached a point where I started writing songs and I realised I loved doing it. I finally said to myself, 'What if I try to make this something that I do?'

I had filled my brain with music. Up to the age of twenty-one, I was a listener and I was going to lots of gigs. Then, at twenty-one, I started writing songs. It became this obsession, this love. I'd think, 'I can be a better musician if I write another song, play another gig.' It became this ongoing journey where I would say to myself: 'Maybe I can achieve the next thing', or, 'Now I've got a band, I can play Glastonbury', or 'Now I think I can get a record deal'. It was like a series of dares, all the way through.

While I was at university, I printed a hundred CD covers and used my laptop to burn CDs of my demos, which I distributed randomly around London. On the tube, in the pages of books at a bookstore ... At the time, we were organising songwriter gigs at the university bar. I was using 'Emmy the Great' as one of my names for these performances – I can't remember why, but it was the title I printed onto those CDs. Those songs spread around the internet faster than I could have imagined, and soon I was being asked to play gigs and support various artists on tour. Emmy the Great became my stage name.

It was an exciting time to be starting out, because of what was happening on the internet. During the MySpace years in London, I swear to god you could play just one chord on MySpace and a hundred A&R people would come to the gig. They were so desperate to be that person who had discovered someone on the internet. So I was having a lot of meetings. I have only understood this clearly in recent years, but it did seem like they wanted to categorise me. They'd say, 'Are you a Kate Bush kind of singer, or a Joni Mitchell? Are you the next Lily Allen? Why don't you try getting more into fashion because that's a really good route to success for a female artist?'

I asked one A&R guy for some notes on the *music* and he said, 'You should get into fashion.' I do wear clothes. I'm already wearing them. Is he saying that he wants me to collaborate with famous designers so I can get into magazines, and that that's my only route to getting into those publications? You can't call up fashion magazines and say, 'I'd like you to send me some clothes and then feature me.' It has to be something that's an authentic result of what you're already interested in.

I am a complicated person. Plus, I am a mixed-heritage person. And, in those early days, I was singing about my love of English nature. When I arrived in people's offices, they would say, 'Why don't we try for something more "exotic"?' In the UK, the fact that I was half-Chinese and had been born in Hong Kong seemed to set me apart – it was confusing to people. They seemed to struggle to relate to me. I think they felt that the only way to address my 'otherness' was to make it a big feature of the music, but when they listened to it, it was so curiously *English*-sounding.

Still, I got offered a few deals in those early days – some

quite big deals, in fact. The offer would come in, I'd go and meet with the person and tell them I wanted to self-produce, I wanted a long career, make ten albums and grow gradually. I would never hear from them again. Nowadays I'm amused by this. Of course no one wants to hear that you don't even want to attempt to make them rich! Amazingly, a few people did understand my plan, and even decided to fund it.

I was twenty-something by that point. Probably twenty-three. I had a manager at the time who only represented me and one other artist, and there was a real sense of us against the world. We were both women in our early twenties and learning the industry together. Maybe, after a while, we built up too much of a fortress against the world. There were a few years when I would only do something if I thought it was unique, if I could do it in my own way. Without that, I couldn't have had that self-belief.

My manager, with whom I later parted ways, always found a way around the mainstream channels. When a deal fell through weeks before my album was supposed to be released, she found distribution. Early on, I signed to an independent publishing company and they were a lifeline. My PR took me on before there was a label to pay her, and my agent worked with me from my first shows in the belief that I would one day bring him commission. Somehow, the belief of a small group of determined people kick-started my career so that I had a foundation to build on.

Recently, I was reapplying for a visa for the States and I had to collect all my press. When I read the early reviews for my first album, *First Love*, I got shivers of such sadness at the way that people described me, because I was just a young girl when those reviews were written. I think we are much better now. These days, critics wouldn't be so quick to use language, make statements or ask questions like this: *Ingénue. Dewy-eyed. She's got a tiny voice. Can she live up to what she thinks she is?*

That was an age of comparing girls to each other, with one always found to be lacking – as though there was only one place at the table. In those reviews there was such a sense of, 'You think you are someone but you are not'. Or, 'At twenty-four, she's a little too old to be singing about stuff like this'. Or, 'All she thinks about is her boyfriend'. *First Love* is a break-up album; what else am I going to be singing about? And then, because I wrote lyrics like this – 'You were stroking me like a pet/But you didn't own me yet/And the tape in the cassette deck was choking/Spat out a broken Hallelujah' – I was also too literary.

I don't think I could have survived that time without this tiny unit me and my manager had built. I had no confidence back then. When you first find out what it's like to be reviewed by strangers, it's a real shock – especially as I was such a young woman at the time. I would have these huge freak-outs: 'At twenty-four I'm too old to be singing about this stuff and I'm too cutesy and they hate my dresses.'

Then I would go into my room, pick up my guitar and forget about it.

One thing I've always been really good at is being forgetful. So I'd just make another album. On some level I knew that my music, and the way I performed, and what I wrote about, was a reflection of who I am, and people enjoyed the honesty. I'm always glad of the instinct I had, as a young woman, that I must stick to my guns. I wouldn't have the life I have now if it wasn't for that.

With the second album, *Virtue*, things got really difficult because just as I was about to record, my publishing company was bought by a bigger company and I had no idea what was going on. Instead of waiting, we financed *Virtue* through crowdfunding. I made up 'incentives' that meant I was travelling the country meeting people for months. Incentives are experiences or personalised merchandise that people can buy on top of pre-ordering the album. I did things like play gigs in people's living rooms, or teach them how to play my songs on guitar. A percentage of their 'pledges' went to a charity called The Enough Project.

It was a hugely positive experience. I still see the core people who supported that album at gigs, and socially. They're a part of my life, and I hope I'm a part of theirs. Crowdfunding should be used sparingly, just so it can be a special and memorable experience. But I would definitely try it again if the right project arose.

Then, in 2016, I released my third album, *Second Love*, through Bella Union. It was nice to be acknowledged finally by a record deal, after years of meeting record company people who I felt severely distanced from in terms of my perspectives on life and my musical taste. It was a relief to suddenly find myself working with people who were on the same page. Their roster doesn't, for example, have a limit on how many female solo artists they sign: they are far more open, and it's been liberating.

The making of *Second Love* was a huge undertaking for me. My first two albums had been inspired by heartache, which, in a way, made them easy to write. I had been so introverted in my songwriting for so long that I finally wanted to look outwards. At the same time, touring had taken me to new places, exciting cities like Tokyo, Salt Lake City, LA ... As I began to write, the world seemed such a promising place. The future felt close to hand.

I ended up working on *Second Love* for three years, during which I moved first to Los Angeles and then to New York. My desire to try new styles meant that I wrote almost a hundred songs, when previously I would write thirteen for a thirteen-track album. I had always relied on other people to work the music software, but this time I downloaded Ableton Live and used it myself. I used internet tutorials, and every time I had a session with a producer, I would watch and take notes. I asked a lot of questions.

With so many things to try, my album budget dried up really quickly. I had to wait long periods for financing to get it finished. But it was worth it. When it was released in 2016, I felt immensely proud of it, and happy about the journey it took me on. Because of it, I was living in America, and getting to know a community of women in New York who inspired and challenged me.

Second Love started out being about technology and optimism, but as time progressed, the modern world revealed itself to be far more complex and insecure. I decided to go back to my roots, which was storytelling through music. That's why I called it *Second Love* – it was a natural companion to *First Love*. The songs now existed in a world of text messages and screens, but they were still about love. In the world that emerged in 2016, love seemed more important than ever.

I'd started recording conversations with friends, as a sort of personal archive, and then, before *Second Love* was mastered, I added my friends' voices to the recordings, weaving them in and out of the music. It had taken so long to get the album out, it made me safer to know my friends were travelling with it.

There was another happy result from *Second Love*. After all that exploration and moving around, I began reconnecting with the side of myself I'd left behind in Hong Kong. I started singing in Mandarin and Cantonese, and released 'Constantly' in both languages. The day that song came out, I felt a sense of relief. I felt completed. I'd also found a way to collaborate with my mum, who helped me translate the lyrics and sat in the studio checking my pronunciation. This is the great thing about music: it can help you come to terms with yourself, and uncover strengths you didn't realise you had.

One of the funniest interviews came out of the 'Constantly' single. The poet and author Jenny Zhang and I had a conversation about growing up between cultures, and discovered that we both used to tell people Jackie Chan was our uncle, as a way to laugh at ourselves before anyone else could. We were both born in China, but she was raised in the US while I was raised in England. It was extraordinary that in our childhoods we'd both found the same silly, idiosyncratic way to survive being 'different'.

At college, I always thought I'd be a music journalist. I was writing for *Artrocker* and *The Stool Pigeon* when I first started playing gigs, and then I ended up writing for outlets like the *Guardian*. I like being busy, I like being independent and I really like writing. The musicians who inspired me weren't making life-changing amounts of money from music. Like them, I need an extra income between albums, and I get this through creative work and writing. I've written scores for film, radio and video games. I've composed for musicals. I've given talks and workshops. Recently I've started combining music, performing and reporting.

One example is a song I was commissioned to write by Radio 3, in honour of the Woodland Trust's Tree Charter campaign. I interviewed members of the Chinese diaspora in the north-east of England about their memories of trees and of the landscapes they'd grown up in. The resulting song, 'Three Cities', incorporated their interviews and told the stories of three trees in China, as they witnessed periods of great change in Chinese history.

Another turning point in my confidence has been working on projects that are led by women. Without thinking about it, it's been the case with all my major projects for the last five years. Each experience was unique, but one common thread is that the women who hired me treated me well. They gave me room to grow as a musician. They made sure I was paid fairly. We looked after each other throughout the whole process, and the work thrived.

It's so liberating. I think it's a myth that women are bitchy. Since the Weinstein story broke, I've been reading a lot about the culture of the 1990s and how it was built by men like him. All those films that were written by men where there's only one special girl, then there's the best friend, then the mother. Now we are breaking through all these stupid myths about who we are. I'm really exhilarated by it.

I've been relatively lucky in the music industry, but I've been groped and disrespected. It's mucky out there.

When the Me Too campaign started, I felt I didn't want to talk about the stuff that is private to me, that only I think about. I felt embarrassed. But a friend who was abused told me that Me Too was really helping her. When British GQ asked me to write about it, my friend's experiences helped me make the decision to say yes. I started off thinking I would write something impersonal, but the moment I began typing, I felt a terrible fury. I asked myself why I'd turned a blind eye to inappropriate behaviour when I was younger. I blamed myself for adding to a culture of silence. The day the article was due to come out, my heart was racing. I thought everyone would be mad at me, but it was the opposite. I experienced a tide of support online and from my loved ones. My dad said, 'I feel sorry for anyone who tried to cross you.' It meant the world.

I felt freer, like I had processed this anger somehow. I don't think everyone should feel pressured to take part in mass revelations, but it certainly helped me. I made a pledge to myself that from this point on I would not take any shit, and I know I'm not the only person who has promised themselves that. I can feel the difference already, in the air, in work situations. I feel hopeful about where it will lead us.

I am lucky: I have other women in the industry that I love and love and love. They are my best friends, my colleagues and my allies. I know that, whatever happens, I'm safe because I have these women. And I'm so proud of them as I see them moving forward, often into positions of power.

In late 2017, I started work on the fourth album in New York; it will be released on Bella Union in late 2019. I co-produced it with the drummer Dani Markham and the producer Beatriz Artola. After the huge process of *Second Love*, it was refreshing to do something immediate – we finished recording in two weeks. It was one of the best experiences of my life. I felt totally in control of my sound, something I could not have conceived of when I was first starting out in studios. Working with Dani and Bea was a dream – we led a team of New York musicians that I met during my time there.

Finishing it felt like closing a chapter on my life, one in which the studio had for so long been an insecure environment. When I first used to go into studios, I would feel so out of place. I would just sit there silently. I knew the sound that I wanted, but I couldn't say it in case I said it wrong and they stared at me.

I really hope that, in the coming years, women will not be intimidated in studio environments. It took forever for me to say things like, 'Could you add some reverb there?' Not because I couldn't explain what I wanted, but because I was frightened someone would turn round and say, 'What *kind* of reverb?' (I think women have already started to overcome this, so I don't want to make assumptions, and would rather use my own experience here and let whoever relates to it, relate to it.)

It took me years to get over that. It wasn't until I watched my female lead guitarist play guitar that it even occurred to me that I too could learn how to play guitar.

I got sucked into *all* the conditioning. The years after *First Love* were some of the most depressed years of my life because I used to just parrot back to myself all the negative things people were saying to me. If you look at pictures of me then, I was turned in on myself. I starved myself as a form of control. I was miserable. I could play a gig and go to work, but I could barely do anything else. I was weakened.

I had to go through a huge process in which I had to give myself permission to make music. Now, I like myself. Gradually, the tone of music criticism has become kinder. Also, the stronger I felt about my own musical abilities, the less I listened to what other people said.

Moving to New York helped. When I was there, it felt like I was living on the island that Wonder Woman is from. Being around other female musicians, I finally started to express myself as a musician.

There's an annual event called The Hum where women are randomly placed in groups, and then you have a night during which you show off your collaboration.

Last year I was placed with these two women and we decided to go through the songbooks of women down the years, women who maybe had been forgotten by music history because of the standards of the time or because they were women. Women like Connie Converse and Karen Dalton, who we felt had paved a step on the way to where we are now. We did covers of their songs.

The process of working with those women honestly changed my life. It felt like I was in some kind of magic circle and it gave me so much strength.

Only now do I feel really confident making music. For me, there was no fast track. It can take ten years or it can take one year. It was a long process, and sometimes it felt like a grind. Then there's a moment of enjoying what you've achieved. Then the grind begins again. Along the way in that long process, there were lots of moments of extreme happiness, especially when playing the music. The more confident I am, the more I write. Now I write every day.

I can look back now and see that I was so trapped by conditioning that pretty much the only thing that redeemed me was the fact that I so desperately wanted to write songs. It's as though I've had this epic journey, only to realise something that's very simple. I felt like I was climbing a mountain forever, but now I'm walking out on this green, open plateau and saying, 'Wow, I can do stuff. After twelve years, I'm allowed to do these things.'

When I was recording the fourth album, I had no idea that another chapter was about to begin. A month after the album was recorded, I discovered I was pregnant – hence the delay in its release. Telling my managers was scary. I thought that my career, the one I had finally got to grips with, would be over. Instead, they were overjoyed. My manager told me his wife had toured when their first child was an infant. They gave me tips that their other artists had learned when touring after a birth. Meanwhile, my tour manager, who had been eight months pregnant when we'd done our last show together, told me that I could do anything as a pregnant woman, and as a mother. She looked over all my plans and told me how to make them happen. I couldn't believe my luck.

It's taken over a decade, but I have finally found a community of people who have understood and accepted me. They have also been willing to help me figure out the surprises that life throws your way. I still think the music industry is a tricky place, for women especially. But if you build a network of good people, people who you trust, you can achieve anything.

DREAM WIFE

London-based punk pop band Dream Wife started as an art project in 2014, when guitarist Alice Go and bassist Bella Podpadec met Icelandic-born Rakel Mjöll at Brighton University. They evolved into a touring band and their debut release, EP1, arrived in 2016. Their eponymous debut album was released at the start of 2018 via Lucky Number Records.

Rakel: I grew up in Iceland, but I have a slight American accent because I spent my formative years in California. It was natural for me to choose a creative life because my family is involved in theatre, performance art and music – apart from my dad, who is the black sheep of the family because he moved to California to become a software engineer. His parents were furious.

I'm fortunate to come from a family of strong women who were very creatively driven. For example, my great-grandmother, a pianist, was one of the first women to be accepted into the Royal Academy in Copenhagen. She lived in Germany during the war and played with the Philharmonic in Hamburg, which was amazing for a woman during that era. She grew up with seven brothers, and so was pretty much one of the boys. She was certainly completely unapologetic and did things on her terms.

It took my family years to transport her grand piano from Hamburg to Iceland during the war. When the piano arrived in Iceland nobody was sure quite how it got there. She never told anyone. I can only think that my great-grandmother must have bribed someone.

Until I was ten, I was raised in California and loved it. When we returned to Iceland, it was like a strange fairy-tale land. There was snow in winter and the sun didn't go down in the summer – extreme weather conditions I hadn't experienced before and the complete opposite to California. My extended family is full of incredible people: I got to see their art, their shows, ran around in theatres and saw all the backstage rooms. When we went back to California for a visit a few years later, the sunshine and beaches had become less familiar.

I have always felt a strong sense of pride in being from Iceland. There are so few of us. Even today, the population of the country is little more than three hundred thousand. We are proud of the island's incredible geographical formation and of the culture it's produced. Iceland, a country of peasants and farmers with no army, declared independence from Denmark in 1944. At this point, Denmark was occupied by Germany – around the same time my great-grandmother's piano was being shipped from Hamburg. There is still a sense of pride in no longer being a colony.

In a way, it's as though we are a new country: we don't have any old houses or structures. Everyone lived in turf houses – similar to hobbit holes in *The Lord of the Rings* – up until the 1920s. I'm always amazed when I walk past buildings in London that were built before the twentieth century. We value our stories, the Viking sagas, the folk tales about trolls and elves. That's our history.

Bella: I'm from a small village in Somerset. It was amazing as a child; we were outside a lot, exploring and being kind of wild. I spent a lot of time with one or two close friends. It was harder as a teenager. I feel I spent my teenage years waiting. I didn't know what I was waiting for, but I think I'm here now. Before Dream Wife, I had only been in one band with two of my best friends. We made costumes and I played the glockenspiel and the harmonium and sometimes the synth, and even made my debut on the bass with a cover of 'Gigantic' by the Pixies.

Alice: I was born in Coventry and moved to Somerset when I was seven. My grandfather had been evacuated to a farm in Lympsham, Somerset during the war and so there was a family link. It was strange moving from the city to the country and, like Bella, I was waiting to leave.

My dad was in 2 Tone bands in Coventry when he was young; he played drums in The Swinging Cats. When he drove me down country lanes to primary school every morning, we'd sit in the car together listening to music. He would play me David Bowie and talk about how he always had the best percussion, teaching me how to listen to each sound carefully. We connected through music in a big way and I always knew I had his support when I started playing in bands. Even better, he didn't mind having a drum kit in the family home. My mum was also supportive and completely wonderful; I'm thankful that they accepted me for who I was and what I wanted to do.

I was close to my family, but I didn't really find my people in Somerset, apart from Bella and a small group of weird boys. I retreated into music a lot of the time, into the creation of it, the enjoyment and love of it. Music was a friend at a time of isolation and loneliness; it helped me express myself and work through my feelings.

It still has that role in my life. Music has made it easier for me to relate to people, in the sense that it can be something we have in common, a shared passion. Most of my teenage friendships were formed with guys I was in bands with. We recorded our own music and learned how to play together. They weren't sexist, but the vibe now – being in a band with two other women – is very different. It feels so much more like a conversation.

I used to go to car boot sales with the boys I was in bands with. We'd buy old keyboards and vintage shiny silver SM57 mics for a fiver, old stuff that nobody cared about, kids' toys that you could circuit-bend and it didn't matter if you got it wrong and fried their brains. We wanted to take things apart and understand all the other sounds you could make with them. There was a scavenger nature to it; we were building our music from the stuff we'd found, understanding different ways to document that sonically. It feels like that attitude of exploring ideas with an open and curious mind is present in all three members of Dream Wife. The way we work together is about growing and exploring things on our own terms.

I met Bella when I was sixteen at Mid-Somerset Battle of the Bands; we were in different bands, competing against each other. In the following years we got to know each other mostly at gigs, then at art college, before we both moved to Brighton to study art. During freshers' week at uni, we mostly sat in Bella's garden doing rituals with hot wax and casting spells. Together, we had a creative space from the start.

Bella: Since Alice and I met Rakel at Brighton University, the relationship between the three of us has been creatively collaborative. Our first venture was breaking into a boarded-up hole, as deep and round as a well, in the grounds of the university. Stashed inside, we found three school chairs facing inwards and some 1980s porn, which led to a complicated incident involving a mysterious handwritten note covered in blood. It's probably our shared sense of adventure and abstract thinking that drew us together.

Rakel: We decided on the band name before we started playing together. It's a cheeky name and controversial in itself. The idea of the clichéd 1950s American dream package: dream house, dream job, dream car and ... dream wife. In the dream scenario, the woman has become an object rather than a human being. Of course there is no such thing as a dream wife, because the so-called perfect woman doesn't exist. Women are such complex characters. We can be funny, sad, sensitive, sexy, angry. That's the beauty of it.

Rakel: When I was thirteen, I got an electric guitar for my birthday and started guitar lessons in Iceland. I'd been on the waiting list for two years and was so excited to start, but I had a tough time with my guitar teacher, who didn't seem to think that girls should study electric guitar. He never once encouraged or complimented me. I wish I had spoken up at the time, but at that age I didn't understand that I was being treated a certain way because I was female.

Alice: I didn't have that kind of terrible experience with a teacher, but I did feel that the male members of the band I was in as a teenager always knew better. Or perhaps they just got on with it without questioning whether they could do stuff or not. As Rakel says, we have to learn to speak out.

Rakel: I've had a very varied education and I've been studying music since I was a kid. But in bands prior to Dream

Wife, I always felt like an extra part. In fact, before I went to Brighton University to study art, I didn't want to do music at all. If anything, I wanted to push it away because I had gotten the idea in my head that I wasn't good enough, that I was inferior. Some people seem to think that if you hit the right note, the song will be good. Which is so wrong: for me, the vocal is about finding its own pattern through the melodies. That's where the magic is. When you experience your words, embrace your interpretation and let go, it's a beautiful moment.

In one of my previous bands, I was suddenly left out of writing sessions and then presented with the music. I was told, 'Here are your lines. And by the way, you only sing the chorus.' There was no discussion. During recording sessions I was being told to sing the same note again and again, because I didn't get it 'right' on the first take. I had to stop every three seconds and try again. This went on for weeks. It was ridiculous. It broke my spirit for a while and made me doubt myself as a songwriter and vocalist.

Shortly after that experience, I was in the studio with a producer who treated me as more of an equal. I did one take, stopped and started again. Stopped and started again. He was baffled. He frowned and said, 'What's going on? Just do the whole take and let's see where the magic is within.' I had to retrain myself. I'd lost my sense of where my melody lay as well as my value as a singer, performer and songwriter. Being belittled over and over was a very insidious thing, especially during those vulnerable teenage years.

It was great when I found my voice again. Now I sing in my own way. I add colour and spice, excitement, and let the note move me. Everyone has a different way of performing and writing. Björk recorded an album, *Medulla*, based entirely on voices. She was fascinated with how voices, even manipulated ones, can overlap with melodies and create a beautiful stream of sound. My piano-playing great-grandma had a great musical ear and, although she could read music, she wasn't into doing so. She could hear a song once and repeat it. I can hear a song and repeat it perfectly, but I always say I'm note-blind; I've tried to learn to read music, but I can't. I had to fake it at school! I faked it well.

Bella: I didn't touch the bass after that shaky rendition of 'Gigantic' at sixteen until my final year of uni when we first started performing as Dream Wife. The band offered a place where you could break the rules, work collaboratively and connect with people. I basically learned to play bass through playing endless shows.

Alice: I learned to play the clarinet and electric guitar as a kid. I did grades in clarinet but, as a teenager, playing the electric guitar was much more fun. The clarinet had too many rules, whereas I could play the guitar freely. It was my thing, and I could do what I wanted with it. It felt liberating both musically and as a creative outlet, particularly at that time. Playing in bands with a small group of friends, writing and recording our songs in our bedrooms and figuring it out as we went along was exciting. I loved punk because it wasn't about playing an instrument in the right or wrong way.

I continued to study music up until college, including music theory. I learned more about composition and production, but figuring things out for yourself and making your own rules always felt more important to me.

Breaking the rules and challenging the status quo is something that we explore in Dream Wife, as three women in music and also just as three friends.

Rakel: Rather than comparing ourselves to other artists, we wanted to find a style that we were comfortable with. I needed to be able to be myself on stage. I'm not going to stand there and be someone else. I won't try to be perfect, but I will be me. It's great to know that Bella and Alice have got my back. Plus, if I screw something up, I know they can go with it. We're not afraid to get things wrong. We embrace it.

Rakel: Alice, Bella and I were talking the other day about getting into music for the first time in our early teens. In the mid- to late 2000s, we hardly saw women fronting rock bands and being loud. Karen O from the Yeah Yeah Yeahs, Le Tigre, CSS. They are the only ones that come to mind. The Icelandic scene was even more extreme; it was full of soft, whispering female vocalists singing so gently you could barely hear them. There were no women *roaring*.

Bella: There was something very masculine about the energy in rock at that time. It was about getting pissed up with your muscular mates, then singing along with the big choruses while waving your muscular arms around.

Alice: I remember the early 2000s as being dominated by commercial pop music. Women were straightforward pop stars and the music wasn't particularly challenging. Maybe there was a lull after 1990s icons such as PJ Harvey, Kathleen Hanna and other more grunge-associated female acts rocking it. By the early 2000s, grunge wasn't so cool any more and the space that had been created for women to be loud and musically aggressive was somehow closed up again. The backlash was a severe lack of women rock stars.

It's also hard not to see the void of women in rock in the early 2000s as just being part of the really complex system that is the music industry. It's difficult to summarise all the ways that it's intrinsically sexist, but it has been very, very sexist. It still is very, very sexist. Women's voices are unheard so much of the time simply because they don't fit within the pre-established canon of what is and isn't acceptable in the mainstream for a woman to be or do.

Bella: It was the era of The Sugababes and The Saturdays. And, of course, Amy Winehouse; I think celebrity culture really tore into a lot of lives while we were growing up. It was a new way of consuming culture, but it was a time before social media was at the forefront. Consequently, only a few specimens were in the spotlight and the women burned the brightest of all.

Rakel: Yeah, but there were *so* many male indie rock bands at that time. We need more role models! Growing up, I think I'd have had a totally different approach to music had I seen more women like Karen O being loud in the mainstream music scene and doing things on their own terms.

Alice: When I was growing up, I listened to the music my parents were into. Blondie, T. Rex, Bowie. I didn't have access to the internet as a kid so I didn't hear that much new music. I remember the way all three of those artists challenged gender expectations and expressed that through image and music.

There was, for example, something incredibly empowering about hearing a woman singing about watching her love take a shower in Blondie's 'Picture This': those words, and proudly taking ownership of her sexuality. I also remember how Patti Smith, the Pretenders and Joan Jett stood out when I listened to my dad's cassette tapes. There was something wild about these women. They seemed free and bold, like they didn't care what people thought of them. Figures like that definitely fed my teenage brain with the idea that, as a woman, you can be yourself, make the music you want to make and say the things you want to say.

It's something we explore a lot in Dream Wife. We want to fly a flag for girls pursuing their passions, regardless of gender.

Bella: We often talk of our twin idols as Bowie and Madonna.

Rakel: David Bowie was *the* rock star. Oh my god, I remember discovering Bowie for the first time. Everything was suddenly possible in music.

Alice: Artists like Bowie stood alone, but Dream Wife is very much part of a scene. It's a creative scene that goes beyond music – it's a creative community as much as a musical community. It's a safe space for us. When we are exploring new ideas and sharing our creative world with others, it's a thing of trust. We are so thankful for the support of the creatives surrounding us, grateful for our friends and collaborators. They have helped us to grow this project in so many new and exciting ways.

Alice: Rakel was living in Brighton with Bella when the three of us first met. We were all studying art and we went on a sober night out. They were saying it would be fun to go to Canada, where we all had friends at the time. Which led to, 'Why not start a band and go to Canada?' I remember getting a Facebook message through from Bella that night that said something like, 'Hey, do you want to start a band with me and Rakel and tour Canada?' It was maybe the best message I ever received. I replied: 'Of course! I'm in.'

We played one of our first shows at our friend Lama's birthday party at The Green Door Store in Brighton, where we had spent many nights dancing on the wonky cobblestones. Another early show before setting out on the Canada tour was in our uni gallery, as part of Rakel's art project at the time. We had four songs, synchronised dance moves and a dream of Canada.

I couldn't figure out what this project was in any shape or form, but it was so exciting to not know. It could be anything we wanted it to be. It felt like such a refreshing approach to being creative, a kind of antidote to the institutional expectations we were experiencing while studying art. I remember thinking: 'These are my freaks'. It's been so liberating to work without limits or expectations. It's been so powerful acknowledging the creative unity and force we have together. Despite starting as an art project, the band has always felt very real to us.

We didn't discuss our political agenda until a while after the band was formed. We felt the project out by doing fairly DIY international tours. We slept on coaches and did our own sound. It felt like those early tours hardened us up somehow. We earned our chops. But we are three women who believe in equality and breaking down gender expectations, so it felt quite natural to be pushing towards something that was trying to break free from even our own expectations of what we could achieve by ourselves.

In fact, it feels like, since we started this project, our fundamental attitude towards it hasn't changed very much. Apart from in the obvious ways: we now have a team of people who believe in this band and support our vision and we are touring more. The band still just feels like the trio of rock chicks we started out as, going on these musical adventures and supporting each other along the way, connecting with the people coming out to our shows.

Bella: Collaboration has always been important to us; there is nothing more fun than making stuff with your friends. The Bad Bitch Club is just one example. We met photographer Meg Lavender in Brighton – she was responsible for Rakel and I moving in together. We've worked with Meg in many ways, from some of our earliest shoots to throwing parties in Brighton and London. For most of our UK tours, we've been able to take her on the road with us, and this is where the Bad Bitch Club was birthed.

Meg started documenting the crowd, taking these incredible, powerful portraits. We want to make people at our shows feel part of what we're doing, put them on the same level. These portraits are of old friends, new friends, bands we've played with, the sixteen-year-old at her first show, the mother-and-daughter unit, the best friends on a night out, the grandmother.

Rakel: The world we have created with our peers is very supportive and close. Today we have an online community to reach out to. I love the music and creative scene that's going on in London right now. There's something so raw and beautiful about it. In a sense, it's like never having left art school. It feels like the right time to be doing this kind of band here and now.

Rakel: I read about Courtney Love being assaulted by men in the audience when she crowd-surfed at a gig in London in the early 1990s. She said those men felt entitled to touch her body because they felt they knew her persona; they assumed that they could access her that way. Because she's loud, she's sexy, she doesn't care what people think. That's so fucking scary.

We love what Kathleen Hanna did when she was lead singer of Bikini Kill. Apart from pioneering the riot grrrl movement, she used to invite the girls in the crowd to come to the front so that they could create a safe space at a rock show. At some shows we do the same: we stop halfway through a show and ask the 'bad bitches' – those who identify as female or a bad bitch – to come to the front and take their space.

Alice: We should explain that our fans call themselves the 'bad bitches' in reference to a line in one of our songs, 'F.U.U.': 'I spy with my little eye bad bitches'. It's empowering to take a word that has been used negatively and turn it around, as women have done with 'slut walk'. A 'bad bitch' is basically a woman who is unapologetic. A bad bitch doesn't have to be a woman or girl, but most of them are. Anyone who is queer, femme or just an outsider might identify with that group too.

Rakel: Getting the girls to the front is empowering. It's a beautiful time when that happens, when the ones you see in the back are now at the front. For some it's the first time they've been to the front or even in a safe mosh pit. They don't necessarily know each other but they are united together with us, having a wild time and supporting each other in a safe space.

Sometimes, if some of the men aren't budging from the rail at the front, I say, 'I know you don't hear this often, but you need to move and make way for the bad bitches.' Nobody wants to be told off by the vocalist.

Rakel: We talk a lot about safe spaces in the show. About how we should be looking out for each other. This is a gig. We all came here to be entertained. We all came here to have a good time. We are supposed to respect each other. We are supposed to watch out for each other. Our song 'Somebody' is about sacking gender norms, and it also addresses sexual assault: 'What you wore and how you bore it so well/What did you expect would happen?' Then the chorus comes in: 'I am not my body, I'm somebody'. When we play it, it creates a special moment.

Bella: I found it really tough starting out in this industry as a woman. Music dudes were – and still can be – very patronising, and it was hard to ask for help. Terms like 'sound guy' and 'girl band' are still thrown around so often and so casually it can be exhausting. This quiet, subtle sexism is true in so many fields; it's inherent in the structures of the world we live in. For me, to get to this place has taken a great deal of internal shifting; it's finding ways to see beyond the structures, and then finding ways to step beyond the structures and build new ones that benefit everyone.

Alex Paveley studied sculpture with Alice and he became our drummer shortly after we released our first EP. Some people are surprised that we have a male drummer, and it can be frustrating because Paves is a genuine gem of a human being, and the conversation we want to have isn't one about excluding men. It's about getting everyone on the same page.

Alice: On an early DIY tour of Germany, we played in this underground bunker in Ulm. After the show, these guys in the smoking area out the back were chatting to us and one of them started asking about my guitar. He very quickly began telling me that I had the riffs but that I didn't really know how to play properly, that I should be learning how to play Spanish guitar; that was, after all, how he played guitar. Then he warned me that I needed to practise more because in ten years my looks would fade.

I remember us all looking at each other and walking back inside. Did that guy really just say that? We went back to a hotel – a rare luxury for that particular tour – and sat on the bed and chatted about how weird the guy was. We were pretty angry. We turned on the TV and *Kill Bill* came on and we sat there together, watching Uma slay. There was something empowering about all being together in that moment, in front of that particular movie. I think it might have been what you would call character-building.

Bella: Women are, finally, beginning to speak up. Me Too

has shown us the global scale of the issue of sexual assault. As a movement, it has united women of every social background, race, sexuality, age. It's a very deep problem, rooted in the way we see women and their bodies – all mixed up with this archaic, subtle but ever-present silencing of female voices. But, finally, social media has provided a platform for women to speak up.

Rakel: Hopefully Dream Wife will inspire women to pick up an instrument and start a band with their friends. Not to strive for a ridiculous level of perfection that's been drilled into all of us from an early age by society. Grow together. Support each other. Make music together. Enjoy the ride. You are enough.

NATALIE MERCHANT

As lead singer and main lyricist with 10,000 Maniacs – a band also including Rob Buck, Steve Gustafson, Dennis Drew, Jerome Augustyniak and John Lombardo – Natalie Merchant recorded five studio albums between 1983 and 1993. She has since released seven solo albums including 1995's Tigerlily, which has sold in excess of five million copies. Between albums, Merchant has devoted her time to a wide range of causes, including anti-racism and anti-fracking campaigns. She was the director of the 2014 short documentary film Shelter: A Concert Film to Benefit Victims of Domestic Violence.

My parents were both teenagers from a small industrial town in western New York when they married in 1959. Four kids and twelve rocky years later they were divorced, but the best memories I have of my intact family all happened around the turntable in our living room. There were stacks of albums everywhere and if we were awake, music was playing in our house, loudly. We had spontaneous dance parties every weekend. My mother was apt to jump on the coffee table and start go-go dancing to The Beatles or The Marvelettes or the original cast recording of *Hair*. On cleaning days Petula Clark would be blaring through open windows for the entire neighbourhood to hear.

The same would go for music in the car – AM radio cranked and windows open. My father's taste was a bit more sedate. He favoured Rodgers & Hammerstein musicals and folk revival groups like Peter, Paul and Mary and The New Christy Minstrels, or vocal harmony groups like The Platters and The Lettermen. He liked to slow-dance, or try to teach my sister and me to jitterbug. No wonder the marriage didn't last!

It was my mother's tradition to buy each of us an album on our birthdays. On my seventh she gave me my first album, *Pet Sounds*. I remember loving the cover photo, The Beach Boys all feeding goats at the San Diego zoo. What an epic opening track, 'Wouldn't it Be Nice' – the tinkling music box sound, stopped by the crack of that massive snare and then Brian and the boys' stack of syrup-sweet voices. Wow! 'God Only Knows' is still one of my all-time favourite pop songs. Other birthdays brought Paul Simon's *There Goes Rhymin' Simon*, Elton John's *Captain Fantastic & The Brown Dirt Cowboy*, Cat Stevens' *Tea for the Tillerman* and every Catholic girl's favourite album of the 1970s, *Jesus Christ Superstar*.

When I was fourteen, I bought my first record with my own money, *The Kick Inside*. I'd seen Kate Bush on *Saturday Night Live*, performing 'The Man With The Child In His Eyes'. She was wearing a silver lamé bodysuit and was crawling around catlike on the lid of a Steinway piano. She was unlike anyone I'd ever seen or heard before. I wanted to know more about her world.

When I was a teenager, I hung out with an elite group of college boys who came home for holidays during the summer.

They worshipped music and listened to it in a highly ritualised way. Coming from families of privilege (unlike mine), they all lived in rambling Victorian houses that had some kind of room over a garage, in an attic or converted basement that served as a deep listening space. For some reason, I was always the only girl in the room. They accepted and mentored me in a kind of musical apprenticeship.

They introduced me to Bob Dylan, Joni Mitchell, Leonard Cohen, David Bowie, Genesis, Roxy Music, T. Rex, The Kinks, Fairport Convention, Brian Eno, Nick Drake, Bob Marley, Peter Tosh, Jimmy Cliff. Initially I wasn't allowed to even touch the records, or the turntable. By the second summer I was trusted to clean the vinyl and was taught how to drop the stylus down perfectly in the groove between tracks. But it would be three summers before I cautiously pulled an album from a shelf and picked my first song to play, 'The Musical Box' by Genesis.

I remember the summer John Mannion came home from art school in Philadelphia with a copy of *London Calling* under his arm. It was like a violent meteor hit. It split the group in half and I tried to look neutral, but secretly sided with the converts. Again, it was unlike anything I'd ever heard and I wanted to know more.

I was an undiagnosed dyslexic all through school. Nobody really understood that I was dyslexic until I was in my forties. I wrote backwards and couldn't do math at school, nor could I learn to read music. There were so many things I couldn't do, but I was excelling in other areas, so the spelling problems were overlooked. I still only look for nouns when I'm reading, and I have to read out loud, otherwise it's all mush. My daughter is dyslexic too, and we have to police each other.

'Five, four, three . . . did you write that down?'

'Yep: three, four, five.'

Despite the dyslexia, I did well enough to be able to convince my high school to allow me into an early college enrolment program. In the fall of 1979 I was sixteen and a freshman at the local community college. There was a student-run radio station on campus and I really wanted to be a DJ. I turned up at the door the first week of school with a stack of records under my arm. (Ironically, the general manager and two of the other DJs ended up being founding members of 10,000 Maniacs.)

Soon after I joined the radio, there was a great event. We wrote to several UK-based indie labels requesting records to play on air. I doubt anyone at 4AD, Factory, Mute or Rough Trade had any idea how small our station was but WJWK was added to all their mailing lists and boxes of records started to come. A direct pipeline was installed from London to our cultural hinterland and it flooded our desert with the sound of Joy Division, Gang of Four, The Young Marble Giants, Cocteau Twins, Bauhaus, Depeche Mode, New Order, The Smiths, Ian Dury. In the predigital days of yore, this sort of cutting-edge music was impossible to come by in a distant corner like Jamestown, New York. It was nothing short of miraculous.

Pretty soon we noticed that nearly all the post-punk songs we were absorbing had something in common: three-chord progressions. We could buy some guitars, amps and drums and play this music ourselves. We rented space in an old factory and started practising and playing at a local dive bar in a rough part of town by the river known for its stripper bars and motorcycle gangs. We made a scene; we were the strange cover band with the girl singer with long, tangled black hair who danced in circles wearing Depression-era dresses. We borrowed films from the local library to project over our heads; we sold vintage clothing out of our cars between sets; we swam naked in the river after the show.

We shook things up in a small town and then bought an old school bus and took what we were making on the road.

I liken the early days of 10,000 Maniacs to being members of a cargo cult. After the Second World War, there were these outposts in the Pacific where the indigenous people never really learned to speak the language of the Americans who were stationed there. These places were basically supply ports during the war. They had warehouses full of Spam and Coca-Cola. After the war, the troops departed and the indigenous people began worshipping Americans who they believed had brought them this cargo in the first place, and they would pray for the continuation of deliveries of goods like Spam. That was the cargo cult.

I joined 10,000 Maniacs at seventeen, just as the world was starting to open for me every which way. I'd never been on an airplane, and I wouldn't until I was nineteen. I knew the world only through books, magazines and films. My mother was a very physical person and really loved being outdoors. She took the television away from us in 1974 because she didn't like what it was doing to us – she was very disturbed at the idea of us sitting still and not communicating. Consequently, I don't have images of a lot of things that went on in the world at that time.

It wasn't long before we started writing our own songs and as the singer, I became the lyricist of the band. I was so young, my life experience confined to the limits of my home town. I looked for inspiration in the lives around me. The 1970s had seen a deep recession in the US, and, like so many other small rust-belt cities, Jamestown was becoming a post-industrial wasteland.

Industry was evaporating and the support system of the town had started to collapse. I was witnessing the death of a way of life. The solid ground under the foundation of the working class was crumbling. In hindsight, it's now easier to understand, but at the time I just saw the decay and the hardscrabble of day-to-day living and the flight of anyone who had the means.

My father barely finished high school, and his first job was as a janitor in a factory. My mother barely finished high school and started having children when she was nineteen. She eventually got a master's degree and my father worked his way up to a company executive position. I feel that that kind of leap – undereducated teen parents to professional class – is more and more difficult to achieve in our country.

In the early 1980s, I had my proper political awakening and started to become aware of the injustices in the world. We lived a hundred miles from Love Canal, where a chemical company had spent twenty years burying barrels of toxic waste, twenty thousand tons. Eventually the land was sold and an entire suburban neighbourhood, complete with school, was built on it. The result was a huge environmental disaster that led to low birth rates, birth defects, miscarriages, leukaemia. The community members rose up in protest and forced the government to purchase their homes and relocate them.

Because of Love Canal, I was waking up to everything around me. It felt like we were reaching a tipping point. There were massive fish kills in the nearby Great Lakes, and a partial meltdown in the nuclear reactor at Three Mile Island in Pennsylvania. I saw the photo essay by W. Eugene Smith of the Japanese village of Minamata that had been poisoned by mercury. I read John Hershey's *Hiroshima* and Rachel Carson's *Silent Spring*, books that exposed the treacherous consequences of scientific development.

The late 1960s and early 1970s were really tumultuous times. I was born a month before JFK was shot and I was only four when Bobby Kennedy was assassinated. I remember the assassination of Martin Luther King and the riots that followed in cities all over America. There were the students protesting the Vietnam War at Kent State who were shot; there was the kidnapping of Patty Hearst and the Manson murders. I can remember that it felt like things were coming apart at the seams. But there was also a real sense of optimism and forward movement at the same time. Peace and love. We were going to take care of the planet and of each other. We were going to end war.

But Reaganomics – the idea that if you make the wealthy wealthier, then that wealth will trickle down – simply made the rich richer.

My interest in politics grew as 10,000 Maniacs started to tour and we met other musicians. Billy Bragg was important to me: he knew more about American politics than anyone I'd ever met. He invited us to do a benefit for the Sandinistas and, backstage after the show, he grinned and said, 'Congratulations! You've just opened your case file with the FBI. And the CIA.'

When the Berlin Wall came down in 1989 and Eastern Europe opened up, Billy took Michael Stipe and me on a tour. We were in Prague when Václav Havel was elected. We went and played in these community centres in East German coal-mining towns. I was learning from Billy that I couldn't just observe and critique. I had to participate.

Even though we always did interviews as a band, the other members of the band were frustrated with me because they weren't as politicised. Nor was the record company. I was very happy with my Depression-era clothing; for years I modelled my look after a book of Dorothea Lange photographs. Farm boots, a cotton day dress from the 1930s. An outfit for five dollars. But the record company knew that, with the right amount of attention and effort, it could tart me up. I could look pretty cute.

As soon as a new record was due, the record company would get the stylist in and the war would begin. The stylist would take me to Barneys. I'd be like, 'This skirt is four hundred dollars. My mother doesn't earn four hundred dollars in a week.' It was all about tighter and shorter. In Britain it would be, 'Right, we've got a band with a girl singer. Let's get her in spandex or latex.'

Then I'd have to talk to the record company about my mission. 'I can't sing about child abuse in a miniskirt, I can't do it!'

It was depressing. It took me a while to realise that instead of the record company instructing the stylist, I could use the stylist directly and so present myself in the way that I wanted to be presented. When I look back, I wasn't overweight, but I wasn't like a model. All the stylists were really skinny and I felt ashamed that I wasn't thinner.

There was pressure on the band to present itself in a certain way, too. If only I could write 'normal pop lyrics', 10,000 Maniacs could be really famous, sell more records. Because I was the lyricist for the band, everything had to pass through me. Eventually, I think they accepted what I was doing. People started writing about us and we actually stood out because of the socially conscious nature of the lyrics.

Socially conscious rather than political. For example, 'What's The Matter Here?', the opening song on 1987's *In My Tribe* album, is about people turning a blind eye to child abuse: 'I'm tired of the excuses everybody uses/He's your kid, do as you see fit/But get this through that I don't approve/Of what you did to your own flesh and blood'.

I called the lyrics 'socially conscious' because I was talking about the abuse of power and how that affected people's lives, whether on an interpersonal level or an institutional level. The bone I was always chewing was power. (For a long time, my argument was that the dominating structures that run underneath everything are always there and so it doesn't really matter who is in power. But it *does* matter who is in power. I've come to realise that, over time.)

There was this general feeling that, to be a rock musician, you had to live this degenerate lifestyle, be narcissistic, have a huge ego. It's a field littered with damaged lives. Rock lifestyles don't really lead to a happy, healthy midlife – that's the point at which a whole new generation of people want to fantasise about someone young and attractive. That's a big part of the entertainment industry: youth, vitality, a certain amount of recklessness.

Since the 1960s there had been this convention as to how musicians and singers were meant to behave, and I never fitted that description. People saw rock music as subversive in itself. To me, anything that was beautiful was a subversive act.

It's almost like I knew that whatever physical attributes I had when I was nineteen or twenty weren't going to sustain me when I was older. I used to tell people that, by the time I'm forty, I'll be done with all this. I'll go and be a teacher or something. I never wanted to become attached to it. I sometimes wish I'd enjoyed being young a little more. But I never smoked. I didn't drink. I was vegetarian for twenty-two years.

I once told *Rolling Stone* that I didn't want to be cast as the Emily Brontë of pop music. I was also called 'the thinking man's Madonna', whatever the fuck that's supposed to mean. Whenever I did a benefit concert, I was the Audrey Hepburn of pop because she did a lot of work with the UN. I was Virginia Woolf for a while, then Emily Dickinson. I was even called the Flannery O'Connor of pop. A lot of the women I was compared to were recluses. Even though I'm not self-promoting on Instagram all the time, I'm not exactly reclusive. I'm around other people all the time. So was Emily Dickinson. She didn't get out of the house all that much, but she had a very vibrant social life with her family and close circle of friends.

I have become even more of a 'goody-goody' in recent years – or at least that's how a male British music writer in the 1990s would no doubt write about me. I'm not making records or appearing on television because I'm leading campaigns against fracking, or making documentaries about domestic violence or getting involved in big community arts projects.

I've been working on one community project for the past year, a collaboration with a hundred impoverished preschoolers who attend a free school. It's been so moving to visit their classrooms every week to sing and dance with them. So moving. I bring in instruments for them. They'd never seen a double bass. The first time I brought one in, they thought it was a very large violin. The next week I brought in a concertina and it all started again. Their mouths drop open. Their eyes get huge. They react as though someone has pulled out a magic wand and turned a tree into a house or something.

My goal is to move people with music. In one old interview I pointed out that I only get forty-five minutes every four years to talk to people, as that's approximately the rate I used to release albums. There's no room for irony in my music. That's not how I want to communicate with people. I don't want to be cynical. I want to be human. I want to connect with people and stay connected all the time. You can't fully empathise with others until you begin to understand people who are living in very different circumstances from your own.

Under the Trump administration, people are being punished for being poor, for being born into the circumstances in which they find themselves. Nobody asks to be born poor, but it's very difficult to crawl out of poverty. You have to possess great strength to be able to do that. You need support and you need love.

Music feeds me in so many different ways, but the essence of it is always the same: it's just sharing music. I get as much satisfaction singing and dancing with these little four- and five-year-old kids as I get from performing at the Royal Albert Hall. Sometimes the responses are quite similar. Wherever I perform in the world, I'll play certain songs and people will run to the stage and they have that joyful expression on their faces, the same one I see on the faces of those children.

I think I have been supported as a female artist. More or less. In the beginning I was young and therefore reticent in terms of demanding what I thought was best for me. I came from a very sheltered, very small town and, by the time I was nineteen, I had a major recording contract. I was in a band with people who were six to twelve years older than me. It took time, maybe ten years, before I was able to say, 'That's not right for me', or 'This is right for me'. I was known as a 'difficult artist' because of that. 'She's so difficult. She won't put the bikini on.'

When I began my solo career in 1995, I completely changed the team of people I was working with. I had a female A&R. I had a female lawyer, who I still retain. I hired an all-female publicity team. I had a female sound person, female lead guitarist and tour manager. When I went solo, I cleaned house and decided that I was going to work with more women. I was tired of being the only woman in the room, which is what it was like when I was in 10,000 Maniacs. Very rarely was there another woman in the room. If she was there at all, she would be a backup singer or string player or stylist or caterer. The only women I'd meet at the record company were in the publicity department or the art department.

It was a significant turning point in terms of me being able to work with people who respected and could understand what I was trying to do. Even then there were times when my publicity people would still say, 'Are you really going to wear *that*?' When I went grey, my record company actually asked, 'Are you going to stay like that? Aren't you going to do something about it?' I was like, 'This is what fifty looks like.' They were like, 'Right. So it's you and Patti Smith.' I'm fine with that. I'm in good company.

I'm at the point now where I don't need to make money. I made more than I ever expected to and I've lived very frugally. When I go on tour now, I'm not going out there because I have to. I'm going out there because I want to. That's an incredible position to be in. I can decide how I'm going out, who I'm going out with, where I'm going to be, what kind of experience I would like to have, what kind of experience I would like the audience to have.

I was raised by a single, struggling mother who said, 'You'll have to get a job that you hate and you'll have to go to it every day.' It's like she tried to condition me to a life sentence, a miserable existence. Because that's what she resigned herself to. At the same time, she spent so much time and effort in my childhood exposing me to theatre, music and dance. She could tell that I responded to music, theatre and dance. She fed me with that. We would go to the library and check out books on art and photography.

It was as though my mother was corrupting me with all this art, sending me to drawing lessons and piano lessons. Then she would lecture me on the importance of getting a skill – be a nurse, be a teacher. I needed to have a practical vocation. I would say that I wanted to be an artist and she would tell me that was impossible. But I managed to do that, and make a living from it. I became independently wealthy and, in turn, a philanthropist – which would have seemed completely out of my realm when I was growing up.

I feel huge responsibility as an artist, but my mother's Catholicism instilled in me the idea that I should serve and that I should find joy in serving other people and giving to other people. And that my life should have purpose – whether that is through work or in my daily life. I really thought that I would become a teacher or a nurse. Instead, I travelled a lot, met very interesting people and had so many rich experiences.

I was able to be an artist.

LAUREN MAYBERRY

CHVRCHES *vocalist Lauren Mayberry co-writes and co-produces the Scottish trio's songs, as well as playing drums and synthesiser. Iain Cook plays synth, guitar and bass and is a co-vocalist while Martin Doherty plays synth and is also a co-vocalist. Their first EP,* Recover, *was released in 2013 and debut album* The Bones of What You Believe *followed the same year. They have released two further albums,* Every Open Eye *and, most recently,* Love Is Dead. *A vocal activist and philanthropist, Mayberry founded the now-defunct TYCI, a feminist collective in Glasgow.*

My parents are not musicians. My father is an engineer and my mother a schoolteacher. I grew up in a household where reading and learning was encouraged, and music was always played. They also encouraged me and my older sister to listen to whatever boy band or teen pop thing was getting everyone excited, while also playing a lot of Fleetwood Mac and Genesis. At ten, Steely Dan and Whitney Houston were my two favourites, which I guess was pretty advanced (and odd).

My mum helped teach me piano when I was little. When I got to high school, I learned how to play drums as part of my music course and, at sixteen, I started playing drums in bands. I loved doing it and it's how I met most of my friends, but I never thought I was good enough to be on that music course. It didn't seem like a realistic option to place everything on that. My parents were pragmatic. They were very much of the opinion that, if you were smart enough at school, you should apply to college and have a sensible backup plan in place and get a sensible day job.

By the time CHVRCHES took off, I was working as a production runner in film and television. Although I wasn't getting to be creative myself in that work, it still felt good to be helping to further something creative. Most people who are struggling in bands don't have that. Both Iain and Martin studied musical composition and performance at university, and they met through a music course in Glasgow. I did a law degree and then a master's in multimedia journalism but I had no formal musical training. I think I used to get an inferiority complex because there were times when I felt like I didn't know what I was doing. I never had any singing lessons until we started touring a lot and I realised that I needed a vocal coach so that I didn't bust my voice out.

I have finally come to the conclusion that, between the three of us, we have a good balance. We have enough understanding of technology and we can understand music in an emotional way that is not completely analytical. I think that's a good combo, and it's what makes our band sound and feel the way it does.

Maybe you think worse things about yourself than anyone else will ever think, but I'd find myself thinking, 'Why the fuck are we playing Glastonbury? We're playing the same stage as bands I love, as people who have been doing this for I don't know how many years. And I have no skill in this area.' When I think about it now, I wonder if that is just impostor complex, probably made worse by the barrage of commentary that was directed towards us – towards me specifically. I wasn't used to it. I don't know if I am now, but I am definitely better at it.

In the autumn of 2013, I wrote an article for the *Guardian* talking about my experiences as a woman in a band that had risen to prominence on the internet. CHVRCHES had formed just two years earlier and in that period we were sent a shocking amount of abusive messages on the band's social networks. The week before the *Guardian* piece, I posted a screen grab of one particularly inappropriate message on Facebook. Within a week, over half a million people responded. As I explained in the *Guardian*, the messages we received in response were in some ways more shocking. This is just one of the many examples of explicit abuse: 'This isn't rape culture. You'll know rape culture when I'm raping you, bitch'.

I don't regret writing the piece. I don't think I'd still be in CHVRCHES if we'd had to put up and shut up. If we'd just let those things happen. Of course there were conversations behind the scenes about whether it was a good idea or not. Not because we weren't all in agreement about it as a moral issue, but because I was sticking my flag in the sand and that was going to piss even more people off, and there was a danger that this thing all of us had been working towards for years would just all go away.

Eventually we came to the conclusion that the people you are going to piss off aren't really people that you want to play shows for anyway. Their connection to your music can't be that pure if they expect you to accept rape and death threats in order to do it. We were prepared for the band to be less popular in return for our overall experience in CHVRCHES being more comfortable.

I look back at it now and can see that the *Guardian* article was an important point for us as a band, and psychologically and emotionally for me. When you're on tour, life can seem otherworldly and it's not a normal way to exist, but being in a band for me has to be authentic. It has to mirror how I think and feel in my normal life. It wouldn't have felt genuine if we had quietly pretended that this abusive stuff wasn't constantly happening to us. It was about trying to take control of the situation. You can't control what other people say, but you can control how you respond and how you conduct yourself.

I don't subscribe to the idea that 'what happens on the internet stays on the internet'. I understand that the way people interact online is different to how we interact face-to-face, but the idea that it isn't 'real' and there aren't consequences doesn't hold water for me. That implies that as soon as someone walks away from a computer, they don't hold those opinions any more. That it's no longer the way they view women, ethnic minorities, the queer community, people from foreign countries or of different faiths. But it is. Of course it fucking is.

There are people behind those keyboards, and they don't hang up their opinions when they log out. The reason we have a security list of names in every venue we play and at every public appearance we do is because those people – in our case, those men – are real. They are not just on the internet, and if anything they are more dangerous in real life, and at this point that is just part of my experience of being a woman in a band.

At the same time, if the internet didn't exist, I wouldn't have connected with and gotten to know people like Tegan and Sara, Hayley Williams from Paramore, Bethany Cosentino from Best Coast, feminist writer Jessica Valenti or Anita

Sarkeesian from Feminist Frequency – all women who have had to deal with these things as part of their careers, and whose work and advice has helped me a lot at times when I felt like I wanted to pack it all in and go live on the top of a mountain somewhere.

Sometimes it makes me feel better to know that this kind of negativity isn't just directed at me, but then it feels worse because you realise again how widespread it is. It is reassuring and encouraging, though, to find other people who can tell you that you're not crazy. Then you have to be able to put your game face back on and pretend you feel as powerful as you could ever possibly be.

As I wrote in that *Guardian* piece, CHVRCHES was born on the internet; if the internet didn't exist, our band might never have been signed. As it was, we were signed from a SoundCloud link that our manager sent to somebody to put on a blog. It was that simple. I'm not a digital native; I can remember the dial-up modem making that distorted whirring noise as it connected and I can recall a time when people weren't glued to their phones constantly. I did, though, spend time on band message boards as a teen so understood how social networks could function as a more modern version of those things. And, since the band had exploded on the internet, it made sense to us to connect with people via the internet.

I remember the day our first album, *The Bones of What You Believe*, came out. We were playing a launch show at a venue called Birthdays in London. We had done a bunch of press during the day and were about to do an interview at Radio 1 with Zane Lowe, whose show I obsessively listened to when I was younger. I would run home from school to see what guests he had on the brown couch on *Gonzo* on MTV. Teenage me would never have believed I would one day be in one of the bands Zane was talking to. But there I was, sitting in a cab, sifting through abusive messages and blocking people on the internet as if it was just part of the daily schedule. At that point I realised the insanity of it.

We often get asked in interviews why we're a political band. For the most part I don't think our lyrics are explicitly political. It's much more personal, with political and social elements infiltrating those personal stories, as they would for anyone. Our albums aren't full of manifestos. But it's funny to me that, just because you say no to something, like we did, it suddenly makes you a political pop band. If that's the rule, I'm fine with it. I'd rather do that than sit down and shut up. What would it look like in another context if I was a guy with a beard? I'm sure I wouldn't be having that conversation.

Oh god, there are *so* many things that wouldn't happen if I was a man fronting this band. But maybe the band would be a very different proposition if I were a man. The vocal would be different, the lyrics, the persona – who knows where we would be. But the incessant trolling would be different, too. I have never once implied that men are not bullied or harassed or called out online, but it is undeniable that the abuse faced by women, LGBTQ people and black/minority/ethnic communities is motivated by something slightly different, and that the content is definitely distinct.

For a time it felt unfair because I thought that, as a band, we hadn't done anything to provoke such disrespectful, degrading or furious comments. But now I know that it wasn't anything we did or didn't do. It was simply because there was a woman occupying a space that some people didn't think she should be in. I wasn't pandering to men and I wasn't apologising, and

I had the gall to speak about the lunacy of the situation. As soon as we'd spoken up about it, we had a target on our backs.

Many people agreed with what we said, but many people didn't. It felt like we were in a moment in time where the wave of feminism in music in the 1990s had been forgotten, so what we were saying was 'new' to a lot of people. I was anywhere on the scale from 'outspoken' to an 'angry feminist bitch', and that is part of the persona that the media have assigned to me now.

I don't think that's all of who I am as a person. In my 'real' life, I really hate conflict. I apologise all the time and cry about pretty much everything, happy or sad. But I'd sure rather that be my persona within the band than be quietly wallflowering it up in the corner, waiting for a certain group of men to deem me acceptable or worthy.

I would put money on the fact that there is virtually never an article that comes out without it mentioning my gender, and the descriptive words and language used are almost always gendered. What am I wearing? I am 'elfin'. 'Petite'. 'Cute'. 'Pixie-esque'. 'Vulnerable'. 'A heartbreaker'. A vacuous, talentless idiot who is only there because two male producers needed her to sell records. An egomaniac with a victim complex who put a band together as a vanity project to give her the illusion of legitimacy.

When we started out as a band, I used to dress pretty much the same whether I was on or off stage: T-shirt, denim shorts, boots. It was interesting to see the kind of comments and bullshit I got because of that. I hadn't even created a stage persona at that point; that was just what I would be wearing anyway. From the photos taken at that time, I can track how I became more anxious, more depressed. I would wear bigger and bigger button-up shirts, with less and less make-up.

I think I reasoned that, if I changed my appearance, then I wouldn't be attracting those comments any more, but now it makes me sad to see those photos: I am literally trying to make myself disappear into the background because I wanted to be left alone. And it didn't change anything.

A man said to me once, 'You wear crop tops and skirts on stage – isn't that inherently unfeminist?' I thought that was interesting because it relies on the assumption that everything I'm doing is for male consumption. For the male gaze.

An artist like Beyoncé has a private life that has more or less remained private, but at the same time her art has remained personal and sensual and sexual and powerful. I think it would be very dangerous if she wasn't allowed to express herself in the way she wants. She's done many, many great things for feminism, specifically for intersectional feminism and the feminism of young black women. I wouldn't be keen on seeing twelve-year-old girls going around in glittery string bikinis, but Beyoncé is not a twelve-year-old girl. She's a grown woman, so why should she not be allowed to dress as she chooses? Why shouldn't any of us? People should be able to dress however they want if it helps them project their art. If you are constantly second-guessing yourself, then you're not really being true to yourself or what it is that you are trying to create. To me, the value of Beyoncé's message far outstrips the potentially negative connotations that people try to put on it. Again, it's about the idea of control and consumption.

In 2012, I set up a feminist collective in Glasgow called TYCI. It lasted till 2017, starting out as a local club night where we booked female musicians and DJs, then evolving into a website and podcast. It felt like an important thing to do because nothing like that existed in Glasgow back then, and the timing is quite eerie in hindsight. I had no knowledge of the misogynist assault course I was about to dive into when the first CHVRCHES songs came out into the world, and I really do believe that it was that community of women, along with my bandmates and our steady-handed managers – Campbell McNeil and Danny Rogers – that kept me sane during that time period. It felt good to be able to get on a Skype call and talk to people who were actually trying to do something useful and who were coming from the same place.

It's really cool to see that the people who were most active in the collective have now gone on to do great things. Amanda [Stanley], for example, now works with Engender, a feminist organisation in Scotland that uses research and analysis to make a difference to women's lives. One of the other women, Anna Hodgart, has worked with the Scottish Green Party. In many ways the climate feels a lot darker than it did six years ago, so we started thinking that it was unlikely we would ever change the world with a club night. Maybe we all needed to do something much more tangible.

There are, of course, occasional moments when I wish more of the conversation around our band was centred on the actual art. What the music is like, what the emotional content is, rather than journalists trying to unpick my political leanings to find the hypocrisy they so desperately seek in whatever comes out of any feminist-identifying woman's mouth. It can be frustrating to think sometimes – rightly or wrongly – that other women in music who have never talked about those things get an 'easier' ride with the media and from the general public.

I never signed up to be a 'female' artist – I just wanted to be an artist, full stop. But if there has to be a discussion around our band that relates to gender, I am glad that we are part of a conversation that feels constructive, and that at least I can feel proud of what we did with our time in the sun while we had it.

A vast majority of the rooms I go into for my work – media offices, radio and TV stations, music venues, festivals, recording studios – are staffed completely by men. There are often tours where I could go virtually weeks at a time without encountering another woman, apart from our tour manager, Cara McDaniel, and our production manager, Brishon Neu. Imagine if my bandmates could say the same. That they had not seen another man in their line of work for a month at a time. As much as the music industry seems to be changing in some ways, in other ways it really isn't.

I guess it irritates me that I've thought about it as much as I have. It is shit to spend so much of my time as a musician talking about men. Why I don't 'hate' them (one of my favourite interview questions to answer, while sitting next to two men – my bandmates, teammates and best friends). Why I see fit to ask that women be treated with respect. But not talking about it won't make it go away. These people need to be called out. From my point of view, it's like looking down the barrel of two different guns. You either fight or you accept that the abuse is happening and say nothing.

I make music because it feels freeing to me, and that's the thing I try to hold on to. It's a place to express things and connect and communicate. Sometimes I worry that everything else that surrounds the music might make me bitter or sad, and I am very conscious of not letting that happen. I've got to the point where I feel it's important to have considered those things and go in with my eyes open and try to find a positive way to be, moving forward. And ultimately, I am very lucky. I have much more opportunity and privilege than other people, and I don't want it to seem like I have forgotten that.

*

Because of Iain and Martin's background, we were able to make the first two albums completely by ourselves, with the two of them producing. It was a really great foundation to build on because we knew what our band was about, what we wanted to say and how we wanted to sound. For the third album, *Love Is Dead*, we wanted a producer to push us out of our comfort zone a little. We tried a few producers out, but most of them weren't gelling. They were either trying to make the music even more 1980s – a kind of clumsy pastiche – or they were making it sound like every other pop song on the radio.

Greg Kurstin was perfect: he wanted to make the melodies bigger, but at the same time make everything else sound gnarlier. We wanted the sweet stuff to be sweet but we also wanted the music to be gritty. If everything sounds cookie-cutter cute, it doesn't feel like us. So it was good to find someone who could fuck up the right bits of it.

When we're writing an album, the music usually comes first. We'll use a kind of nonsense lyric and a vocal melody. On the last two records, I went into another room completely, wrote stuff, then came back in. Sometimes I'd have a lyric I loved and the boys would have a melody they loved, but when we put them together, they wouldn't quite fit. On *Love Is Dead*, we were focused on trying to make the lyrical hooks fit with the melodies – so that when we went into our own little corners, we all knew what we were working on.

Sharing an idea with the others as soon as it comes up is something I've never done before and it's been a good bonding exercise. I have to feel connected to my lyrics, but the lyrics also have to resonate with Iain and Martin, which can feel exposing. Still, working so openly with them was better than writing on my own and looking at their blank faces when I handed over the lyrics.

Martin, Iain and I often talk about what makes a great singer or a great vocalist. Someone can be an amazing vocalist and do lots of wonderful technical things, but their voice might not connect with you in a meaningful way. Some of my favourite singers of all time are people who, on paper, don't have good voices. They wouldn't impress at an *American Idol* audition but, when they sing, it's heartbreaking and connects people immediately simply because of what they are singing about and how they are singing it.

When I was a teenager I felt very connected to Bright Eyes and Alanis Morissette – artists who you might say haven't got technically great voices, but who make you feel something, and that's definitely more where we're trying to be at when we're making music. There's nothing more boring than turning on the radio and hearing one type of vocal style, with the same tuning on it and the same kind of effects. It's hard to come away with any sense of what the song is about and what the emotion behind it is. To me, the weirder and more character-driven a vocal is, the better.

It seems to me that women who write from an autobiographical perspective are looked at in a certain way. Female artists who are as open and vulnerable as Alanis are regarded differently from, say, Bob Dylan or Bruce Springsteen. Bob and Bruce are two of the greatest poets of our time, but they are never judged as hysterical or criticised for oversharing.

Journalists often ask me in general rather than specific terms about my lyrics. 'Is that song about a man? Which man? Is this album a break-up album?' I struggle to believe that a man in my position would have those same assumptions made about them. People always assume that I am writing about romantic entanglements – which I have done, as so many songwriters do, but it is definitely not exclusively all I write about – and people have also commented on the lack, from their perspective, of explicitly feminist lyrics.

I suppose it has, inevitably, changed the internal dynamics of the band. At one point we felt quite helpless because we didn't know what to do about the abuse. But now that we have decided on this stance where we don't take any shit, it makes it easier for me to handle. It became clear that we had to adopt a zero tolerance policy not just for our own sanity, but also because of our audience. There are a lot of young people who listen to our music, and more specifically a lot of young women. If a teenage version of me came to one of our shows or read an interview with us or came across the comments directed at us online, I like the idea of her seeing the comic book superhero version of us dealing with it. As opposed to how we would actually deal with it as normal people who sometimes feel vulnerable.

I don't suppose CHVRCHES' relationship with the internet will ever be straightforward. It has given me a lot of grief, but it's also given me a platform to make music and forge a community. I try to see the internet as a place where I can share things with people. For every person that hates us, there are all those who appreciate our music, and have found a place to belong within it.

I think that's all any of us want, really: something to believe in and somewhere to belong. I want to show our fans that you don't have to abide by a narrative that's just handed to you. If you use it constructively, it can be a very powerful thing. Maybe I'm trying to show myself that, too. To prove that all of this was worth something more.

POPPY AJUDHA

Poppy Ajudha grew up in south London and studied social anthropology and music at the School of Oriental and African Studies. Since 2015, she has released a series of singles, including 'Love Falls Down'. In 2017, Ajudha played her first headline show and the following year released an EP, FEMME, including the tracks 'Spilling Into You', 'Tepid Soul' and 'She Is The Sum'.

As a kid, I used to go on long car journeys with my mum at weekends to visit various members of our family. Mum had an orange cassette that she kept in the car with singers like Al Jarreau, Al Green, Luther Vandross and Marvin Gaye on it. It was all rare groove, soul and Motown. When I was older, Mum played CDs in the car, including artists like Lily Allen and P!nk, whose rebelliousness I loved. I was obsessed with the Pussycat Dolls, although I can't believe I was allowed to listen to them! I can't imagine Mum enjoyed them, but I really did love them. During early adolescence I was really into Jill Scott, Erykah Badu and Lauryn Hill and then, during my teen years, I listened to Amy Winehouse's first album *Frank* over and over again.

My parents separated when I was really young and I've only got one or two memories of them together. My dad was a DJ and then a nightclub owner, so I grew up between my mum's house in New Cross and my dad's club in Deptford. I didn't come from a formal musical background, but I grew up around music. My older twin sisters Sophie and Lauren went to the BRIT School and their band, Fluff, was taken on by the managers of S Club 7. I don't think they wrote any of their own music, but they represented exactly what I wanted to do when I was young.

When I was about eleven, Fluff's manager bought them two plastic Yamaha learning guitars that I used to play around with. I remember crying in the car in Surrey Quays car park, telling my mum that I needed a real guitar. That Christmas, Dad bought me my own fake plastic guitar from Toys R Us (so unhelpful), but I also got the Michael Jackson CD box set, which literally made me cry with happiness. I was completely obsessed with him.

I finally got an acoustic guitar for my thirteenth birthday and started teaching myself how to play, using an internet site called Tabs. I could never afford lessons, but I was always in the music room at lunchtime, forcing my friends to listen to my songs. I thought the songs were all terrible and that my enthusiastic friends were lying to me. It was a paradox: I had this strong creative streak, but at the same time I was a typically insecure teenager. My best friend at the time told me I could be the next Adele. When we were growing up, we loved Adele so much that I was blown away by her comment and I've never forgotten it.

And then my inspirational music teacher Mr Dottridge came into the music room one lunchtime and said the song I was playing was actually really good. He had great taste, playing us music like Buena Vista Social Club. He was the first person whose opinion I actually believed. He heard something in my voice and my music that was unique: maybe because my ear lends itself to jazz and I tend to write jazz-influenced chords, even though I was never a big jazzhead as a kid. Years later, I bumped into Mr Dottridge on the train and I really wanted to tell him how inspiring he'd been, but I was too shy.

Like my twin sisters, I applied for BRIT School, but in the end I was too scared to go to my audition. I was freaked out by the idea of doing a theory test because I've always struggled with dyslexia – and I later found out that I'm also dyspraxic. Lewisham is a poor borough so not many kids got tested, probably because the exam is so expensive. I finally got tested in my final year at university for free, after years and years of being told I wasn't 'dyslexic enough'.

After failing to turn up for the BRIT School audition, I started to think that being a musician was beyond me. I was convinced I couldn't do it. I didn't have access to things that other, more middle-class musicians had. I didn't know that you could study music, had no idea that conservatoires existed or that you could be taught how to sing jazz. I only knew about the pop side of music. I guess intellectual families discuss things around the dinner table, but I didn't have that kind of upbringing. I learned a lot from my mum, but she never said, 'Here are all your options'.

I did A level psychology, and for a while wanted to be a psychologist. Understanding people cognitively comes to me very naturally: I spend most of my life teaching men to be emotionally intelligent! My mum said I had to do something worthwhile as a degree and not just music. She was right: I ended up studying social anthropology and music at the School of Oriental and African Studies (SOAS) and was amazed by how diverse the discourse was around anthropology. I focused my course on philosophy and gender, and also on West African anthropology because I wanted to understand my Caribbean roots.

I signed as a model in my third year, so I was making music, modelling and studying for my degree all at the same time. It was pretty hectic and meant I didn't ever have much of a social life.

Had I got into the BRIT School, I might well be an established artist now, but I wouldn't have done my degree, which has informed all of my writing. Years after I howled for a guitar, it all worked out okay.

As I was growing up, I always fitted the stereotype of a pretty, feminine woman. My mother's family is British and my father's is from St Lucia and India, so lots of people see me as 'exotic'. From an early age, I knew what it was like to be objectified as a mixed-race woman and it definitely informed how I perceive myself.

When my hair was long, I was acceptably mixed race and fitted into European beauty standards: my hair is straight and my skin quite light. I looked like I thought other people wanted me to look, and I valued other people telling me I was beautiful. As I got older and went to university, I wanted to move away from that, so I cut my hair short a few years ago and then shaved my head completely. I didn't want to be judged solely on how people perceived me physically.

I'm an intelligent woman. I left SOAS with a first-class degree. Of course there are more important things than the way you look. Adhering to constructed ideas of how a woman should look or behave only ever hindered me in my interactions and I realised how important it was to keep rewriting the narrative of womanhood.

That's what I wanted from the artists I admired: women and men who were happy with who they were. I've never been big on icons; I never had posters of celebrities on my bedroom wall. I take lots of things from different people. As an artist myself, I want to empower other women as much as I can. The notion of women being in competition with each other is old sexist rhetoric which only divides us and disables us from succeeding together.

All the women I know are intelligent enough to realise that we work better together. I have a creative network of incredible women who are all doing amazing things and who inspire me on a daily basis. I have a film-maker friend who is as busy as I am, but when we find time to meet I always feel so good afterwards. She works at a million miles an hour, is so enthusiastic about life and so appreciative of our friendship and the value of growing with another woman within creative industries that are dominated by men.

It's particularly important for me to be around other women in a male-dominated music industry. I always try to include them. I recently organised a panel talk in which women of colour talked about their experiences in relation to the topics and themes surrounding my first EP, *FEMME* – namely race and gender identity. I try to get a gender balance on stage. I book female support acts where possible. I collaborate with female directors like Ali Kurr on my videos. I work with *gal-dem*, the magazine and creative collective of women and non-binary people of colour.

I think things are moving in the right direction, albeit slowly. Look at the films that have come out in the past few years: *Moonlight*, *Get Out* and *Black Panther* are some of my favourite films because they are so intelligent and powerful. And the music: *A Seat at the Table*, Solange's game-changing

2016 album. Childish Gambino's video for 'This Is America', which is an important and radical piece of performance art.

Black intellectuals and communities are finally being recognised for writing their own narratives and are thus seeping into commercial culture (for all the right reasons) and, in turn, changing the way people think. This process of changing stereotypes around blackness and openly talking about the difficulties and hardships of people of colour through creative media will mean these discussions are steadily integrated into our social fabric.

I am very much an independent artist. I wanted to sign to a major label when I was young and have everything done for me, but I pretty quickly realised that it didn't really work like that. Everything comes at a cost. I like to be in control of all the aspects of the work I put out, so from the visuals to the sonics, it has to be a reflection of my own vision. At the very start of my career, I was invited to meetings at a number of major labels, but the guys were all complete idiots. They just wanted to change what I wanted to do; they didn't trust my vision. I'm not into having loads of white men tell me what to do and I never have been.

Of course, I can never be truly independent, in the sense that I have a team supporting my career. For me, it's just about not signing over everything you own to one company. Having your eggs in different baskets means you have more control, more flexibility and the possibility to change your mind because you're not tied into long-term deals. However, I might want to sign a publishing deal or work with bigger companies in the future.

I have learned to look after myself. No one else is going to. I guess watching my mum bring me and two sisters up as a single parent taught me that everything is possible as a woman, but that at the same time it's not always easy to be heard as a woman. I became politicised while I was studying at SOAS and then *A Seat at the Table* came out just as I was starting to write my first EP. It really helped me to articulate in my lyrics how I was feeling politically and emotionally.

When I wrote the lyrics for 'Tepid Soul' as a response to the work of Gil Scott-Heron and James Baldwin ('Whiteness, blackness/Swallows me whole'), I wondered if they were too much. I'd always been so concerned with being liked when I was younger, and the idea of stepping into this controversial space was scary. The last line, 'Am I the right shade for you?', felt a bit on the edge the first time I sang it.

My mum was in the audience and I'd never spoken to her about my fragmented identity as a mixed-race woman. But I just sang it. I learned to get over the initial discomfort that saying what you think brings. I have to be bold. I have to say what I feel at that time. It might not be how I always feel, and that's fine. People change and develop. But you can't be afraid to think.

I'd say it's pretty clear that I write my own lyrics because they are so personal to my experience. And yet people, mostly men, still don't expect female artists to produce or co-produce their own music. Or even write the chords. A guy will touch a record – for example, he will do some post-production – and suddenly he's made the whole thing. I want to shout out to the world: 'I did everything before that!'

It's like someone forgetting to write down my name when they list the producers on one of my tracks, when I co-produced the song. If it's not written down then everyone will assume that I didn't have any input on it.

I have learned the hard way that, in order to be heard and

acknowledged in the studio and to push my ideas through, I have to be really thick-skinned. I no longer care about being liked. I don't avoid confrontation just because it makes people feel uncomfortable. I used to feel uncomfortable the whole time because I didn't like what some guy was doing but I didn't want to upset him. It's time we had open and fair dialogues. How do we get men to be more emotionally intelligent if we don't include them in the conversation?

From a political point of view, I think it's important that artists like Cardi B are coming through. I don't listen to her music, nor do I follow her closely enough to have a really informed opinion, but I like her as a personality. She takes up space and claims everything within her reach. She says whatever the fuck she wants and doesn't care how people might respond. There's something very powerful about seeing women in popular culture doing this.

Her loud and sometimes unashamedly 'grotesque' behaviour completely flips the stereotype of what a woman should represent and what her place is in society. Whether she's a feminist or not, she illuminates a more modern way of expressing the female voice and, in doing so, moves us away from older, more conservative types of feminism. Cardi B ultimately shows us that not all women have to behave in the same way. That's something women need to learn to be: themselves. As long as you're not hurtful or discriminatory, being yourself is good enough.

It is, nonetheless, a weird balance. As there isn't one way to be a woman, so there isn't one way to be a feminist. It's one of the problems people have had with the word feminism. It's been homogenised by the media and the people who feel threatened by it and now it's seen as a dirty word as opposed to a way of allowing women to be free in so many different ways. If used in a way that relates to your personal politics, feminism will help you realise that you aren't alone.

Feminism is also very intersectional. If you want to be a conservative feminist, a womanist or an Islamic feminist, that's your choice. It's about respecting that choice instead of imposing your Western ideology around freedom and liberty on to someone else's culture. It's about respecting that everyone's history and experience is different. It's something that was discussed at length at SOAS, and it really opened my mind.

Cardi B's presentation of herself is hypersexual. People get upset because she used to be a stripper, but women have the right to do whatever they want with their bodies so long as they ensure it's not the only way they value themselves. As I said, there are different types of feminism: if everyone else objectifies you, why can't you take pleasure in your sexuality? Why can't you own it and enjoy it? Or use your sexual power to get what you want? After all, men have used it to oppress women for years.

Many people can't deal with how sexual women can be. But if that makes you feel empowered, then it's your right to use it. It's your choice to use that power. It's a tool. Maybe that's why I was drawn to the Pussycat Dolls as a kid: I've always been quite a sexual person and it was refreshing to see women own their sexuality rather than being submissive. At least, I'm assuming that was the critical reading made by my ten-year-old self when I first encountered the Pussycat Dolls!

In spring 2018, I put a link to the new video for 'She Is The Sum' on Instagram and beneath it wrote a long post. 'As a song, "She Is The Sum" is aimed at reminding you of your infinite power, a power that you have been taught you don't possess but that has always been there deep inside you . . . there is no one way to be a woman . . . like myself, the woman [in the video] is queer-identifying, and through the video she navigates her sexuality. Being open is something I've struggled with all my life, and this video is my first public portrayal of my sexuality . . . I hope LGBTQIA men and women will see this and learn to accept themselves sooner than I have.'

It was a stressful thing to write. I still cringe a bit when I see it and I'm going to be working through it for a while. But my sexuality wasn't something I felt I could be open about until going to uni, and so it still feels quite uncomfortable. Then I started my gender course and everyone was using this new word 'queer'. I didn't have to label myself lesbian or bisexual. I am already heavily objectified as a mixed-race woman, and being labelled bisexual was another element I wasn't comfortable with.

At uni I got used to the term 'queer' because of its ambiguity. I felt I could be more open, more confident. I only told my mum and dad about my sexuality towards the end of 2017, which was weird at first but fine once they got used to it. My dad is quite traditional, but we're really close and quite similar as people. As he lives in St Lucia now he's not so connected to the media, but my mum's on Instagram and sees what I post.

Some people are comfortable with themselves from an early age, but I never knew anyone like me. I always just wanted to be normal. It's something I really struggled with as a kid. I hated being attracted to women. When I got older and met all these queer women who were open and in relationships, it became really normal. I was suddenly in a very liberal, creative community both at uni and later within my creative networks.

I know what it's like to feel alone, so I try and make people feel that they are not alone with my music. I wanted people who can't say how they feel to watch 'She Is The Sum' and see that queer love can be beautiful.

For me it's about representing what I do with honesty. Everything I do relates back to my experience. I do give a lot of myself; some artists don't say anything about themselves. My art is my therapy, so it's just as important for me as it is in terms of reaching out to other people. Ask me again in five years' time. Although, if I haven't made it by then, I might quit and become a yoga teacher. There's only so much you can give this business without getting something back!

KALIE SHORR

Kalie Shorr left her home town of Portland, Maine for Nashville when she was a teenager. Her first independent debut single, 'Fight Like A Girl', was released in January 2016. Later that year, Shorr released The Y2K Mixtape, *an eight-song collection of some of her earliest music, that became the second bestselling debut female in all of country music that year. In 2017, she released a second single, 'He's Just Not Into You', and in 2018 came a third single, 'Two Hands'. She is part of a weekly song-writers' event in Nashville called Song Suffragettes that showcases female singer-songwriters.*

I grew up in Portland, Maine, the youngest of seven, all of us brought up by my incredible single mom. My dad hasn't been in my life very much, but for my ninth birthday he gave me tickets to see the Dixie Chicks at Madison Square Garden in New York. Like all my favourite artists, they stand for something. They aren't afraid to speak out. I can't see the point in being an artist if you have nothing to say.

As soon as I got a new Dixie Chicks CD, I'd rip it open and

pull out the booklet to see who wrote the songs and read the notes about each song. There's a track on *Fly*, the Dixie Chicks' fifth studio album, called 'Goodbye Earl', which is about poisoning a man who was abusive to his wife. In the notes was a funny disclaimer along the lines of, 'We don't condone murder, but it's okay to sing a song about it'.

There's another song on *Fly* called 'Cold Day in July' which is about a relationship break-up, but when my grandfather passed away in 2001, I needed to think the song was about losing my grandfather. It was the first time I found a song to see me through a difficult time. I was only young, but that song was so, so important to me.

In the same year that I saw them in New York, the Dixie Chicks' lead singer Natalie Maines told a London audience that, given George W. Bush's stance on Iraq, she was ashamed to be a fellow Texan. The band were immediately dropped from radio playlists across America and, even though all three members of the Dixie Chicks were articulate and respectful, fans kept on burning their CDs in the street.

My mom is a lifelong Republican and was a big fan of Bush, but she wasn't against the Dixie Chicks. She was very clear that free speech is to be celebrated, and she's always been a feminist. I don't really care what her politics are because she's a good human being and she believes in equality for women. She was in the Miss USA pageant in the 1970s – she's a total babe – and she was asked if she believed women deserved equal pay. She said, 'Hell, yeah!' That might sound like the expected response now, but back then it was a lot more edgy to talk about the pay gap/Women's Lib.

My mom had to work non-stop to support us. I make more money now than she did when I was growing up, but she taught me how to work hard for what I want and to never expect anything to be handed to you. It's a pretty valuable lesson.

I can't remember a time when I didn't want to be a singer. I was writing songs from the age of six. Everybody likes music when they're growing up, but I *loved* it. Shania Twain, Faith Hill, Reba McEntire – basically modern country. My mom used to book the national anthem singers at local sporting events in Portland, and she had a beautiful voice so sometimes she sang the 'Star-Spangled Banner' herself. I used to go to work with her because day care is expensive. I'd sit there with my pens and colouring book, listening to the national anthem being performed over and over again.

When I was two and a half, I said, 'Mom, I want to sing it.'

She was shocked. But I stood there and sang it to her. So she let me sing it at a local basketball game. I got all the way to 'And the rocket's red glare' and I couldn't go on – Mom had to finish it for me. I'm sure she knew then that I was going to be a handful.

When the notorious American gossip blogger Perez Hilton first got in touch with me in 2011, I didn't initially believe it was him. I'd been posting cover versions of songs on YouTube; I did a take of 'Friday' by Rebecca Black, which he saw and loved. He flew me to his birthday party in Nashville and I opened for the Backstreet Boys. I was sixteen and I thought I'd made it.

But Perez shot it to me real straight. 'It will take six years to make it. It very rarely happens more quickly than that. If it does, it'll probably be the kind of success you don't want. You could get a deal really quickly and be shelved for not fulfilling your potential.'

It was great advice: I'd been thinking that I was going to move to Nashville and blow everyone away. 'Watch out, suckers!' Like Nashville had been waiting for me to show up. I think everyone thinks like that, whether they care to admit it or not. But Perez gave me a reality check, and reminded me of what my mom had said about hard work.

I also had to graduate from school and save up enough money to move to Nashville. The week of my eighteenth birthday, I moved into a small apartment down the road from my mom's place. I needed to figure out how to pay a utility bill, how to shop and cook for myself. I didn't have a car, so I had to get the bus to school, and the bus system in Portland isn't great. I'd get to school for 7.30 a.m., take two classes and leave at 10 a.m. I'd be at my first job by 11 a.m. and I'd stay there till 4.40 p.m. My second job was from 5 p.m. till 9 p.m., after which I'd go home and do my homework.

I did this for four or five months, while my friends were going to parties and football games. I had to check out of any social life and focus on my plan. Looking back, it was a really crazy time. I definitely missed out on some normal teenage experiences, but I wouldn't trade any of them for the place I'm at now in my career.

I arrived in Nashville within days of my nineteenth birthday with a good mix of optimism and realism. I worked at a hot dog stand, serving canned chili out of a crockpot. I worked every day from 6 p.m. to 4 a.m. and I was exhausted, but at least I could write during the day and take meetings.

I had to keep reminding myself that Faith Hill used to work at McDonald's. 'If she could do that, I can do this!'

I started singing in hotel lobbies downtown and eventually quit all of my other side jobs to do that. It changed my life because it finally meant that I could do music full-time. I was just barely getting by, but I was so thankful to get to sing every day that nothing could bring me down. Eventually, I signed with management and released my first single, 'Fight Like A Girl'. I then signed a publishing deal and starting working with a booking agency, which in turn led to cutting records with other artists, and plenty of touring. I'm thankful that 'Fight Like A Girl' was a breakthrough single, simply because it opened so many doors for me.

I'm still independent, so I practically run my own record label. My team is amazing, but, at the end of the day, I'm the one who says yes or no and I really like that. I might be a control freak, but I'm also a team player: I don't want to be this person who marches around saying, 'Do this! Do that!' I've put together a team I trust and I'm very transparent. When they say to me, 'Maybe you should step out of your comfort zone and do this', or 'Hey, that's not quite the right look', they are usually right.

I try to manage my own narrative as much as possible. I run all of my social media so that I can control who I want to be and what I want to sound like. It's very empowering. I have to remind myself not to take it for granted because ten or fifteen years ago artists didn't have Twitter or Instagram as platforms, and they couldn't post their own thoughts or regulate images online.

Image is everything. I care about how I represent myself because I want to feel that I'm expressing my sexuality without having to be sexy all the time. I would never judge another woman's way of manifesting her sexuality because it's always beautiful, right? There is a way for me to be sexual that is authentically me, which is not the way Beyoncé does it, nor the way Taylor Swift does it. Which is great, because we shouldn't all be doing it the same way.

I find it comfortable talking about that side of myself in

songs. It doesn't even have to be about sex. It's more about connecting with someone physically. We write about love, and sexuality is such a big component of that. I don't think you can disagree with that.

When I was growing up, Alanis Morissette was one of my biggest inspirations. She was like the queen for me – she still is. I've never met her. I would die! Most teenage girls will know what I mean when I say that I felt Alanis was there for me. Country is my path, but I grew up with rock 'n' roll, too. My first band, when I was thirteen, was a Nirvana cover band. But Alanis's music was all I wanted to hear. I was going through a break-up and I hadn't even done anything with a boy at that stage, but I remember hearing 'You Oughta Know' and it hit me hard because it was just so visceral.

I related to it because I was thinking, 'I want to go and make out with someone else just to make this guy mad about it.' That line might make you squirm in your seat a little bit because it's so honest, but it's something that people feel, and you should sing about stuff that people relate to. There are plenty of teen girls going through break-ups who need to hear their less-than-poetic emotions represented.

I've always tried to channel Alanis's unabashed honesty in my music, especially with 'Fight Like A Girl'.

I didn't realise that sexism was an issue until I got to Nashville.

It started off slowly and subtly. I'd show up in someone's office with a guitar and they'd look surprised that I even played.

Or I'd be setting up a meeting or a co-write and suddenly it became clear that it had nothing to do with work – it was a date. Oh my god! How weird is that? Get me out of here!

Then I noticed people becoming ballsier and much more openly sexist.

I'd walk into an office and have people say, 'You're a star, but you're a girl and we already have one of those on our roster.'

It was unbelievably direct. Casual, everyday sexism.

One of the hardest encounters I had was with a woman who I admired and respected. After a meeting with her label, she told my manager, 'We're a little burned out on women right now.' They have over forty acts on their roster. Eight of whom are solo female artists. If that's what burned out looks like . . . oh my god! Fifty-one per cent of the population is female.

I just had to smile and say, 'Thank you for your time.'

Now that I'm slightly more successful and in a position to give less of a shit, I've become more outspoken about it. I don't want to whine about those sexist attitudes; I know those people are just trying to do their jobs. We all know the music industry is in turmoil now and no one wants to go out on a limb. If it doesn't pay off, that's a million dollars they flushed down the toilet. I knew from day one that this was a business. It's not summer camp.

Equally, I do think that, if record companies invested in women and put their power behind those acts, it would pay off long-term. As Steve Earle said in the *Guardian* in 2017, 'the best stuff coming out of Nashville is all by women'.

The female voices in Nashville are so diverse, both sonically and lyrically. We all have our own lane. I think women are being unapologetic in their experiences and are owning those parts of their story. Marriage, divorce, sex, children, youth, change – so many perspectives that the world needs to hear. Not every girl in country is blonde-haired, blue-eyed and standing in a field. I'm especially intrigued by women and men of colour in country music and their experiences being shared within our genre.

We can't, however, wait for change: the only thing us women can do is pull together to make it work for ourselves!

Which is why we started Song Suffragettes: each week, five female songwriters perform three songs each and the show finishes with a cover performed by all five women.

It was something my manager Todd Cassetty thought of in 2014: since it started, more than thirty performers have got publishing deals and seven have got record deals. We've been trying to round up female producers and engineers, but there are literally about five in the whole of Nashville. It's not that the female engineers aren't getting work – there simply aren't that many because women aren't encouraged to pursue it as a career. Hopefully we can help change the musical landscape and encourage young girls to get involved in music in all sorts of ways.

I'll be super-honest here: there was a time in high school when I wasn't a feminist. I was fifteen and I didn't know anything. When I became an adult, I suddenly got it – it can be harder being a woman in all sorts of ways. And now I speak out about it. I certainly don't need to put up with men coming up to me at airports because I'm carrying a guitar and mansplaining to me about everything. How I should make my music, even though they most likely haven't heard it; how to produce it, ditto; how to avoid getting ripped off when signing a contract . . . I could go on.

I'm a better woman because of Song Suffragettes, for sure. It's made me proud to call myself a feminist. My first three singles, 'Fight Like A Girl', 'He's Just Not That Into You' and 'Two Hands', were co-written with women I met at Song Suffragettes – it wasn't planned, but it made sense. These women are my friends. We drink wine together. We're in our early twenties. We love working together, so why the hell not?

We went out on a bit of a limb with Song Suffragettes. When we first started, we tried to make a big splash of it and I saw a tweet about us that said, 'If you packaged five average female artists together, they are still average female artists. Putting them together doesn't make them any shinier'. Then some dude who owns a big company in Nashville talked some shit about it. Seemingly, he wasn't keen on the feminist angle.

But it blew up pretty fast after that. And you could see the cynics thinking, 'Oh shit, we're probably going to have to be nice about this because it's going to get bigger real quick.'

It's a totally inclusive space. Guys are welcome. Families are welcome. We love it when girls who don't want to sing come along just because they love what we do.

It's incredibly competitive in Nashville. There are far more unsigned singers than there are potential record deals. But hard work, kindness and patience go a long way.

Young women have been pushed together by misogyny. We have realised that everything is so skewed against us that we literally have to be in it together. Trying to shoot another girl down is not going to build you up. It can be really hard in Nashville, and I need my girlfriends.

When I was growing up and my mom had to go to work, her best friend would watch me; she literally helped raise me. I always thought I wanted female friendships like that when I was an adult and, here in Nashville, that dream has come true.

TRACEY THORN

After releasing two albums and three singles with the Marine Girls in the early 1980s, Tracey Thorn formed Everything But The Girl with Ben Watt when they were both at Hull University. Their first album, Eden, *was released in 1984. Before disbanding in 2000, EBTG released nine more albums and enjoyed their biggest success with Todd Terry's 1995 remix of the single 'Missing'. Thorn's solo career has yielded five solo albums. She wrote and recorded the music for Carol Morley's 2013 film* The Falling *and has also collaborated with artists such as The Style Council and Massive Attack. Her 2013 memoir,* Bedsit Disco Queen, *was a* Sunday Times Top 10 *bestseller. It was followed in 2015 by* Naked at the Albert Hall.

I was seventeen when I borrowed a copy of Patti Smith's *Horses* from a boy up the road. The first time I played it, I was profoundly shocked, but also excited. I'd heard some outlandish things on punk records, but nothing like the opening lines of 'Gloria': 'Jesus died for somebody's sins but not mine'.

And there Patti was on the cover, in a white shirt, a black

jacket slung over her shoulder. It was as though she was saying, 'I'm not trying to look pretty. I don't care.' Boyish but clearly gorgeous. I was still a tomboy and very aware that I couldn't fit into the 1970s notion of what girls were supposed to look like. Flicky hair and lip gloss weren't really my thing.

Patti Smith was otherworldly. I felt I had a handle on punk, but not on this woman who had appeared out of nowhere. I was only a teenage schoolgirl and I didn't know anything about New York. Now, of course, I'd simply have typed her name into Google and within a few minutes I'd have read her Wikipedia page. I'd know that she came from the New York art scene and that she was close to Robert Mapplethorpe, who took the cover photo of *Horses*. I think it would have reduced the experience; as it was, there was just the music and the cover shot. I played *Horses* over and over again and sang along with it obsessively.

Up until that point, I only sang along to male artists – I had the same range as Elvis Costello. I wasn't trying to copy Patti or Elvis, nor was I trying to be them. It was rather that I didn't fit the rock template, so I couldn't really learn vocally from powerful female singers like Janis Joplin.

I'd started going to gigs seriously when I was sixteen. I sought out the other girls at my suburban girls' school who were into music. When a cluster of approachable girls attached themselves to the cool alpha girls who were already going to gigs, I started to go with them. We went to St Albans to see XTC, Ian Dury, Siouxsie and the Banshees, Buzzcocks, Boomtown Rats and Tom Robinson Band – anyone who came through town.

I joined a local band called Stern Bops when I was seventeen, playing the Les Paul copy I'd bought a few years earlier. It had felt audacious for someone like me to buy such a masculine icon like a Les Paul. I hadn't seen that many girls playing guitar – even within punk, girls tended to sing. I wasn't one of the cool, rebellious girls at school. I didn't get into David Bowie first, or have a great haircut before anyone else. But I saved up from my Saturday job, found a small ad in the back of the *NME* or *Melody Maker*, got the train to London Fields, found this guy's flat in a tower block, handed him £60 and proudly carried the guitar back home. I surprised myself. It was a rite of passage.

I found it was quite difficult to compete with the boys in Stern Bops. They had that boy confidence that I found quite daunting and they seemed to understand technology better than me. How they acquired that knowledge, I do not know; I suspect they were winging it much of the time, in the way that boys do. And I took it for granted that they knew more than I did.

When I left Stern Bops to form the Marine Girls with my school friend Gina Hartman, it was absolutely in defiance of local boys. I very much wanted to form a band with girls, to show them. Jane Fox and her sister Alice joined the band and we did better than the boys. We were the first local band to be offered a gig in London and to be written about in the local papers and the music press.

Although we wrote our own songs, we didn't think of ourselves as a band; after Gina left, we really were three schoolgirls making records incredibly primitively for very little money. It cost £36 to make 50 cassettes. It's hard to explain how small-scale it felt at the time, but I was proud of our achievement because I didn't feel like we were trying to copy the boys. We were almost wearing our lack of expertise as a badge of honour. We were writing interesting songs and we didn't sound like everyone else – even if that's only because we weren't technically proficient. It was about being individual.

I started as a backing singer. I'd write a song for Alice to sing and I'd sing a few lines myself. I started to sing more and more and then it became difficult; as I acquired more confidence, I began to resent having to give my songs to Alice, especially on record. I still wasn't crazy about singing live. It's one of the reasons the band split up. As well as for geographical reasons.

There was no sense in my mind at all that this could end up being a career and it never occurred to me not to go to university, if only because I wanted to leave home. When I started at Hull University, Jane went down to Brighton. It became really hard to keep the band going and we lasted another year, if that.

Writing for the *NME* was the dream. I wanted to be the next Julie Burchill. It seemed like a reasonable goal. I can't remember if there were any other female journalists writing at that time, apart from Vivien Goldman and Caroline Coon. They must have been ploughing a lonely furrow. I would have been fine going to gigs and writing in a notebook or reviewing records in my bedroom, but I'd have been hopeless at hanging around bands who didn't want to be interviewed, asking them impertinent questions. I'm far too shy.

Back then, when I was growing up in suburbia and the Marine Girls were still together, I read the *NME* every week; it was the way I found out about music. I'd read the singles reviews and order records by post, sending off a postal order to pay for them. Waiting for the record to arrive in the post was *so* exciting. It's hard to convey how precious it seemed compared to this world of instant gratification. I was crazy about the music press, and then suddenly I found myself in the position of being written about in the music press as a member of the Marine Girls.

Some of the early stuff that was written about us was really irritating. I admit that we were partially to blame because we used to make seaside jokes around the 'Marine' Girls, but journalists would nearly always take it too far. The interviews would now seem incredibly patronising. We were girls, we were still at school and we didn't know anything about the things you were supposed to know about.

We were completely out of our depth. We weren't one of those bands who had a manifesto. Some bands had clearly sat down and thought about it. They knew which bands to name-check, like Velvet Underground and Big Star. I do think it's a boy thing; they arm themselves with all this information and context that places them perfectly, so that journalists can then neatly pop them in a slot.

The three of us were also very disparate. Alice, at fifteen, was three years younger than us. A child. She was also a goth; she was shaving her head into a massive Mohican and going to see Spear of Destiny. Jane loved The Slits and Pigbag and then she got into jazz – she was more experimental, whereas I was following a path of jangly pop: Orange Juice, Aztec Camera. When Jane and I went off to university, we were pulling in increasingly different directions and because we were so young, we didn't have the language to sort out our issues or to resolve them.

Interviews have rarely been easy for me. When I released my first solo record, A Distant Shore, in 1982, I was asked who had influenced the record. The journalist – a man, as they nearly always are, even now – mentioned a folk singer called Bridget St John, who I had never heard of. I got very arsey because I didn't want to be thought of as a folk singer, but I also felt intimidated because it made me think that the journalist knew more about the music I was making than I did. It was disempowering.

I felt as though someone else was telling my story.

*

As a teenager, I wanted to be in bands for all sorts of reasons. I loved music. It was a laugh. And I thought it would be a good way to meet boys. As it turned out, it was an absolutely useless way to meet boys! Well, that's not strictly true. My first boyfriend was the bass player of the band I was in. But when I started the Marine Girls, it all went wrong: being in an all-girl band frightened the life out of boys. I thought they would be so impressed that we'd beaten them that they'd want to go out with us. Ha! Did I know nothing about the male psyche? Do they want to go out with girls who have shown them up and beaten them at their own game? Of course they fucking don't!

In the year I was in the Marine Girls, I had hardly any male attention. I'd have done better if I'd have carried on buying the *NME* and saying in a demure tone, 'So which single do you think is the best one?'

But then, of course, I met Ben Watt on the day I arrived at Hull University. I had signed to Cherry Red in 1981, asking my dad, an accountant, to look at the contract. He said, 'That's probably all right.' Ben was a labelmate, a solo artist who'd played guitar in a few bands. He was, without question, a better musician than me. It was almost a relief; we each sensed that the other one had strengths the other lacked.

We formed Everything But The Girl in 1982 and our first album, *Eden*, was released on Blanco y Negro two years later. The brilliant idea behind Blanco y Negro was that it would be funded by Warner Music but the artists wouldn't have to compromise. Rob Dickins, the chairman of Warner Music, was known for being very hands-on. He didn't seem to understand why I had no interest in being the new Sade, winning best album at the BRIT Awards and selling millions of records.

Instead we were being 'awkward', because we made a series of records that all sounded so different to each other and we could easily have lost our listening base from one record to the next. We were simply following what was exciting us, which made it harder for the record company to sell us. Let's ride this new wave of British jazzy pop! Let's make a record with guitars and miserable lyrics!

Working with a major label – and there was no hiding the fact that Warner had ultimate control – I did feel the awkwardness of being a woman who didn't want to play by any of the rules. I made it so clear that I wasn't going to be told how to pose for a record cover or how to dress/behave in a video, and we didn't agree to have a stylist till the 1990s. I look back now and think, 'My god, you were so pig-headed.' I was so rigid. So uncompromising. So dogged about everything. I certainly didn't suffer in silence. So I can't look back and say, 'Oh god, they made us do this or that.'

I don't think anyone ever said to me, 'Put more make-up on, wear a shorter skirt.' It's intangible, really – a feeling that you know the record company is a bit disappointed in you. That you could be more successful if only you tried a bit harder and you weren't so ... uncompromising. You end up internalising people's dissatisfaction with you and attempting to rectify the 'problem' with yourself.

When Ben was seriously ill in 1992, we both got very skinny – Ben because he was so ill and me because I was so worried. Because this was the era of grungy fashion, of 'heroin chic' and of Kate Moss being photographed by Corinne Day in *Vogue* looking wasted, Ben and I looked very rock 'n' roll.

The way we both look in the 'Missing' video in 1994 is quite shocking. We did play it up; we quite enjoyed the extremity of it. We were sick of the nice little cosy image we had before Ben's illness, which didn't suit us at all; we're both slightly prickly characters, not very cosy at all. Suddenly, post Ben's illness, we looked a little bit ravaged and very, very skinny. No one would have known why. It could have been anything.

For me it had nothing to do with 'a woman can't be too rich or too thin'. It wasn't about feeling more beautiful – it was almost the opposite. 'Look how ugly I am, I'm so thin.'

I look back at images from the early 1990s, not just of us but also of other people, and it's clear that creating an idealised version of a body that is so starved was a dangerous thing to be playing with. People watching the video might have assumed that we had eating disorders, but the reality was that we'd just been through a massive trauma.

When 'Missing' was remixed by Todd Terry and became an unexpected worldwide hit in 1995, I wasn't thinking, 'Fantastic, we can really build on this . . . ' Ten years earlier I might have done, but subconsciously I knew I was approaching the end of Everything But The Girl. I had done an MA in 1990, and was considering how a PhD might be ultimately more fulfilling than being in a band. I was never the keenest of performers. I'm not a natural show-off; standing on stage often makes me feel anxious and I have a fairly soft voice that doesn't fit brilliantly with live music. Ben would have been horrified to hear that; he was ready to roll up his sleeves and capitalise on our success. He is a musician through and through. It was all he was ever going to do.

Which is not to say I turned down opportunities during this period. Working with Ben had been quite easy and safe. He understood me very well and we communicated very easily. I worked with The Style Council very early on in my career – I sang on 'The Paris Match' in 1984 – but otherwise I'd never collaborated with other artists. When Massive Attack asked me down to Nellee Hooper's studio in Bristol to do the vocal on 'Protection', I was very much stepping outside my comfort zone.

I got the gig because Björk told Nellee how much she loved A Distant Shore, he listened to it and in turn played it to Massive Attack. I never knew how much the band were into me doing the vocal. 'Protection' was one of Mushroom's tracks and he barely even spoke to me, which made me wonder if he wanted me to do the vocal. For someone shy and self-doubting, I had to keep forcing myself to go through the process. As soon as I sang over the backing track of 'Protection', at least I knew it was really good, which gave me the confidence to push on through. But it was awkward sometimes. Perhaps Massive Attack were used to being like that with each other – I don't think they spent much time congratulating each other.

It was a relief to write with Ben again, and in 1996 Walking Wounded became our most successful album. It was great for me because it meant I could go out on a high.

I wanted to have kids. I'd started thinking about it in the late 1980s, when we were still working very hard. I was happy to put it off, but then Ben was very ill and very nearly died. It was shocking. You think you've got all the time in the world and actually we nearly had no time at all. In the immediate aftermath of his illness, I was very keen to have a child, but Ben protested, 'I'm only just recovering from not being dead.' Completely fair enough.

When he was strong again, he felt a profound need to make a record. He had a lot to write about. A drive to feel he was alive. But the years were ticking by and after Walking Wounded, I put my foot down. It was almost ten years since I'd first thought we would have kids and I was reaching my mid-thirties. We turned down the U2 tour because it would have meant another deferral. We were doing well at that point and another offer was always going to come in.

When I got pregnant, with twin girls, I told people that I wasn't retiring, but I don't know how honest I was being. I became so absorbed in motherhood that there was no way I wanted to go back to it all. We did make another album, *Temperamental*, while the girls were really small and we took them on tour with us when they were eighteen months old. I did the tour with the best intentions – I was very aware it was Ben's career too, and we'd been a partnership till then. He hadn't decided to retire, why should he? I was trying to please people. It wasn't a long tour, but I didn't enjoy it at all.

I agreed to do one gig in New York and went out for the day on Concorde. I was away from the girls for about eighteen hours. I just couldn't bear to be away from them. What if something happens when I'm not there, let alone on a different fucking continent?

I got pregnant again and that made the decision for me. No more records, no more tours. Not for a while, at least.

I was very happy.

I come from a fairly conservative urban background. Mum worked until she had children and then became a housewife and mother and was always conservative in her thinking. There weren't great expectations on me to achieve: I did well at school and I was brainy and that was great, my parents were pleased with me. They were thrilled when I became the first person in the family to attend university. What I might then do and what my aspirations might be wasn't a topic at home, and it wasn't something anyone thought that deeply about. We weren't a madly ambitious family. Ben came from a much more boho background – his parents were a jazz musician and an actress.

I've been shy but opinionated for as long as I can remember. I was aware of feminism without having a word for it – I intuitively knew boys shouldn't be allowed to be in charge of the music scene. Some of the early lyrics I wrote for the Marine Girls have got that defiance in them, despite being small-scale and localised; I was writing about boys and the way boys think about girls, about the expectations that are being placed upon you and the way in which boys treat and view you.

I didn't learn the language of feminism until I got to Hull and did a Women in Literature course. I hoovered up the Brontë sisters, Sylvia Plath and Charlotte Perkins Gilman's 'The Yellow Wallpaper'; they made complete sense. And then I started asking questions. Should I be in a band with my boyfriend? Should I even have a boyfriend? And more realistic questions such as, Can a man be a feminist? I definitely talked to Ben about relationships and the way they worked and the power structure within them. I found my voice.

By being opinionated in interviews pretty much from the first interview I did with the Marine Girls, and then with Everything But The Girl, I got a reputation for being a bit of a harridan. In the way that opinionated women do. In the 1980s musicians were asked a lot about politics, and while Paul Weller and Billy Bragg would be celebrated for talking about Red Wedge, I'd say something not dissimilar and be portrayed as a *humourless* harridan.

It felt unfair. I didn't know how to put my opinions across with any degree of humour or warmth, and maybe I did come across as being cold and unforgiving about things. But I do think men don't have to worry about those kinds of things. It's back to the issue of having to be likeable. If women are expressing a controversial opinion or trying to assert power, they lose their likeability.

When I joined Twitter in 2009, people kept saying, 'You're so funny! You're so likeable!' It made me realise that no one had ever had any inkling that it might be the case. They thought I was dour. They had no idea that I have always had a sense of irony and can be self-deprecating. No one ever captured that side of me when interviewing me. They created a version of me. A female pop star with no sense of humour about myself. My public persona was constructed for me and was beyond my control.

As soon as I was back in control, I was able to convey another, more realistic image. My image after joining Twitter and post-*Bedsit Disco Queen* is entirely different. Everyone was shocked that I watched and enjoyed *X Factor*. That I had any hinterland or breadth. Because I had a penchant for writing sad songs, I therefore had to be melancholy all the time. Or the fact that you care about feminism means you can't watch certain things on the telly. That I can embrace low as well as high culture. It's bizarre. I thought we'd dispensed with all that twenty-odd years ago.

There are, of course, plenty of negative sides to social media. You have to face backlash and feedback. I can't believe some of the shit that women in public have to put up with now. I was at least spared that. No one had any direct access to you in the 1990s. Trolls didn't write anti-fan letters. Every time I tweeted about *X Factor*, some knobhead would have something clever to say about it, so I learned to mute people, ignore them or block them if they were being idiotically rude.

I don't engage. I try to turn away from it. It seems pretty fruitless to me to have any kind of in-depth argument on there.

Having a voice as a woman has always created problems of one sort or another. I went through awful anxiety before writing both *Bedsit Disco Queen* and *Naked at the Albert Hall*. I wondered if I had the authority to say those things. I was commenting – and, unavoidably, passing judgement – on the music business.

In the first book I worried that I'd get something wrong about some detail of the indie scene. I fact-checked obsessively, thinking I might, for example, misdescribe a B-side. It's back to that thing of expertise: there will be boys out there who know everything and I'll get it wrong and misquote someone and I'll be outed as an impostor.

With the second book, I had this terrible fear that I didn't have the authority to make all these claims about singing or to describe people's voices. It's such a female thing. I think guys assume they are just omniscient. Whereas they almost always get it wrong in the way they overestimate their own abilities and knowledge, women do the opposite.

It's not just men writing about men; they will happily show the same 'authority' when writing about women and women's experiences.

It's about confidence. It's about living in a culture that thinks you're right from the day you open your mouth. Women, on the other hand, are constantly apologising. It becomes ingrained. When I showed *Bedsit Disco Queen* to my agent, Kirsty, she said I had used 'perhaps' way too much. Now when I write I make sure I remove all qualifiers. But I still have to remind myself that I can have my opinion. More women need to write about and tell their stories. It's the only way things will change.

As I get older, I get angrier about the way in which men have somehow seized ownership of music – of all art, probably.

I find myself wondering when and how it happened. And then there is the difficulty of seizing it back: the likelihood is that it will only be discussed in the context of gender. Even in the days of the Marine Girls, I longed for the day when we weren't rounded up in an article on women in music. That day hasn't yet come.

Women can be really successful in a particular era of music, yet when the story is retold even a few years later they have disappeared. So you feel you do have to keep making a case for women – all women – just to ensure we are not relegated to the sidelines. Ideally we'd just be enmeshed in the story of music and art and everything else, but so long as the story is retold and women are erased, there is a need for a book like this.

MITSKI

Now known mononymously by her first name, Mitski Miyawaki released her first albums – Lush in 2013 and Retired from Sad, New Career in Business in 2013 – while studying at the Conservatory of Music at the State University of New York at Purchase (referred to in the chapter simply as SUNY Purchase). She has since released three further studio albums: Bury Me at Makeout Creek (her breakout album), Puberty 2 and Be the Cowboy.

I had a peripatetic upbringing. I was born in Japan, to a Japanese mother and an American father. I'd rather not disclose my parents' work, but it involved travel. My mother flew me to the Democratic Republic of Congo right after I was born and from there we went to Washington, DC for a stint, before going to Taiwan and on to the Czech Republic. Or maybe it was the other way around. And then China, Malaysia, Japan, America – I went back and forth between Japan and America for a while. After graduating from high school in Turkey, I went to college at State University of New York at Purchase.

I went to Japanese-speaking elementary schools and then, in the seventh grade, I was put in an English-speaking school, which was a drastic change not just in language, but in educational culture. The Japanese and English/Western education systems differ fundamentally and their expectations for students are different.

I suppose that, while English might not be my first language, I am more fluent in it now; it's what I work in and what most of my friends speak. The truth is that I don't think of any language as my first, simply because so many languages are jumbled up in my head. I have a dictionary in my head of many different words in many different languages, and the word that pops up into my head at any given moment might be Japanese or it might be English. In a way I'm always in translation.

I can now see that my upbringing was an advantage, but when I was growing up it was very frustrating not knowing anything for certain. As an adult you figure out that there are no real rules and nothing is black and white, but as a kid you need a basic set of rules to follow. Every year I moved to a completely new environment with a whole new set of rules, so I never had any routines and I never knew what was acceptable – or not – and that messed with me. By 'acceptable', I mean when something that is right in one country is wrong in another. Social cues vary wildly from one country to another.

From quite a young age, I had to decide for myself what I thought was right or wrong and who I was because there were no external markers to tell me. As I moved from one environment to the next, I didn't know anybody and a different language was being spoken. By the time I got used to a place, I'd have to leave again.

I never learned how to make proper friends as a kid. I never knew what to rely on or what to believe. I became self-sufficient and independent, to the extent that I've had to undo those tendencies as an adult. When I settled in New York – and I have stayed here longer than I've ever stayed anywhere – people would get mad at me in ways that I couldn't understand. I didn't know that you had to work at maintaining friendships. I'd get into a casual argument with a new friend and I'd stop talking to them and just disconnect. Since my experience of friendships was that they never lasted, in my eyes a disagreement simply signalled the end of the friendship. I wasn't going to be around for much longer anyway. If it wasn't fun to hang out with them in that moment, then what's the point?

Everyone else had learned that if you have an argument, you make it up with your friend and move on, but I had never learned how to invest in anything. Everything was disposable. No wonder people got mad at me.

Moving around as much as I did gave me the freedom to explore my identity. This period predated social media, so I got a clean slate every time I went to a new school and I took advantage of the fact that I could be a different person every year. But, again, that made it hard when it came to creating lasting relationships. I never knew which version of myself to be. Everyone has these conversations in their head about identity, but in my case, every aspect of it is exaggerated.

The one constant I had during those itinerant years was music.

Music wasn't just something I loved. It was who I was at my core. It was an anchor for me. It was part of who I was, the part I could always carry with me. Music is portable. You don't need anything to hear the music in your head. Material things come and go. We never really had old photos in our house – nothing with much history. But each time we moved somewhere new, I had music. I could sing to myself. It was familiar to me.

I made songs up to entertain myself, influenced I'm sure by the music I listened to. Living abroad and being rootless, I was never part of any local scene. For example, I'd be in Malaysia and a selection of major-label music from the UK and US would arrive a year or two later. So that's what I grew up on: Top 40 pop. Mariah Carey, Britney Spears, Backstreet Boys, Spice Girls, Christina Aguilera.

On occasion I'd find a record that was in some way life-changing. When I was in the eighth or ninth grade, I was living in Kobe in western Japan and waiting for a friend in a combination book and CD store. I saw M.I.A.'s debut album, *Arular*. I didn't know what it sounded like, but for some reason I picked it up and bought it with the allowance I had at the time. When I got home and listened to it, it blew my mind. What's always been so interesting about M.I.A. is that she will make music that sounds like nothing else that's happening in that moment, but then three to four years later, you'll start to notice major-label artists catching on and doing the same thing.

Arular was like a door opening for me. It didn't make me want to be a musician – I didn't reach that point till I was seventeen, eighteen. In that moment, it was just pure discovery. I'd seen so much of the world and yet, as I listened to that record, the world just got bigger. Not to be too nostalgic, but imagine feeling things the same way you did as a teenager. Everything is vibrant. It's like the Allison Reynolds character says in *The Breakfast Club*: 'When you grow up, your heart dies.'

I first heard Björk's *Vespertine* at around the same time, in a Tower Records store. There were these little listening stations where you could listen to some albums for free. The first time I heard Björk, the music terrified me. I don't really know why, but to this day no other music has terrified me like hers did. I swore off her music until a few years later, maybe junior or senior year of high school, though I don't remember why I decided to give her another chance. Maybe she just seemed too interesting to ignore. When I came back round to her, I got hooked. Her music taught me to pay attention to detail.

It was through *Arular* and *Vespertine* that I discovered music co⎯⎯⎯⎯⎯ than the ⎯um of its parts. For me, it was always v   nalities behind i   didn't even oc   neone's life stor

I still   so now that I a   as like for musi   le want everyth   h. The visuals   want to know th   r from? What a   ? That kind of   le have come t   l. They don't ju

The   o write songs r   r, but it doesn't   ght and wrong   n to get the fac   t fucked up. Th

So what happens if, as an artist, you decide you don't want to give that? People's response is simple: 'Fine. The person next to you is offering that to me, so I'm going to take that from them. I don't care about you any more.'

There are so many artists out there trying to get attention that, if you don't do the same thing, if you don't take a picture of yourself on the toilet, then someone else will and people will listen to their music instead. I love how little we really know about Bob Dylan, for example. The fact that he doesn't Instagram his life doesn't in any way detract from his music. I used to hate it when artists explained their lyrics. Oh dammit, now they've taken that song from me!

I have had to learn to make Twitter work for me. I've had to make my page worth visiting. But I'm not always in the mood to be entertaining. As I said, it's not just about music any more: you are labouring 24/7 as an artist. You are always entertaining. You can't turn it off. But the internet has also worked for me in that I can promote a show without going through all the traditional channels.

I make Twitter interesting so that, when I have a show to promote, there are eyes on that post. If I don't build my Twitter up to be something worth following, then no one will see that post about how I have a show in London. I don't know what promoting tours was like before the internet, but I have more access to people in the way that people have access to me. People can access my music in a more democratic way because I don't have to go through all these different channels to get my music to an ear. I can just post it on the internet and people can access it. As soon as someone hears one of my songs, it's no longer mine, it's theirs. I want them to attach their lives to it. I don't think it matters what I experienced, or even who I am.

Social media is, as we all know, a double-edged sword. You have to turn off the infinite scroll of criticism in order to be able to write freely and genuinely. Except now you can't escape that because it's all around you. One moment being a musician can be very discouraging – you want to write, to make music, and you have to keep doing this other shit – but the next, you can hear first-hand that what you do actually matters and it motivates you to keep doing it.

People call me 'Asian-American', so now I've started calling myself that too. It's a very specific term. When I'm in Asia, I'm not Asian-American. When I'm abroad, I'm just American. When I moved to the US to go to SUNY Purchase, everyone called me Asian. I feel like people don't realise how big Asia is.

Women of colour are expected to work harder than white male musicians. I read somewhere that when a white male looks in the mirror, they see a person. When a woman of colour looks in the mirror, they see a woman of colour. It beautifully encapsulates how you're not allowed to be a full person.

You have to be a very specific genre of person, and that genre becomes your musical genre. I'm in so many 'Asian-American artists' playlists, even though the music on that list varies wildly. I understand that it's important to bring forth voices that haven't been heard before because of how the musician looked or where they came from. I get the positive intention of it. But the flipside of it is that you're not allowed to be more than Asian-American.

There are so many articles about me that don't even reference my music. They just discuss the fact that I'm Asian-American. I do interviews in which I'm trying to promote my album, but all that is asked of me is to display some sort of struggle (you could call it 'struggle porn'). How hard is it for me to be both Asian-American and female in the music industry?

I've been thinking about this for a while now: in the beginning when it was asked of me, I would very sincerely and earnestly try to express my feelings as an Asian woman in the music industry. I genuinely thought it would be helpful and I wanted my story to be told. I found over and over that the publication then sold the article with that angle. And then they'd congratulate themselves on how they'd just featured an Asian-American woman artist. Look at how diverse we are!

The readership of the magazine in question, which is usually white and male, think they're doing something good just by reading about me. 'I'm learning about an Asian-American woman. I am a good person because I agree with what she's saying. I feel good!' They go about their day and everyone pats each other on the back and I'm still here with my same life. Nothing has changed. I've just given you my story again and I feel like a monkey that was asked to dance. I did it, but I wasn't even paid for it.

It's a very weird time in history; no one seems to know what the correct opinion is and whether they're allowed to have it. The positive intention to ensure that these voices are heard is there, but it can so easily backfire as well.

I didn't write my first song until I was eighteen. Early one morning I came home drunk, and sad. I went to my room, plopped down at my keyboard and started hammering at the keys, when a song spilled out of me so urgently that I could hardly keep up. This would become my first song, 'Bag Of Bones'. I'd written simple phrases of music before, but never with such intention. It felt like the world had flung open its doors. It was a great scream and, for the first time, I thought to myself, 'God, I am glad I'm alive.'

But I also understood then that I was doomed to love music and follow it to the end, because how can you feel the whole world pass through you like lightning, then go on with your life as if nothing has happened? So I kept writing . . .

Writing and performing is the easiest aspect of making music. I'm not going to lie. Trying to be a musician while trying to live was very difficult at the start. When I graduated from SUNY Purchase, I lived in Brooklyn and Queens and shuttled between places. I often slept on floors or couches. I learned to survive on three hours of sleep every night for months on end. I'd try to pursue my music career while just surviving. My living conditions were horrible.

I felt like I didn't have anything else in my life. I hadn't learned to make friends, I didn't feel close to anything. I didn't feel like I had any worth outside of music. Not pursuing music was never an option, and it never occurred to me to pursue a different profession that might have allowed me to be a healthier person. No one needs you to be an artist, and it's so fucking hard that you can only do it if you really feel there's no other option for you. That obsessiveness and single-mindedness is necessary, especially in today's creative climate.

It's almost an act of desperation. People ask all the time what I'd be if I wasn't a musician. I wouldn't be who I am. It's not an option. That's why musicians take so much abuse and allow things that are unhealthy to happen to them and endure horrible working conditions – because we can't not. No one needs my music like they need doctors or plumbers, but I can't imagine not doing music. What would I do?

Worse, I'm probably even more of a control freak than other artists in my position. I make my own album artwork,

which is why it's not as cool or hip or nice-looking as other artists' album artwork. I have this stubborn need to be the creator.
My stage show is very pared down, which is intentional; I want
people to listen to my music. Equally, I don't know how to put
on a good light show, and I don't have enough trust in people
to just hire someone and say, 'Do something pretty.'

I wish I could just let go. I feel like I'd be more of a success if I did.

I'm bad at letting people help me. Curating is another skill.
Curating your team and the people you hire is a whole other
skill that I have to learn. If I hired people who were good at
their job, if I hired a creative director who actually understood
me and knew how to translate my music into something visual,
it would probably enhance my music.

Lyric writing is a challenge in its own right. It comes naturally to me and I'm passionate about it. I approach it as a craft.
You can't just say what you feel. The whole point of lyrics,
in my mind, is that you put together words that immediately
create an image in someone's mind. It has to be something that
creates an image, idea or emotion upon hearing it once. Often
when you read lyrics out loud they sound stupid because they're
supposed to be heard and not read. It affects word order, syntax,
rhythm. The rhythm of the words is so tied into the melody. I'd
often write lyrics first and then put a melody on top according
to how the sentence felt on its own.

Obviously I can't control how people react to my music once
I put it out there. But almost all criticism of my music contains
words like 'raw' and 'confessional'. I can't remember how many
times writers have said some form of the sentence, 'listening to
her music is like reading a diary entry'. I understand that this
language is intended to express that the music is emotional and
direct, but I don't think there would be such an emphasis on

the music being 'confessional' if I weren't a woman. This very gendered language ends up making me seem like an emotional vessel; it implies lack of refinement, lack of control, lack of autonomy. It's as though I'm a fevered priestess who's gained access to some deeper, holy well of creativity and it flows through me without my really knowing how or from whence it came. I am at its mercy and I have no autonomy.

It's funny the lengths to which people will go to make sure they don't have to think of me as an artist and a creator, practising a craft. Or more importantly, the lengths to which people will go to reframe what I am doing as anything other than labour.

I want to be heard, but equally I want to be invisible. I think about this a lot, about why I do what I do, because I don't enjoy strangers looking at me and forming opinions of me, and having access to my life without my consent. I've always been the different one, the one on the outside, and it was incredibly lonely, because I love and need people. So I think I make music not to stand out, but rather to say, 'Look, I may seem different, but we're actually the same, because you have felt exactly how I've felt. Now let me in and accept me as your own.'

I deeply crave connection. But I've been confused lately, because it seems the more I do this, this being a public figure of some sort, the more I have to stand apart, and the more I'm disconnected. I want to be seen, but now that I'm seen I'm just looked at like The Other. I don't know how to solve this problem.

There's a Japanese word, 'ikigai'. It basically means 'something to live for'. I decided that I'm going to live for and dedicate my life to making art, even if my work will likely just reiterate what other humans have already said before me, because I just need something, anything, to live for. And I think that in order to honestly call myself an artist, I need to be in constant pursuit. I don't really know what exactly I'm pursuing, but I know I can't stay the same – I have to keep changing and evolving. It wouldn't be making art if I kept repeating the answer to a question I've already solved.

I don't think that's being hard on myself. I want so badly to be useful. To be useful is to be necessary to others, so I guess it's really just a need to be needed, and to have proof that I should exist after all. The thing is, I've never really been good at anything other than music – I can't really be useful in other ways – so, when I figured out I was really good at music, I latched on to it, thinking, 'This is how I will be needed. This is the reason I will stay alive.' So I decided I'm going to live for making art.

Music truly is the deepest, most complicated love I've ever known. It's my great romance, my affair of a lifetime. It's my family, my sibling and my own true self. It's all of my loves, and my one true love.

CATHERINE MARKS

After completing a master's degree in architecture, Catherine Marks moved from Melbourne to London in 2005 to train as an assistant producer with legendary producers Flood and Alan Moulder. As a record producer, mixing engineer and audio engineer, she has worked with Wolf Alice, St Vincent, PJ Harvey, M.I.A., Foals and The Killers. In 2016, she was named Breakthrough Producer of the Year at the prestigious Music Producers Guild Awards. Two years later, at the same awards, she won UK Producer of the Year. She was also Grammy-nominated for her work on Wolf Alice's 'Moaning Lisa Smile'.

Like most kids, I grew up listening to my parents' record collection. They had pretty obscure tastes. Musicals like *Chess* and *The Phantom of the Opera*. The Fureys. Paul Simon's *Graceland*, which is still one of my favourite albums. Bonnie Tyler. ABBA. Laura Branigan. Mum still has a photo of me singing Branigan's 'Gloria' when I was two.

In 1995, when I was fourteen or fifteen, I fell in love with *Nirvana: MTV Unplugged in New York* and The Smashing

Pumpkins' *Mellon Collie and the Infinite Sadness*. I remember hearing the Nirvana *Unplugged* album at a party on the beach in Lorne (a seaside town on the south coast of Victoria). My friends and I were probably underage drinking, discovering boys and stuff. It was a pivotal time in my life, and those two records were the soundtrack of that summer.

I played piano from the age of four – I think it was fairly common for young Australian kids to go to piano classes back then. I wanted to give it up when I was eleven, but my parents encouraged me to continue. I'm glad they did. By the age of fifteen, having completed most of my grades, I travelled around Europe with my piano teacher and other music students. We stayed in youth hostels, attended masterclasses, performed to small audiences. Contemporary composer Sonny Chua wrote some epic interpretations of 'Three Blind Mice', lasting twelve minutes, to be performed with three pairs of hands playing simultaneously. The experience was incredible and inspiring, although I was probably too young to realise that at the time.

As I was never very good at sight-reading music, my teacher would give me recorded versions of the music I had to learn for my exams. I could do everything by memory and through imagery. I would create little films in my head to remember what the music was. I'd also change stuff. I'd think, 'This isn't quite right', and tinker with it. I'm sure I was a nightmare student.

When I was maybe twelve or thirteen, my teacher suggested that I have some lessons with a local composer, who was quite avant-garde in terms of what he was writing. The composer told me that there is no right or wrong way to create music; it's about whatever feels right. Learning this was a game changer. In my later teens, I was listening to the commercial pop of the time and trying to write songs that were along the lines of Robbie Williams' 'Let Me Entertain You'. I would try to break down the songs, analyse them, work out the chord progressions.

Understanding that there are essentially no rules helped me better understand the framework of more 'conventional' songwriting. The way certain chords can feel satisfying, or the way certain song structures feel familiar. Ultimately, it was about what felt right. I apply this to the way I produce music now. Trying to create those satisfying moments, whether it is through the familiar or the unexpected.

In the house I grew up in there was a piano in the living room and an old-fashioned serving hatch between the living room and the kitchen. When my mother was cooking dinner, I'd yell through the hole: 'Pick a key!' And I'd make up a song in that key. I would do many other dorky things, like have a *Phantom of the Opera* party when I turned eight.

Clearly I loved music, but I wasn't thinking beyond the teenage fantasy of one day being a pop star – I wanted to be Britney Spears. It wasn't until I was in my early twenties that I seriously considered pursuing music as a career.

I was studying architecture at university and, in 2001, had a compulsory year out in the workplace. There were so many architecture students looking for jobs in Melbourne that I decided there was no way I was going to get a placement, never mind a job. My mum is Irish, so I figured I would get a dual Australian-Irish passport and live abroad for a year. I'd also been dating a guy whose cousin Nick Seymour was in Crowded House; I'd visited Nick and his girlfriend in Dublin the previous year and they seemed to have an amazing lifestyle.

The Irish economy – the so-called Celtic Tiger – was still booming and everything and everyone seemed to be on a high. It felt as if everyone was in a band or working with bands and they were very open to a new face in town. I started playing rounders in Phoenix Park with DJs, musicians and comedians, all these older, inspiring people. Everyone was sharing books, music, ideas. I remember Glen Hansard from The Frames gave me Klaus Kinski's *Kinski Uncut*. Someone else gave me Anaïs Nin's *Delta of Venus*.

It was the first time I'd really hung out with musicians, and it was so exciting. It was a totally rock 'n' roll year, but also incredibly isolating being away from home for the first time. I was only twenty-one, and young for my age.

One night I went to a Nick Cave concert and was introduced to Flood. I didn't know he was a famous producer who had worked with artists including Nick Cave, New Order and Depeche Mode. Someone mentioned that he was working on the next U2 album and I thought that was cool.

We were in a box with a lot of other people and Nick Cave was singing 'The Weeping Song'. I'd never heard Cave's music before and thought it was called 'The Weetabix Song'. I turned to Flood and said, 'It's so funny he's singing about a breakfast cereal.'

Flood looked at me as if to say, 'You absolute nutter.'

I certainly didn't, as has often been reported in the press, go up to him that night and say, 'I want to be a producer. Can I come and work with you?' Life isn't that simple!

In fact, the turning point came when I met an engineer called Tom Rixton, who was working in Nick Seymour's studio just around the corner from my flat. I could actually get from my place to the studio by walking across the roof. Tom was working with three quarters of Elastica – Justine Frischmann wasn't around – and we got really drunk one night. They were talking about writing an ambient song and I said, 'Oh, I could write one for you.' Tom said, 'Okay, why don't you? I'll see you back here tomorrow.'

I remember going to bed, kind of out of it, and thinking, 'What have I got myself into?' But somehow it all worked out. I dreamed up this piece of music, went into the studio the next morning and started playing it. Tom was reading the paper, paying no attention. But then he listened and thought it was amazing. The band seemed to really like it too. It turned out to be this really beautiful piece of music. Elastica guitarist Paul Jones put lap steel on it and they added some other guitars and the noise of fire crackling. I don't think anything came of it apart from my friend Tom and his wife Trish eventually using it for a website.

It was only at my 'bon voyage' party that I talked to Flood seriously. Well, seriously for a twenty-one-year-old: I asked him if he thought I had what it takes to be a pop star. He said, 'Well, no. But if you want to work in the music industry, go back and finish your degree and then we'll see what we can do. Figure out what you want to do. Join bands. Write songs. Record in a studio. Try things out. Although you may not want to do what I do. It's hard work.'

I returned home from Ireland to Melbourne totally inspired, and announced my plans to my parents. 'I am going to finish my architecture degree, move to London and be a record producer.' Can you imagine their faces? But I did the right thing in the end: I finished my degree and did a master's. I even worked for an architecture firm for a while. But music kept pulling me back in.

After returning to Australia, I joined a few bands, including one called The Harlocks. The guys were brilliant musicians, playing 1960s rock 'n' roll-inspired pop. I can't believe they let me in their band. We went into the studio to record an album; I was playing piano. I didn't understand any – well, barely any – of their musical references, so they staged an intervention.

They set up a projection screen in the studio, sat me down and played a Rolling Stones concert, a Led Zeppelin concert and a Stone Roses concert. I was thinking, 'God, I've been missing out on this stuff for so long.' I was blown away.

I asked the studio engineer, 'How do you make the music sound like it's being recorded in a big room?' He told me it was reverb. I couldn't believe it was as simple as it sounded. So I looked it up on the internet and printed pages and pages on all the different kinds of reverb. I was fascinated by this one little thing. But I still needed the guys in the band to plug my keyboard into my amp because I didn't understand anything about recording music.

During this period, Flood and I talked regularly. I'd call him up, tell him I'd joined a band, done my first gig. Every year or so I'd visit him and his wife-to-be. I kept thinking about producing. The people who ran the architecture firm told me to go away for six months to get the music out of my system. I didn't know if I could afford to do a production course in Melbourne; it was very expensive and I knew that hardly any women applied. I also knew that getting a job in a Melbourne studio was almost impossible.

In the end, it seemed that the easiest option was to move to an entirely new country and start making tea in a studio.

Finally, Flood said he had a job for me. I didn't think twice. I packed my bags and left for London.

The first time I turned up at Flood's studio I was handed a Hoover. This wasn't Flood indulging stereotypes, it's what every runner has to do. It was brutal, but it has to be that way. I'm the same with interns now – we don't need to know what a compressor does after we've been in the studio for just a day.

Hoovering and making the tea is important. It's teamwork. A clean floor in the studio puts the producer in a good mood. A good cup of tea instils trust. It's caring about the little things that makes a difference as you move forward.

Everything is more relaxed now, but when I first started, interns had to be the first to arrive and the last to leave. You had to be paying attention all the time, not scrolling up and down your phone. If you were caught checking it, you'd have been chucked out of the studio. Blow something up and you'd be sacked. Though I blew plenty of things up.

I can say all this with hindsight. When I was hoovering and making tea, I do remember thinking, 'I shouldn't have to do this!' I'd been working in an architecture firm and wanted to enter the music business at the same level. I'm not sure what I expected. But then everyone who starts at the bottom thinks that they should be doing more than the seemingly menial roles they are initially assigned. I remember feeling utterly useless, like I wasn't contributing anything. I had to be stubborn and determined. All day, every day.

I'd go and have a cry in the bathroom and tell myself, 'C'mon, you have a dream. It's going to take a while.'

I remember asking Flood, 'So how long do you think it's going to take?'

He said, 'Probably about ten years.'

Wow. A decade.

After about three years of interning and assisting, or even engineering, you think, 'I should be in the producer's chair now.' But looking back I can see that it took about the right amount of time.

At the start, I didn't even know the difference between a producer and an engineer. The former is more about emotion, the latter about the sonics. Another engineer had a good way of putting it: the producer is the heart and the engineer is the head. But I do both and, to my mind, they are largely interchangeable.

I learned by observing; or sometimes a producer would take the time to show me how something worked. I taught myself a lot. How to uncoil a cable. Signal flow. For some reason, I found the difference between input and output really confusing. I didn't understand the difference between 'send' and 'return'. I still sometimes have to stop and think about that. There were other more complex things, like how to program a modular synth, that I figured out straight away by reading a manual.

I was given really amazing opportunities, and I definitely made the most of those. I knew I had to really prove myself. Whether that was because I was a woman or not, I wouldn't know. It's always been my personality to prove myself, even when I was at school. I wanted to show people that I was serious. Even if I was sometimes a bit of a bumbling idiot in the studio, I was always enthusiastic.

After about six months, Flood gave me the keys to his project studio in Kilburn because he was going to America to work with his long-time collaborator Alan Moulder on The Killers' second album *Sam's Town*.

This was where I learned the most about equipment and began my understanding of the more technical side of the studio. Everything was a mess, and so I literally unplugged and rebuilt the studio so that any engineers or producers coming in would know where everything was. Alan Moulder, famous for working with artists like Nine Inch Nails, Smashing Pumpkins,

Jesus and Mary Chain and My Bloody Valentine, told me later that he was impressed with me for doing that; nobody could find anything before I reorganised it.

After a few years of working in the studio in Kilburn for various other producers and engineers, as well as being the in-house assistant at the recording studio that is now called Assault & Battery 2, I started working for Alan Moulder. By this point, I'd engineered for artists like Kelly Rowland and Kanye West and I'd worked with a lot of other artists. I had a lot more confidence in what I could do, but I'd never really been involved in the mixing process before. Alan was the one who took the time to explain a lot of the technical stuff. He taught me how to 'finish' a project. To focus on the detail. To use the technology to create the emotional picture. We have a very similar work ethic and we worked really well together. I think he liked the fact that I was super-efficient, too.

I don't think I properly finished my apprenticeship until I'd engineered *Holy Fire*, the 2013 album by Foals. I don't mean I was still making tea in 2012; I was learning to deal with pressure and responsibility as well as how to cope with artists. I didn't feel ready to go it alone until after *Holy Fire*.

Even after that, I remember doing mixes and always having Alan or Flood in the back of my mind, wondering what they would be doing with the sound. Sometime in late 2013, early 2014, I ran into Alan and said, 'Do you mind if I don't mix with you in my mind any more?' He laughed and said he'd been waiting for me to say that for years.

I'm very comfortable with who I am in the studio now, but it's taken a long time to reach that point. When I was struggling with confidence in the beginning, I used to dread going into the studio. When I started producing on my own, I'd think,

'How am I going to navigate these complex emotional situations?' It took time to understand the dynamics of it, to learn to manage those personalities and egos, to deal with management, with pressures from the record company, to get my head around massive budgets.

If an artist says, 'I'm not feeling it today,' and walks off, how are you going to bring them back? You've got something you need to deliver. If it doesn't work out, it's all on you.

We are not saving lives, but a lot of money is involved. You have to come up with a really good product and make people feel this is the best possible outcome. Meanwhile, you have to deal with everyone else's doubts and fears. I might have moments when I think, 'Shit, this sucks. How am I going to turn it around? How am I going to pull this one out of the bag?'

I used to get butterflies and feel really nervous before I started a project. I used to think that the project wouldn't go very well if I didn't have that feeling. Now I don't need to have that feeling in order to get it done. It's a different kind of excitement: 'I have no idea how this is going to end up.' It's so exciting to see how a project starts and where it leads.

Before I start working with an artist or a band, I like to spend some time with them, to see what the chemistry is like. We usually both know. It's like going on a date; you know pretty quickly whether it's going to work out or not. Or sometimes it's a bit of a slow burner; you're just feeling each other out, but you might have similar ideas about making a record.

So by the time they come into the studio, I'll have established some sort of relationship with the band and they will have decided that I'm the right person to work with. I've learned that, if they show vulnerability, I should show it too. Maybe this is just me. I don't think this is a requirement for the job. It's just how I relate to music and the process of making music. I want to be able to feel something, whether it's elation or complete despair. A man might feel that too, but he might not show it in the same way. I might be teased a little if I get over-emotive, but I don't care because it's about the result and I'm putting everything into that.

Because I'm so transparent and I completely wear my heart on my sleeve, it's really hard for me to shut out the external part of my life and then walk into the studio like the two things are separate. If there are things going on in my life, they will invariably seep into the project. Of course, it depends on each project as to how much of that I reveal, and on the age group I am working with. Male or female artists, it makes no difference to me. I am always myself.

I learned so much from working with Flood on *White Chalk* in 2007. Polly Harvey was enigmatic at the start, but so clear about what she wanted to do. She's very particular about her work. Very controlled. And yet her performances were so emotional. She'd really go there. Seeing her so open and vulnerable, and so strong at the same time, I decided it was how I wanted to be too. She was comfortable letting go; particularly with Flood and [long-time PJ Harvey collaborator] John Parish. The three of them had worked together as a team for so many years that they had a very comfortable relationship.

I'm never star-struck. But at the end of *White Chalk*, I looked at Polly and thought, 'You're incredible.'

The energy in the studio is obviously different if I'm working with a female artist. There are probably female musicians who want to work with me because I'm a woman, which is great, but I hope it's not the main reason. I've built this awesome relationship with record labels, artists and management. All those people know what I can do. They know what I deliver. I'm just Catherine Marks.

Younger women who have been inspired by me and want to be producers and/or engineers sometimes write to me. The first time I got an email like that, I was so embarrassed. I got into a panic because it felt like such a massive responsibility.

I didn't think I deserved it. Then I was like, 'Hang on a second!' It was kind of what I always wanted. When I first started I knew I was one of only a handful of women, but I also knew that it was going to be my point of difference. I was going to exploit that fact, but also become awesome at my job.

It would be nice if there were more women around that I could share my experiences with. Because we are different. We have a different perspective on things. While it's fun hanging out with guys all the time, it's also great when there are other women in the studio. But neither one is better or worse.

When I first started out I would sometimes be employed by a studio rather than a band, as an engineer, to record demos or whatever. I do remember one experience where the band rocked up and they were like, 'Ah, you are a girl. We weren't expecting a girl.' I didn't take it personally, I just wanted to do a good job. It's their problem if they have that attitude. By the end of it, that wasn't an issue. They soon saw past my gender.

I'm not saying that being a producer/engineer is always easy. There have been so many things that I haven't been credited for that I've spent months on. This had nothing to do with being a woman; it happens to all of us! I was pretty pissed off about it, but I know what I did and the people who matter know as well.

I've said a few times in interviews that, at the start, I cut off my hair and wore drab, boyish clothing. The decision to do so related to my initial understanding of what was required from the job of an assistant. I understood it to mean that I was there as part of the operation of the studio. Kind of invisible, so that no one really noticed I was there if I was doing my job properly. But I would be noticed if I wasn't. I embraced that concept and took it very seriously. I didn't want to be noticed. I just wanted to put my head down and learn what I needed to and do the best job possible. No one told me to change the way I dressed or cut off my hair. Those were my decisions I made to show to myself how committed I was.

I have had to adapt to working in a studio as the only woman. Whenever I have flirtatious clients, I have to find a way to deal with it; I still have to work with them and I don't want to make it awkward. I can't make them feel uncomfortable, even if I've been made to feel the same.

One time I was in the studio with a male producer. I was climbing up the stairs and he was looking down. He said, 'I can see down your top.' I was like, 'Yeuch. Gross. Whatever.' I think in this situation he was probably stating a fact.

It's taken some women a long, long time to voice their experiences of sexual harassment without fear. The Me Too movement has given those women a voice. But I think it's also okay if my perception of one situation is not what someone else's might be. One person might view the producer's comment as sexual harassment, while another finds it simply irritating. It's certainly not flattering. But each of us has to find our own way of dealing with these kinds of remarks.

I know that, early on in your career, you don't really have a choice about who you work with. I'm lucky in that the men I've worked with closely have been respectful, supportive and encouraging. I have never thought that things haven't worked out because I'm a woman; at the time, I simply thought other people were better suited to the job or that I probably wasn't good enough.

There was a period quite early on when I felt I could be myself around men, but, when I was around women, I'd find myself putting on this bumbling idiot persona because I didn't want to step on anyone's toes. I didn't want to be the alpha. Inevitably, those women would put me down – I didn't appear to know what I was doing! I really needed the support of another woman and that's when I started working with Alan Moulder's manager, Karen Ciccone. She is a little older, wiser and way more experienced than me and the initial respect was already there.

Over the years, she has believed in me and listened to me. She has always been very clear about her thoughts, but never condescending. I couldn't have done it without her.

When I was nominated for Producer of the Year by the Music Producers Guild (MPG) in 2018, I really didn't think I stood a chance of winning. I made up a little speech in my head, in case I won. Then, in the three days leading up to the awards, I decided I needed to get that speech out of my head. Surely I didn't stand a chance. I thought that, if I did win, I'd ask all the other female nominees up on stage for a group photo. However, I was so overwhelmed when I won, the photo completely slipped my mind!

After I'd won the award, and in a state of semi-shock, I bumped into Tony Platt, MD of the MPG Awards. I blurted out, 'Oh, you were just wheeling out the token chick.'

He frowned and said, 'Catherine, it wasn't like that. I was there on the judging day. You won it because you deserved it.'

The same night another producer said to me, 'You add glamour to this industry.' He wasn't in any way denigrating my work, he was simply stating a fact. I was wearing sparkly earrings and high heels. I can see what he means. I'm different to what has gone before in this industry, and I'm embracing that. This is not meant to sound cynical. I love the fact that the industry is changing. And if my profile, glamorous or otherwise, encourages more women to get involved in production, then surely it's a good thing? Men and women are fundamentally different and, in this creative industry, it just makes sense to me that you have access to all these different perspectives.

I had so much work coming in prior to the award that I don't know if it's changed anything for me personally. It was certainly an honour, and nice to share texts with bands I'd worked with, like Wolf Alice and St Vincent, who were proud of me – even though they are the ones who got me to that point. And being recognised by fellow producers and MPG affiliates, all so talented and creative, was pretty awesome too.

Most importantly, it raised the profile of female producers. In 2017 the MPG estimated that only around 6 per cent of its members were women. Only a handful of women have ever been nominated for the Producer of the Year Award at the Grammys. I used to think that being the only woman in the studio was my point of difference, but now, finally, there are a lot more of us – women such as Olga Fitzroy, Steph Marziano, Manon Grandjean and Marta Salogni. It's great to have that kind of network now, and we are all encouraging and supportive of one another.

GEORGIA

Georgia is a multi-instrumentalist, songwriter and producer. The daughter of Leftfield's Neil Barnes, she began drumming at an early age before exploring other instruments while studying ethnomusicology at the School of Oriental and African Studies in London. After graduating, she collaborated with rising stars Kwes and Kate Tempest. Georgia released a debut EP, Come, in 2014. Since signing to Domino, she released her eponymous debut album in 2015 and her sophomore album will follow in 2019. During her teens, Georgia played for Queens Park Rangers youth team.

I was surrounded by music when I was growing up, but I always wanted to find my own stuff. My dad never said, 'Sit down and listen to this record because it changed the face of music.' He was always very encouraging in terms of me finding my own way. As was my mum. I remember buying a Slipknot CD, playing it at home and saying to my parents, 'This is the future of music!' My dad raised his eyebrows and said, 'Yeah, okay. Go through your little heavy metal stage.'

It was quite daunting at times, though. I was aware of

Dad's musical stature even if I didn't understand it when I was younger. In fact, I recently came across some old press clippings of Leftfield from the *NME* and saw that what they were trying to do was all very creative, really dark and mysterious. The dance music pioneers weren't visible in the usual way – they weren't singers with a spotlight shining down on them. Nor did people know them as individuals, only as the brand and the music.

The first gig I went to was, inevitably, Leftfield. They always took me on stage; I was like their little mascot. At T in the Park in 2000, one of the live players in the band walked on with me on his shoulders. There was a sea of fans in this huge tent; in my mind, there were at least a million of them. I made a gesture and the entire audience made the same gesture back. Once I started doing gigs myself, I really believed every show would be like that for me. How wrong could I be?

I've been to so many gigs that it's hard to recall specific ones that made me want to be on stage myself. Perhaps the Radiohead gig my mum took me to in 2001. Or Missy Elliott in Victoria Park. She was headlining and we were right at the front, almost close enough to reach out and touch her when she walked onto the stage. The crowd reaction was mixed – at one point people were throwing stuff at her. She had to stop and say, 'Whoah! What's going on?'

Missy had created her own aesthetic world and she was exploring all sorts of visual narratives which perhaps didn't translate on stage for some people. But I was totally there. Sometimes it can be quite cool to see an artist divide an audience. Those can be the most exciting shows.

I forget the exact year, but I saw The White Stripes in their early days and it remains one of my favourite shows of all time. The energy on stage was incredible. I've always been interested in artists who are on the edge of chaos; you never quite know where they are going, especially when they play live. It was heightened with The White Stripes because Jack and Meg White would never say if they were brother and sister or husband and wife. So there was all this tension on stage, something awkward and odd about them. Is Jack going to walk off the stage? Are they going to *fight* on stage? Because they sure do look like they hate each other.

Later, of course, it emerged that they had been husband and wife and had divorced before The White Stripes took off. But I liked the fact that, for a long time, their relationship was unexplainable.

When people ask about my favourite drummers, I always mention Meg White. For some reason, people are surprised. But for me, she's like Ringo Starr. She's not the flashiest of drummers, nor is her technique the best. But it worked brilliantly with The White Stripes, and I don't personally think Jack has been able to do anything else as good without her. As with John Bonham and Led Zeppelin, the music is so influenced by the drumming that you can't recreate it or better it without that person.

I started drumming myself when I was six or seven. There wasn't a drum kit in our house, but Paul (Daley), my dad's partner in Leftfield, had one round his flat. One day he put me on the chair in front of the kit and said, 'Do what you want.' I enjoyed having a good whack on the drums whenever we went to see him, but I never took it seriously. I think my mum quite liked the idea of me playing drums because I had so much energy as a kid.

I finally decided to ask for my own drum kit when I was fourteen, but before that I used to play on the school kits. I was always wary of the boyish culture of music rooms, and I didn't know if I could get involved. If I was allowed. Having said that, I was always quite daring. I never really had a problem getting involved with boys' activities.

But still, there were times when it was like, 'Hmm, the boys are in there. Maybe later . . .' Perhaps I thought they'd be a bit judgemental, a bit piss-takey, maybe quite competitive. Sometimes I couldn't be bothered with stuff like that. But it never stopped me. If anything, it drove me to be a better drummer.

It was the same when I started playing the bass. I've always been a fan of instruments; I can never play them to a high grade, but I really enjoy playing. I once said to a school friend that I really wanted to play bass with him and he started going on about Jaco Pastorius and all these other virtuoso male bassists, and it put me right off.

For a long time, it seemed that men felt the need to lord it over women with their in-depth knowledge of music and what they considered to be 'cool' and 'uncool'. It seemed like everything needed to be categorised, pigeonholed. But I think that's changing now. We're getting to a better, healthier place. With things like Spotify, you can see that people's playlists are really eclectic. They say that streaming sites are killing music, but there is a positive side to listening to music in this way.

It's great that kids are getting access to all sorts of music, jumping from one genre to the next, cross-referencing as they go. I had to go to record shops to do that; when I was sixteen, I started to become really immersed in the spider's web of influences, going from folk to Joni Mitchell to Prince. That's the time I started thinking seriously about being a musician and writing my own music.

I found myself at a crossroads when I was sixteen.

Football or music? Music or football?

Football was an obsession for me. I grew up in a flat in central London and I played football in the courtyard with other kids, most of whom were boys. I was always made to feel, 'This is Georgia, she's a really good footballer'. It didn't matter that I was a girl. I was just good.

I played left wing, slightly in front of the midfield, slightly back from the strikers. But I could play with both feet. I don't know how, but I could. I started playing in local parks. One day, when I was ten or eleven, a scout came up to me and my dad in Regent's Park and said, 'I'm from QPR. You should take your daughter along to a training session.' I was super-excited; I ended up playing for QPR for four years.

But I didn't get a proper opportunity to play at school – I went to a co-ed school and the teachers didn't make any effort to include me. There wasn't a girls' team at the school, so when I was thirteen, they put me in the boys' team. I sat on the bench the whole time. They always promised to put me on for the last ten minutes, but it never happened. I know that the boys' game is tougher at that age, but why pretend to include me? I'd pack my new boots and always come home disappointed.

Meanwhile, at QPR, I started thinking that I wanted to play professionally. But my coach died when I was sixteen and the team disbanded. Back then, once you reached sixteen or seventeen, you had to start training with the women's team. There was nothing in between. And it was awful because you were suddenly playing against forty-six-year-old women. It didn't feel right to me. Something I'd loved so much became a chore and generally not a good experience.

So I stopped playing. From 2005, I had been travelling all the way to south London to go to the BRIT School and training had become a bit of a logistical nightmare. So, feeling a little sad to turn my back on football, I chose music.

I got a lot of stick for being a girl who was really into football, but I didn't feel inhibited about picking up a guitar and singing for friends or, later, performing in public. With music, I never thought 'I can't do this because I'm a woman'. It simply never entered my head that this was something I wasn't allowed to do. Maybe because I was encouraged by my friends and family to just get on with it. There was a lot of love around it. I felt like, 'Fuck it. I don't need permission. I just need to go out and do it.'

I was lucky that I had two parents who were always supportive and who always encouraged my interest in music. Maybe my mum was slightly more realistic because she had seen Leftfield's ups and downs. When it became clear that I was serious about doing music, my dad was all right with it. My mum might have been a little more cautious, but she never said, 'Don't do it.' It was more a case of, 'Prepare yourself.' She knew how hard it could be.

Anyway, by the time I left the BRIT School in 2008, I was fed up with popular culture and probably in a bit of a rebellious phase. My attitude was very much 'all pop music is shit. I want to go and learn about music that has come out of different cultures'. Later, my love for pop music returned and I was reminded that a lot of pop music is simply great. But back then I was more interested in the way that hip-hop, for example, uses samples from African or Indian music – again, it comes back to that idea of cross-referencing.

A friend of mine suggested a course in ethnomusicology at the School of Oriental and African Studies (SOAS). It sounded interesting; I was up for it. The first year was great because I got to play an instrument of my choice – I chose the kora, a West African harp – and I did a few performances, met new friends and took drugs for the first time.

When my best friends Joy, Jess and Hayley invited me to go with them to Cuba, I didn't think twice. I'd been studying Cuban music at SOAS, already had some musical connections in the country and really wanted to experience Cuban culture and musical history first-hand. A few months later, I was standing on the Malecón in Havana, a beautiful sunset behind me, looking on as Cubans embraced one another and music filled the air.

During the month we were there, I played Cuban bata drums in compounds in Havana, swam in waterfalls, drank rum, formed a new Cuban family and, best of all, had those memories to share with my best mates. It was a formative trip, one that I'll remember for the rest of my life.

I did a lot of crazy things at SOAS. I played the kora in an African band with all these amazing musicians. I performed for the Thai queen in a Thai music ensemble. I played in a gamelan, a traditional Indonesian instrumental ensemble. I played in a salsa band.

The final year was far more academic, and I found myself spending endless hours in the library. That's not something I ever thought I'd do, not in a million years; academia was never my strong point. But I did all right, I got a 2:1. And the course turned out to be really fascinating and the contacts I made were brilliant.

The course offered me plenty of opportunities, but it was pretty wild. I experimented with lots of instruments, but I wasn't formally trained in any of them. I didn't have the grades to go to Guildhall or any of the other top music colleges. Maybe I was too eclectic. But the course definitely influenced my music; it made me realise how much I love music that is unpredictable.

SOAS has also influenced my life in ways that I didn't

expect. I decided to go there partly because of Africa Express, an amazing organisation that brings together Western and African musicians in a nominated African country where they then make a collaborative album. At the start of 2018, I went to South Africa and I'm now a member of the Africa Express collective. We even got tattoos to commemorate the trip!

I've always worked – I was a nanny while I was at SOAS – but as soon as I graduated, I went to Rough Trade West and asked for a job. Luckily someone had just left, and by this point I had a pretty good knowledge of all kinds of music. Customers would come in asking really specific questions about a particular type of country music, or about some obscure artist who had collaborated with another obscure artist, and you had to have at least a vague idea of what they were talking about.

I loved working there: I was learning more and more about music. And the more I learned, the more I wanted to play.

My mum used to be a social worker back in the 1980s. Her best friend is Kate Tempest's auntie, Gill Calvert; they met through a social worker scheme and have been mates ever since. Mum has known Kate since she was a baby and I've known Kate all my life.

I'd been working with her producer, Dan Carey, and he called me up one day and said, 'We're putting a band together, Kate wants you to drum with her.' I was flattered, of course, but I'd been in and around the same scene as Kate for years.

When I was at the BRIT School, I became really good mates with Elan Tamara and Elan introduced me to Kwes, a producer and songwriter who was later signed to Young Turks and who has worked with Micachu, Kelela, DELS, Damon Albarn and Solange Knowles.

Back then, when he was making a name for himself, we all

played together. First Kwes and I were in Elan's backing band and then Elan and I were in Kwes's backing band! Through Kwes and Elan, I became really good friends with Mica Levi and her band, Micachu and the Shapes. We played some shows together and went on tour as the support band.

Mica was friends with Kate, too, and so we all hung out after her shows. They were part of the south-east London MySpace generation, connecting through the internet – and I suppose Kwes, Elan and I became an extended part of the scene.

In 2013, I went to see Jeannette Lee, who co-owns Rough Trade Records and manages artists like Jarvis Cocker. I'd written, performed and produced an EP in my home studio and I didn't know what to do next. I was going through some tough family stuff and I felt a bit adrift. I asked Jeannette for advice and we ended up working together.

Jeannette has always been one of those people I've really admired. As a woman, she's just smashing. Like me, she is drawn to artists that are a bit chaotic, a little unpredictable, not too easy to define or categorise. And she has always encouraged those qualities in me. Her advice has always had an element of, 'Fuck it, do it yourself'.

Soon after Jeannette became my manager, I signed to Domino Records. They felt like the right label for me and I knew I would be able to develop as an artist while relying on them to be supportive and to provide me with some platforms on which to work. That's all I ever wanted. Because, by this time, I'd already recorded my debut album, I was already on my own path and I had a vision of how I wanted the music to be.

Neither Jeannette nor Laurence Bell, owner of Domino, wanted to tamper with my first album, *Georgia*, because it's a good introduction to my music. It's an album of experimental pop songs and it documents everything I'd learned about music up to that point. 'Kombine', for example, was based on a Pakistani qawwali sample a London taxi driver played me when I was on my way to a session. 'Move Systems' was inspired by Brazilian baile funk that I mixed up with punky riot grrrl vocals. There are love songs and break-up songs. The album shows my love for cross-referencing music and refusing to be defined by one genre. I was inspired not just by world music, but by Kate Bush, whose music has never been easy to define.

It's been different with my as-yet-untitled second album. I wanted the songwriting and production to be a step up from simply experimenting. I wanted to go back and listen and study classic pop songs – particularly the work of Depeche Mode's Martin Gore – and see how it could develop my writing.

I always ask my record company for advice, but they've never dictated the direction I should go in. Which is why I wanted to be on an independent; as much as major labels try to convey a sense of the artist maintaining their control, there are inevitably constraints. There are, of course, cons to being on an independent label, too, but Domino is a good home.

I'm proud of the fact that I write the music and produce my own records. My parents encouraged me to be in control; they said I could only ever really rely on myself.

And because I'm so in control of the music, there's not much space left for anyone else to come in and direct where it's going. When my music was first released, people were often surprised that I do pretty much everything myself. I was frustrated that such a strong emphasis was put on me creating it all. Why couldn't they be more matter-of-fact about it? Why did I have to answer endless questions about being a woman producer?

As far as I was concerned, what I did was normal. I'd been hanging around with Kate and Mica for years, alongside plenty of other women who just got on with it. I was in awe of Kate; she inspired me to think 'I can do this' when I was playing with her. Of course I've noticed people's faces when I turn up and I'm the drummer and I'm a woman. And yes, I've been asked to mime for a pop gig. Oh, do fuck off. It's why the video for 'Feel It', which came out in 2017, shows dozens of women drumming. In fact, we were sent so many clips that we could have made another video and still not have used them all. It's amazing how many girls and women are out there, of all ages, playing the drums.

Since I signed to Domino, it does seem that things have moved quickly. Maybe we are reaching a stage where it's no longer so surprising that women write the music, produce the records, do the artwork, all of that. It feels good.

The 'fuck it, do it yourself' advice has served me well. It's such a strong, no bullshit message. I always think of what my mum and dad told me, too. Be self-sufficient. Don't rely on anyone. Don't wait for permission.

CLARA AMFO

Clara Amfo joined Kiss FM as an intern and ended up staying there for six years before finally being offered the drive time show in early 2010. In 2012, she earned a nomination as a Rising Star at the Sony Radio Awards. The following year, she left Kiss FM to host the weekend breakfast show on 1Xtra and, in 2015, became only the second woman to host the Official Chart since Radio 1 launched in 1967. The same year, she left 1Xtra to take over Fearne Cotton's mid-morning Radio 1 show. She is the first black woman to front her own show on Radio 1's daytime schedule.

My mum and dad were such an interesting couple. My dad always used to tell people how he came to this country with just £25 in his pocket. It's true: he came on his own and my mum came afterwards. They're both from a village in Ghana called Gyakiti, which is about two hours from Accra, the capital. Both Mum and Dad were part of large families.

My dad died in 2015 and I miss him badly, but I like to talk about him as a way of keeping his memory alive. Nobody's perfect, but my dad was a wonderful person. Very logical, pragmatic, handsome, charming and charismatic. Everyone loved him. He came to England to 'better his life' and further his studies – he became a microbiologist. He had a thirst for knowledge and was obsessed with education and learning. He bought a set of encyclopedias, made us read chapters and then tell him what we'd learned. Whoever did the best got ten pounds, which is a lot of money when you're nine or ten.

My mum isn't necessarily academic, but she too has a thirst for knowledge and is still a very hard worker; she was a secretary before leaving Ghana, a dinner lady when I was at school and she's been working as a janitor at our local hospital for the last fifteen years. She loves it. Since dad passed away, she likes to keep busy.

My parents weren't unusual in wanting the best education for their kids; it's the story of so many immigrants and their children. All my black and brown friends, whose parents came to the UK with nothing, are similarly obsessed with education. I'm one of six: I have four brothers, and a sister from Dad's previous relationship. I'm sure Dad would have loved us all to have been pharmacists, doctors and lawyers, but none of us are. My brothers do very different things: one is head menswear stylist with a big high street brand, another does voiceovers, a third works in alcohol and cigarette branding and the fourth works for an agency that books after-dinner speakers for events.

Dad was strict, but he was also as liberal as they come, at least by the standards of other Ghanaian parents that we knew. He really just let us be ourselves. When we go to family functions and see certain cousins or other second-generation Ghanaians and hear how hands-on their parents were, I am reminded that we had it pretty sweet.

My mum and dad were like chalk and cheese. My dad had a sense of spirituality but didn't insist on us going to church every Sunday. Mum is very religious. I had so many arguments with her about the kind of outfits I should wear for church. She would nearly always make me go and change into something 'more suitable'. I stopped going to church when I was thirteen or fourteen. The congregation would be speaking in tongues and I just didn't get it. Faith is a beautiful thing, but religious dogma has never been my thing.

Everyone in Ghana is into music and my parents were no different. Highlife came out of the twentieth-century music scene in Ghana. At the start it included traditional African music and hymn singing, but as the century progressed, it absorbed jazz, swing, blues and Latin music; soul and funk; disco and finally hip-hop. The Afrobeat and African-style music that you hear in the charts is often inspired by highlife.

So I listened to highlife, but also to my dad's pretty eclectic vinyl collection, which included the Police, ABBA, Hot Chocolate, Status Quo. Country music. He had a copy of the Carpenters' greatest hits, which me and my neighbour Katie listened to a lot – that and Boney M. Dad was mostly into vinyl and he used to get furious with us when we used his vinyl albums as Frisbees. My dad loved us, but there must have been times when he couldn't stand the lot of us. He had five of us in one house, driving him mad.

I was also influenced by my brothers' musical tastes. My eldest brother was really into Guns N' Roses and U2. Another brother was into ragga, jungle and garage. Another brother was into French house music and alternative hip-hop. Then my little brother and me were into R&B and grime. I listened to a lot of rock music as well.

Our house in Kingston (in the London burbs, not Jamaica) was always flipping noisy. The telly would be on. The radio would be on. Music was blaring out of my brothers' bedrooms.

We had this next-door neighbour, Mrs Chapman, who despised my second-eldest brother because he'd be playing his house and his garage and his jungle from 7 a.m. until midnight. She'd be banging on the wall, but it never stopped him. He loved his music and was involved with local pirate radio. His music was his life.

Kingston is not as posh as people often think. Lots of the kids in our local primary school grew up in poor-quality social housing, and certain parts of the town are still deprived. When I was growing up it was a predominantly white area, but all the brown families knew each other so there were all these friendly nods. We didn't segregate ourselves; we hung out with everybody.

As a kid, I was happy to spend three hours in the middle of a Thursday or Sunday afternoon in my room, listening to the radio and making up dance routines. I was in a state of bliss. I still do it now, only I'm doing the washing-up at the same time. During all those hours alone in my room, I not only got an ear for the music I liked, but I also started to prefer certain broadcasters. Trevor Nelson, who is one of my best friends now. Sara Cox, Vanessa Feltz, Angie Greaves, June Sarpong and Lauren Laverne were all huge influences on me.

I listened to lots of commercial radio: Kiss FM, Capital and Choice, which is now Capital Xtra. I listened to the local pirate stations when I could. Most weekends my mum and dad would drive us to Balham or Tooting to go to the food markets, because African-Caribbean food isn't the easiest to find in Kingston. On those journeys, we'd start picking up pirate radio as we headed towards south London. My dad would complain; he wanted Classic FM or Smooth instead. But we insisted and I'm glad. It was so valuable for me to hear that mishmash of music.

But the best day of my life as a kid was when my parents got Sky TV. I was in year eight and these two salesmen called Harry and Gary – yes, really – came to the door and gave us a big pitch. Me and my little brother stood behind my dad, begging him. 'Please, please, please!' He was into current affairs, so eventually he was sold on the offer of twenty-four-hour-news.

I was ecstatic. We had MTV! I was glued to the music channels from the minute I got back from school until I went to bed at 11 p.m. I didn't even bother taking my uniform off. R&B and hip-hop is pop music now, part of everyday culture, but it wasn't when I was growing up. Black music has always fed the world in an immeasurable way, and whether in its purest form or appropriated, I believe it will continue to form the basis of popular culture.

I loved music and I loved to dance, and once I had access to MTV, I started to mimic the hosts. I wasn't thinking, 'This could be my career.' I was just drawn to presenting. I knew I was good at talking. I liked to write. I loved reading. I wanted to do something creative.

At fourteen, I started buying my own CDs. My older brother Andy had a friend whose uncle worked at Virgin Records so he'd get freebies like N.E.R.D, Beck and Daft Punk. The very first time I saw a promo CD was when I crept into Andy's room after he'd gone out clubbing with his mates. I had my own CD player so I would take his CDs and listen to them, then slip them back, being careful to remember the order they were in so that he'd never know I'd borrowed them. Later on, he told me that he knew what I was up to.

Me and my two brothers Andy and Chris really bonded over N.E.R.D's album *In Search Of*. That album is still in my top five albums of all time. Obviously, that was the point at which Pharrell was introduced to the world. I told Pharrell when I interviewed him that it mattered a lot that he was aware of black kids like us. For me it was essentially, 'Oh my god, Pharrell likes rock. He likes hip-hop. That's us! He likes to skate; I work in a skate and surf shop and hang out with skaters.' Arguably tenuous links, but given the lack of representation at the time, we were truly enamoured with him.

I had plenty of role models when I was growing up, but I had to seek them out. Representation is so vital, especially for women of colour, because you don't often see yourself reflected in a way that is not negative or stereotypical. When I started seeing black women on TV or in movies, especially dark-skinned black women, it was a big thing. I remember seeing Whoopi Goldberg in *The Color Purple* and in *Sister Act*, then seeing Lauryn Hill for the first time in *Sister Act 2*. Those women were my role models, along with Oprah Winfrey. Every time I saw a cute black girl in an American sitcom I'd be like, 'Yeah, she's great. She's my favourite.' Because you just want to see yourself reflected.

Those people were so vital and I clung on to them. Because everybody else around me, in my real life or on telly, were hot blondes or hot brunettes with blue eyes. That was it. I never really struggled with my weight but everyone on television was one body weight. There was basically one generic 'hot girl' look and that wasn't me. So women like Whoopi and Lauryn were vital to my coming of age. Even when I felt horrendous about myself in the way that teenagers always do, I could look to those women.

To this day, I look for role models, for women who inspire me. I could talk about Beyoncé all day. She is the best entertainer on the planet right now. I've seen her live more times than I can even remember. I first saw her on the I Am ...

Sasha Fierce tour in 2009. I lucked out and got a front-row seat with a mate. Beyoncé just has it. She's got the tenderness of a Diana Ross, so she can be quite gentle, really graceful. She can stomp like a Tina Turner. There's a touch of Michael Jackson. She's got that work ethic, and she'll dance until her feet bleed.

Beyoncé has really evolved as a public figure in the past two or three years. Her superpower is what she doesn't say, what she chooses to sing about and what she chooses to 'show up' for. She may not be out on the picket lines shouting about the fact that black lives matter but she will do 'Lift Every Voice And Sing', the alternative anthem for the NAACP, to a predominantly white audience. She knew what she was doing by singing that at Coachella. It was implicit: 'I know you are watching, world. Here I am. I'm visibly here for you all.'

For me, one of the biggest and most important things she has done was to give Colin Kaepernick his Muhammad Ali Legacy Award in 2017 in the wake of the whole 'taking a knee' controversy. Of course he wasn't protesting the flag; he was peacefully protesting police brutality against black people. Predictably, in Trump's America, it was taken the wrong way. Beyoncé had been out of the limelight for ages, but then she turned up to give him that award. Again she was saying, 'I'm here for you lot.'

It's about talent and authenticity. It's about being real. Artists like Beyoncé, Cardi B and Adele all have it in abundance and they manage it very well. Off stage, they might be the loudest person in the room, the quietest or somewhere in the middle. Beyoncé makes fucking great music and considered choices, whether it's giving Colin Kaepernick his award or about liking her 'negro nose with Jackson Five nostrils' in 'Formation'.

I love Cardi B. She will run her mouth off every single day and everything that comes out of that woman's mouth is her, and you just know that. She's the girl from the hood, the immigrant's child who did good. I became aware of her when she was making her little Instagram videos, back when she was still working in the strip club, talking about blocking guys' phone numbers when they weren't acting right, making hilarious observations about life and just really being herself. Then she did the reality show, *Love & Hip Hop: New York*. When she left, I stopped watching it for my sanity because that show is problematic. I was a huge fan, but, over time, felt that it didn't contribute positively to the perception of black people.

I still love her, Cardi B. She presents herself in such a truly unapologetic way. Yes, she used to be a stripper, but she also vehemently tells young women not to make that their career choice if they can help it. At the same time, I see that she is also supportive of those who are still living her old life. People dismiss her as being too loud, too 'ghetto', but that is her charm.

Then there's Adele. If she doesn't want to make an album for five years, she won't. There are so many charlatans in the music industry, the people who aren't the best singers, who are very aware that they are getting by on their looks or whatever their gimmick is. It's clear that Adele chooses not to talk to the press when she doesn't have to. She plays the game strictly on her terms.

My mum has been a different kind of role model. I don't even know if she is a feminist. She's a very traditional Ghanaian woman of her generation. She was a dutiful wife who was happy to support her man and look after her kids. Equally, she's one of the most stubborn, forthright people you will ever meet in your life. If she says she's not moving, then she's not moving. If she decides she doesn't like someone then it's not likely to change. Once she has made up her mind, that really is it. Does that make her a feminist? Or does that just make her a strong woman?

Either way, I inherited some of her stubbornness. I was so pig-headed growing up that it never occurred to me that I wasn't equal to my brothers. If they could do something, so could I. I was adamant about trying to wee standing up for about a week when I was eight. Sometimes I'd bump heads with my mum or my dad about why I wasn't allowed to do certain things or wear certain things because the boys were. If they were wearing trousers to church, why did I have to wear a dress?

Ironically, I love dresses and skirts now, and my mum will chastise me for wearing short skirts, so I can't win! Sometimes, when I'm going out to a special event, I'll send her a photo of my outfit and her text responses are so funny that I post them on Instagram. My recent favourite being, 'The photo does not look like you. The skirt is too short. You actually look nice in a good length skirt. When Meghan [Markle] got married, she used less make-up, like I did ... I know you will not be offended. Have a blessed week. Shalom!'

I left high school at sixteen to go to college. By the end of year eleven, I couldn't wait to leave. It was an all-girls school and, while I made some lifelong friends there, at times it was very toxic and I just remember thinking, 'Get me away from these bitches!' I went to Richmond College, where we were given a lot of freedom, and I wasn't the best student. I just about managed to scrape A levels in Communications and English. It was a novelty to be somewhere where you could wear your own clothes every day and be around both sexes. I enjoyed college, but mainly because of the friends I made.

At that point, I'd decided I wanted to do something in the media. I was going to a lot of gigs and club nights, and it was a really pure and lovely time. There was a hip-hop night in Camden called 'Kung Fu' that was great. Deal Real Records off Carnaby Street was another favourite haunt of mine – it's where I saw Amy Winehouse sing for the first time. At sixteen, seventeen and eighteen, the energy you have is nuts. I'd be somewhere like Fabric until 4 a.m., then turn up at college at 10 a.m. three or four times a week and not feel it.

When I was eighteen, I did a six-month stint on CBBC – I was remembered from an old audition that I did for a BBC talent scheme. I was gutted when my contract wasn't renewed, but at least it prepared me for the industry.

Shortly afterwards, I joined Kiss FM as an intern and was only supposed to stay for three months, but I ended up working there for nearly six years. I made myself bizarrely indispensable by being very good at doing all the unglamorous things! Once, the morning after a Kiss club night at Ministry of Sound, I had to peel all the branded stickers off the windows. Or I'd stand outside Topshop for hours with a dictaphone, persuading people to record bits for station jingles, putting up with being ignored by people as they rushed past.

I slowly made my way up, promotion by promotion, until I was station coordinator. I loved being in the office, but at the same time I was thinking, 'Fuck this. I want to present.' It became a running joke with my boss. We'd play this game called Name That Tune. He'd line up songs on his computer and I could *always* name the song in a few seconds. We'd have this thing: 'three in a row and you get a show'. I'd always get three in a row. But no show, not at first.

I'd do voiceovers for clients and internal adverts for the station and, much to my boss's annoyance, I was saying, 'You should be playing this song or that song.' Eventually I was given an overnight show to present. I'd work in the office Monday to Friday, then pre-record the 2 a.m. to 6 a.m. slot with all my links and the show would go out while I was sleeping. Then I'd come in live on Saturday mornings and do the 6 a.m. to 10 a.m. show. So Friday nights I'd be in a club with my friends and I'd have to leave at 10.30 p.m. because I was so obsessed with sleeping and not oversleeping – although I did oversleep a couple of times and got into big trouble!

Over Christmas 2010, people were away, so my boss said, 'Do you want to do a full show? Pre-record it for Christmas Day?' Of course I did!

Shortly afterwards, I was offered Kiss FM's drive time show, which I did for about three and a half years. It was really liberating because I was no longer ordering stationery or doing admin. I was coming in to do a radio show, then going home.

Towards the end of my drive time stint, I sent Radio 1Xtra a demo because I love their broadcasting style. They got me in around eight times over an eighteen-month period to do pilot sessions. In 2013, I was finally offered the weekend breakfast show on Radio 1Xtra and, after six years, left Kiss.

I got my first stint on Radio 1 because my workmate had a dodgy tummy and couldn't make his afternoon show, so I was asked to step up. I had covered for Fearne Cotton a couple of times and naively hadn't thought anything of it, but I guess I was being auditioned for my current radio slot. When it was first announced in 2015 that I was taking over Fearne's 10 a.m. to 1p.m. slot, the response was 90 per cent positive, which I was appreciative of and relieved about.

I was a rarity in national radio simply because there aren't many black women on the airwaves. It was all I was asked about when I was doing press for my new show, and, as proud as I am of my heritage, and as much as I love being a woman, I didn't want those things to define every aspect of my career.

Since I started doing the mid-morning show, I've become more accepting of what people – especially the black community – expect from me in my role, but that doesn't mean I *have* to be what they or anyone else want me to be. Clichéd as it sounds, I have to stay true to me; I am *a* voice, not *the* voice.

There were people who weren't happy with my appointment, and there were a few ill-informed tweets accusing the BBC of box-ticking. I remember getting a tweet from a guy called 'UKIP Dave' who wasn't impressed with me, and I hadn't even started.

I just got on with the work. Radio 1 daytime shows are playlisted by the music team, but I am allocated a couple of free plays every show and I'm really passionate about them. They are a chance for me to really show off my personal taste, and sometimes a chance to break an act. I get so excited if a band I love is on the playlist. It could be Little Mix or Christine and the Queens. I'm not snobby about pop music. If you come from *X Factor* and you're good, then great. There are Little Mix songs I love as much as Lauryn Hill's.

Christine – or Chris – is the real deal. She is so exciting: Edith Piaf, Michael Jackson, Serge Gainsbourg and Madonna mixed up in a lab. She has it all. She came into the Live Lounge on my show in the summer of 2018 and I was blown away by her. We're lucky to have artists like that. A proper, old-fashioned pop star.

*

I encounter casual racism and sexism all the time. Micro-aggressions are crazy, even if they sometimes come from a place of ignorance rather than a hateful place. I could give you so many examples. I was filming a TV show and the host shook everyone's hand, but when it was my turn, he wanted to fist-bump me. I had to make a decision in a split second: was I going to halt a TV production and try to explain to this man that his behaviour was microaggressive, stereotypical and really patronising? Or was I going to grin and bear it? I did the latter, but I did stand there with my hand resolutely out for a handshake.

But I felt dehumanised. Why wasn't everyone else being fist-bumped? Don't dehumanise me by what you think you need to do to be down because I happen to be a black person. Fuck off.

It happened when I had my big Afro. I had an artist come into my show a couple of years ago. The hands went straight into my hair. I had to say, 'You don't get to do that.' It was awkward. But even now that my hair is relatively short, people still put their hands on it. 'Can I touch it? Do you wash it?' Do *they* wash *their* hair?

My hair is not exotic, but people are obsessed with the Other. Look, Afro hair is incredible. It's so diverse. You can do so much with it. But you don't need to put your hands on it. People literally regard you as a pet.

They say, 'You're quite pretty for a black girl.' Or, 'I went out with a black girl once.' Yeah? What's she got to do with me? I don't care. So what?

The list is endless. I've had comments like that my whole life, not just in my professional life.

It really helped when Solange released *A Seat at the Table* in 2016, including the brilliant, brilliant song 'Don't Touch My Hair'. It's such an empowering track for black people.

One of my best memories from the summer of 2017 was seeing Solange at Lovebox and, when she performed that song, the black and brown girls crammed into the tent were screaming the lyrics at the tops of their lungs. 'You know this hair is my shit . . .'

A Seat at the Table is, to me, the most important album for black women since *The Miseducation of Lauryn Hill.* It's an incredible piece of work. And, since 'Don't Touch My Hair' came out, people don't seem to be reaching to touch my hair as much as they used to. I guess that's the power of music.

People absolutely see me as black before they see me as a woman. One hundred per cent. A lot of the time, how I look determines how someone communicates with me. Hence, I will get a fist-bump rather than a handshake. Because that's what that person thinks I want. Well, not necessarily.

I have a friend who was at work recently. A white guy who was working on the same project came up to him and started rapping 'Straight Outta Compton' at him.

My friend said, 'Sorry, I don't know that song.'

The white guy frowned and said, 'How can you not know that song?'

My friend explained that he was into rock music. It totally threw the other guy. He thought he was being really cool. It happens, man. Every day. It's so patronising. And if you question it, you get accused of playing the race card.

As a person of colour in this country, especially as a woman, I have been shown that our opinions are either one of two things: weaponised against you or completely ignored. I see that more and more as I navigate my life. I try to choose my battles wisely. If I went online and sought out examples of inequality every day, I'd never get anything done and it would drive me crazy.

People talk about progress being made, but it's at a snail's pace. We've only got to look at the evolution of the world as it is. People say, 'I can't believe the Holocaust happened. It was so horrendous. How did people allow that to happen?' Well, look at what is happening in America in 2018 – immigrant children as young as two years old are being separated from their parents, who are only trying to get into the county for a better life.

I am hopeful that things will change for the better, but will there be true equality between men and women in the next fifty years? I don't think so. Will there be true equality between women of all races? Not as quickly as we would like, sadly. I believe that all we can do is keep talking and keep doing what we say we're going to do. There have been some important books published in recent years: *Why I'm No Longer Talking to White People About* Race by Reni Eddo-Lodge and *Slay in Your Lane: The Black Girl Bible* by Yomi Adegoke and Elizabeth Uviebinené are being widely read, which is encouraging.

Slay in Your Lane refers to #BlackGirlMagic, which was contentious at first. People would tweet and say, 'Isn't that a bit racist? Aren't all girls magical?' Missing the point, the whole point of why it is there. Yes, it's a celebration, but it's combative, too. The truth is that we live in a society which doesn't tell us that black girls are magical.

Anyone who considers themselves an ally should read *Slay in Your Lane*, because we have to have these uncomfortable conversations. People are scared and the fragility of privilege is real. There is an innate fear of saying 'racism' or 'racist' out loud because people think it's as simple as somebody standing very close to a stranger, screaming a slur at them, followed by the inevitable retaliatation. If only it was that binary!

White male privilege won't disappear overnight. But it's getting called out. I have heard and read white guys saying, 'Oh, being a white male is treated as a crime these days.' It's not a crime, but guess what? The world has been created inherently in your favour. People who are not white or male are finding their voices amplified louder than ever and using them to level the playing field.

We've got a long way to go, but who knows what might happen? There are always anomalies. Exceptions to rules. I never thought I'd get to see someone like Obama elected President of the US in my lifetime. Oprah is the perfect example of an anomaly – she started out as a poor, dark-skinned, overweight girl from the Southern States of America and is now one of the most powerful women in the world.

Being a woman in 2018 is so complex. It's certainly not a monolithic thing. I'm excited and hopeful. I interact with girls on social media who are way smarter than I was when I was fourteen, fifteen, sixteen. They have access to so much knowledge. It's there for them to be greater. When I was their age, I didn't know any other young girls talking about intersectional feminism and inclusive feminism or going on marches. There are plenty of girls obsessing about being the next Kim Kardashian and pumping their lips full of shit, but some of them are also going on women's marches. You don't have to be defined by one aspect of who you are.

The girls who are coming up have got amazing tools to enable them to genuinely be great. There are thirteen- and fourteen-year-old girls who are reading Me Too news stories who will go into the workplace with a 'don't you fucking dare' attitude.

They will, I hope, speak up. And the world will have to listen.

A–Z OF ACKNOWLEDGEMENTS

Ailah Ahmed; David Bamford; Riccardo Berna; Todd Cassetty; Karen Cham; Karen Ciccone; Jack Delaney; Toby Donnelly; Ros Earls; Rhian Emanuel; Georgie Gibbon; Lennie Goodings; Tim Hampson; Bonnie Raphael Irvine; Jon Lawrence; Matthew Rankin; Carol Raphael; Ben Skerritt; Laura Snapes; Sarah Strickland; Becky Thomas; Steve Warby; Jon Wilde; Leah Wilson. Thank you!

CREDITS

Photograph credits

Christine and the Queens – Jamie Morgan
Ibeyi – David Uzochukwu
Kate Tempest – Hayley Louisa Brown
Alison Moyet – Steve Gullick
Nadine Shah – Julia Romanovskaya
Jessica Curry – James Pike
Maggie Rogers – Olivia Bee
Emmy the Great – Alex Lake
Dream Wife – Hollie Fernando
Natalie Merchant – Jacob Blickenstaff
Lauren Mayberry – Danny Clinch
Poppy Ajudha – Lennon Gregory
Kalie Shorr – Samantha Klose
Tracey Thorn – Edward Bishop
Mitski – Bao Ngo
Catherine Marks – Al Parker
Georgia – Hinako Omori
Clara Amfo – Adama Jalloh

Lyric credits

Lyrics from 'Ash' and 'Deathless' by Ibeyi by kind permission of Universal Music Publishing France.

Lyrics from 'Other' by Alison Moyet by kind permission of Mega Music LTD. All Rights Reserved.

Lyrics from 'FUU' by Rakel Mjöll Leifsdóttir, Isabella Cornelia Podpadec, Alice Gough, Alex Paveley and Vigdís Howser Hardardóttir by kind permission of Cannibal on behalf of Universal Music. Lyrics from 'Somebody' by Rakel Mjöll Leifsdóttir, Isabella Cornelia Podpadec, Alice Gough and Alex Paveley by kind permission of Cannibal on behalf of Universal Music.

Lyrics from 'What's the Matter Here' Robert Buck and Natalie Merchant by kind permission of Words & Music, a division of Big Deal Music, LLC on behalf of Christian Burial Music for the writers Robert Buck and Natalie Merchant.

Lyrics from 'Tepid Soul' by Poppy Ajudha by kind permission of Poppy Ajudha.